Black American Women in Literature

This book is dedicated to:

my mother, Sylvia Monis Cohen
my close friend, Maxwell
my colleagues at Eastern Michigan University

for their limitless patience

Black American Women in Literature
A BIBLIOGRAPHY, 1976 THROUGH 1987

by
Ronda Glikin

McFarland & Company, Inc., Publishers
Jefferson, North Carolina, and London

British Library Cataloguing-in-Publication data available

Library of Congress Cataloguing-in-Publication Data

Glikin, Ronda, 1945–
   Black American women in literature.

   Includes index.
   1. American literature — Afro-American authors —
Bibliography. 2. American literature — Women authors —
Bibliography. 3. American literature — 20th century —
Bibliography. 4. American literature — Afro-American
authors — History and criticism — Bibliography.
5. American literature — Women authors — History and
criticism — Bibliography. 6. American literature —
20th century — History and criticism — Bibliography.
7. Afro-American women authors — Biography — Bibliography.
8. Afro-American women in literature — Bibliography.
9. Women and literature — United States — History —
20th century — Bibliography. 10. Authors, American —
20th century — Biography — Bibliography. I. Title.
Z1229.N39G57   1989   016.81'08'09287   88-43488
[PS153.N5]

ISBN 0-89950-372-1 (lib. bdg. : 50# alk. paper)

Printed in the United States of America.

McFarland & Company, Inc., Publishers
   Box 611, Jefferson, North Carolina 28640

Contents

Acknowledgments

I would like to thank the following people for their help: Randy Wright, who introduced me to the bibliographical software used to compile the book, and who offered not only technical support, but also encouragement and praise throughout the three years I spent compiling the bibliography; Keith Stanger, a coworker and friend, without whose expert advice in buying and using computer hardware and software I would have had a much harder time compiling my citations; Dr. Naomi Long Madgett of Lotus Press, Detroit, and Becky Birtha, a writer from Philadelphia, who provided much-needed assistance in verifying some of the women I included; my mother, Sylvia Monis Cohen, and a coworker, Diane Eimer, who helped me type the index; and my friends Birdie Travis, Glenn Ruihley, Marian Hampton, and Ron Colman, who provided shoulders to lean on at stress points.

I am grateful to the staff at the Schlesinger Library, Radcliffe College, Cambridge, Massachusetts, for providing me with hard-to-find literary and feminist journals during the upheaval of their move into new quarters. I was able to travel to Radcliffe with the assistance of the Keal Fund, established at Eastern Michigan University for the benefit of women faculty members. The Keal Fund also enabled me to purchase my software.

In addition, I used the resources of the following libraries: Eastern Michigan University, Ypsilanti, the University of Michigan, Ann Arbor, and Michigan State University, East Lansing. I would also like to thank the staff at the Ann Arbor Public Library, who are responsible for the special Black Studies Collection, from which I retrieved a number of recent publications unavailable elsewhere.

Beverly Guy-Sheftall, Eloise McKinney Johnson, and Terri Jewell sent back questionnaires I had distributed at the Black Women and the Diaspora conference in East Lansing in 1985, and, although I did not use all the citations they submitted, I am very pleased that they took an interest in my publication.

Introduction

The purpose of this book is to facilitate research on the work of Black American women writers, specifically to update bibliographical resources and to provide a reference tool for not only Black studies but also women's studies and American literature. The book includes the poetry, short fiction, novels, essays, and plays by, and criticism on, approximately 300 women whose work has been published in periodicals and anthologies between 1976 and 1987, and is the only multi-genre bibliography on Black women authors that has citations for both original works and literary criticism. Over eighty periodical titles and two hundred books have been searched to gather the material used. Science fiction and children's literature are included. Excluded, in general, are audiovisual works, newspapers, dissertations, and reprints. Citations are mainly in English.

The focus of the bibliography is on women writing creative literature, but the publications of women known primarily as literary critics are listed if they have written creative literature as well. Most of the women listed in major bibliographies are well known (Alice Walker, Gwendolyn Brooks, Nikki Giovanni, etc.), but a number of productive writers are not mentioned in those sources. Rita Dove and Colleen J. McElroy, for example, have produced a large body of work which has, up to this time, not received much critical attention. Certain subjects have also been neglected; an area which has not been treated widely is Black feminism. Authors such as Barbara Smith, Audre Lorde, Becky Birtha, and many others are prolific representatives of the feminist viewpoint. In addition, only a small number of the authors listed in this book have been published by large presses. Most of them have been published by small literary and feminist presses, which are struggling to survive the competition. The compiler hopes that this bibliography will serve as a catalyst to encourage literary critics to publish more books and articles on the work of all the authors appearing in this publication.

The arrangement of the book is alphabetical by author, with a list of general articles appended. Works *by* the authors are categorized by topic, such as Poetry, Drama, Essays, etc.; works *about* the authors and their publications are listed under the heading "Textual Criticism." This heading includes literary criticism, book reviews, interviews, biography, and bibliography. Sometimes a separate heading appears — for example, "bibliography," if a book or article is, in its entirety, a bibliography. At times, categorization of publications is a challenge, especially when such terms as "prose poem" or "choreopoem" are used to describe an author's work.

A section on the authors arranged by genre is provided after the bibliography to serve as a guide to the total body of literature. The book, then, is not only a bibliography but a guide to Black women writing creative literature for the past twelve years. (Since a criterion for inclusion is an article or book *published* from 1976 on, not only are contemporary women included, but the name and work of any woman who has been of literary interest may appear. The book takes, therefore, a historical view of the literature as well.)

Birth and death dates provided are, of necessity, approximate because of either the lack of information in current sources or the appearance of contrary information (sometimes in the same source). The names of the women included were verified in many publications and by several people in the literary field. Some writers, unfortunately, had to be left out because the compiler was unable to verify that they were both Black and female. (In one case, a person was identified as a man in one source and a woman in another.) The compiler hopes that more research will be done in Black women's studies to bring to public view the women that are not included in this book.

The citations should be easily readable. The abbreviations used are listed at the back of the book. A brief note is provided if the title of the article does not clearly identify the contents.

Books published by the authors included are listed by title, place of publication, publisher, and date.

Articles in books are listed by author, title, and a four-letter abbreviation for the book indexed, followed by a colon and inclusive pages. A list of the abbreviations appears at the end of the book.

Articles in periodicals are listed by author (if one was cited), name of article, name of periodical, volume (or number) followed by a period and then the number of the volume (if one exists), date, and pages.

Since this book includes citations from a large number of journals that are not indexed (small literary and women's periodicals), as well as those that appear in widely available indexes, the book may be used not only by researchers using the resources of small libraries, but also by those using large and specialized library collections. Extensive examination of literary bibliographies, in general, and Black literary bibliographies, in particular, published since 1976 has revealed that until now there has been no publication representing, on a wide scale, the achievement of Black women in literature. This book is not comprehensive, but it fills a decade-long literary void with a critical guide *in one volume* to the work of these women. With the increased number of publications about Black women writing creative literature appearing in just the past few years (consult Appendix A, "Works About Black Women Writers"), perhaps the gap will close. There is so much more to be done.

Bibliography

Ada

Poetry

1 "Lines, suggested on reading 'An appeal to Christian women of the South' by A.E. Grimké." In STET: 17–19.

2 "Lines, on the suppression, by a portion of our public journals, of the intelligence of the Abolition of Slavery in the British West Indies." In STET: 20–21.

3 "To the memory of J. Horace Kimball." In STET: 21–22.

4 "Untitled [Oh, when this earthly tenement]." In STET: 19–20.

Janus Adams

Drama

5 *St. Stephen: A Passion Play* [Excerpt]. In BARA: 29–46. Play was written in 1981.

Jeanette Adams

Poetry

6 "Langston Hughes attends the Festival." *Steppingstone*. Wint. 1984: 18–19.

7 *Love Lyrics*. Elmsford, NY: Published by author, 1982.

8 "Love lyrics no. 2." *Essence*. 16.10 Feb. 1986: 133.

9 *Picture Me in a Poem*. Elmsford, NY: Published by author, 1980.

10 *Sukari*. Elmsford, NY: Published by author, 1979.

Textual Criticism

11 Banfield, Beryle. *Interracial Books for Children Bull*. 13.4–5 1982: 28. Rev. of *Picture Me in a Poem*.

12 Kazi-Ferrouillet, Kuumba. *Black Collegian*. 15.1 Nov.–Dec. 1983: 26. Rev. of Adams' three books.

Kenyette Adrine-Robinson

Poetry

13 *Be My Shoo-gar*. Cleveland Heights, OH: Kenyette Productions, 1987.

14 "Let's go." *Essence*. 18.6 Oct. 1987: 144.

Fatimah Afif

Poetry
15 "Tanka." In BARA: 47.

Ai (1947-)

Essays
16 "Memories." In HEYE: 2-3. Prose piece accompanying poems published in the anthology.
17 "On being one half Japanese, one eighth Choctaw, one quarter Black and one sixteenth Irish." *Ms.* 6.11 May 1978: 58.

Poetry
18 "Before you leave." *Essence.* 16.12 Apr. 1986: 188.
19 "Blue suede shoes." *Iowa Rev.* 11.4 1981: 87-91.
20 "Blue suede shoes (a fiction)." *Callaloo.* 9.1 Wint. 1986: 1-5.
21 "Conversation." In GAES: 26-27.
22 "Conversation (for Robert Lowell)." *Paris Rev.* 77 Wint.-Spr. 1980: 116.
23 *Conversation: For Robert Lowell.* St. Paul, MN: Bookslinger, 1981.
24 "The émigré." *Agni.* 23 1986: 98-100.
25 "The expectant father." In HEYE: 8.
26 "The expectant father." *Ironwood.* 4.7-8 1977: 21.
27 "Father and son." *Antaeus.* 23 Aut. 1976: 130-132.
28 "Four haiku by Issa." *Ark.* 14 1980: 155.
29 "The German army." *Ironwood.* 6.2 1978: 25.
30 "The gilded man." *Antaeus.* 30-31 Sum.-Aut. 1978: 51-52.
31 "Guadalajara Hospital." *Virginia Q. Rev.* 54.4 Aut. 1978: 704.
32 "The hitchhiker." In HEYE: 5-6.
33 "I have got to stop loving you." In HEYE: 4-5.
34 "Ice." *Chicago Rev.* 29.4 Spr. 1978: 4.
35 "The journalist." *Missouri Rev.* 9.1 1985-1986: 66-69.
36 "He kept on burning." *Antaeus.* 23 Aut. 1976: 128-129.
37 "The kid." *Antaeus.* 23 Aut. 1976: 133.
38 "The kid." In HEYE: 7.
39 "Killing floor." *Paris Rev.* 75 Spr. 1979: 281-282. Corrected reprint. Originally published in the same journal, 74 Aut.-Wint. 1978: 186.
40 *Killing Floor: Poems.* Boston: Houghton, 1979.
41 "Kristallnacht." *Poetry.* 135.6 Mar. 1980: 340-341.
42 "The man with the saxophone." *Amer. Voice.* 1 1985: 66-67.
43 "The mortician's twelve-year-old son." In HEYE: 6-7.
44 "Nothing but color (for Yukio Mishima)." *Paris Rev.* 74 Aut.-Wint. 1978: 184.
45 "One man down." In HEYE: 5.
46 "Pentecost." In GAES: 25-26.
47 "Pentecost." In HEYE: 8-9.

48 "Pentecost (for myself)." *Tendril.* 9 1980: 17.

49 "The priest's confession." *Agni Rev.* 17 1982: 53–56.

50 "The psychiatrist." *Poetry.* 135.6 Mar. 1980: 338–339.

51 "The ravine." *Ironwood.* 4.7–8 1977:20.

52 "The ravine." *Ms.* 6.11 May 1978: 59.

53 "Salome." *Antaeus.* 40–41 Wint.–Spr. 1981: 252–253.

54 "Salome." *Ms.* 11.6 Dec. 1982: 74.

55 "She didn't even wave." *Ironwood.* 4.7–8 1977: 19.

56 *Sin.* Boston: Houghton, 1986.

57 "The singers." *Antaeus.* 30–31 Sum.–Aut. 1978: 49–50.

58 "Sleep like a hammer." *Chicago Rev.* 29.4 Spr. 1978: 6.

59 "Talking to his reflection in a shallow pond." *Michigan Q. Rev.* 17.4 1978: 505–506.

60 "They shall not pass." *Iowa Rev.* 11.1 Wint. 1980: 103.

61 "Twenty-nine (a dream in two parts)." *Ms.* 6.11 May 1978: 59.

62 "The wake." *Virginia Q. Rev.* 54.4 Aut. 1978: 703.

63 "Why can't I leave you?" In HEYE: 3–4.

64 "Winter in another country." *Poetry.* 135.6 Mar. 1980: 336–337.

65 "Yellow crane pavilion." *Paris Rev.* 77 Wint.–Spr. 1980: 117.

Textual Criticism and Interviews

66 Connelly, Kenneth. "New books in review." *Yale Rev.* 68.4 Sum. 1979: 566–569. Rev. of *Killing Floor.*

67 Jahns, T.R. *Ohio Rev.* 25 1980: 108–113. Rev. of *Killing Floor.*

68 Kearney, Lawrence and Michael Cuddihy. "Ai: an interview." *Ironwood.* 6.2 1978: 27–34.

69 Seidman, Hugh. *N.Y. Times Book Rev.* July 8, 1979: 14. Rev. of *Killing Floor.*

70 Wojahn, David. *N.Y. Times Book Rev.* June 8, 1986: 38. Rev. of *Sin.*

Nanina Alba (1915–1968)

Textual Criticism

71 Bogle, Enid. "Nanina Alba." In DL41: 3–8. Includes biography and bibliography.

72 Redmond, Eugene B. In REDM: 332, 333. Biography and brief commentary on her writings.

Alexander, Margaret Walker *see* Walker (Alexander), Margaret

Fareedah Allah

Poetry
73 "Cinderella." In STET: 167–169.
74 "Funky football." In STET: 170–172.
75 "The generation gap." In STET: 174–175.
76 "Hush, honey." In STET: 164–167.
77 "Lawd, dese colored chillum." In STET: 175–176.
78 "You made it rain." In STET: 173–174.

Donna Allegra

Essays
79 "Butch on the streets." In DELA: 44–45. On being a lesbian.
80 "Some personal notes on racism among the women." *Heresies.* 4.3 1982: 33.

Poetry
81 "Before I dress and soar again." *Conditions 5.* 2.2 Aut. 1979: 100.
82 "Before I dress and soar again." In SMIT: 166–167.
83 "A prayer for my soul." *Essence.* 9.5 Sept. 1978: 24.
84 "A rape poem for men." *Heresies.* 2.2 1978: 49.
85 "Up in the sky." *Conditions 5.* 2.2 Aut. 1979: 101–102.

Short Fiction
86 "The electrician's girl." *Sinister Wisdom.* 32 Sum 1987: 33–36.
87 "She knew ways." *Sinister Wisdom.* 16 1981: 15–19.

Fayola Kamaria Ama

Poetry
88 "For 'Mamie'." In BARA: 48–49.

Johari M. Amini (Johari M. Kunjufu)

Poetry
89 "Ceremony." In STET: 192–194.
90 "The promise." In BARA: 51.
91 "The promise." In STET: 195.
92 "Return." In STET: 194.
93 "Story for the remainder." In BARA: 51–53.
94 "There is no title: only echoes." In BARA: 50–51.
95 "Untitled [On the naming day]." In ADOF: 242–243.

Textual Criticism

96 Brown, Fahamisha Patricia. "Johari M. Amini." In DL41: 17–23. Some biography and bibliography included.

Kathy Elaine Anderson

Poetry

97 "Ahmos." *Obsidian.* 5.1–2 Spr.–Sum. 1979: 106.
98 "Derrick." *Obsidian.* 5.1–2 Spr.–Sum. 1979: 106.
99 "For Mulaaka." *Essence.* 11.6 Oct. 1980: 25.
100 "The Grandpa." *Obsidian.* 5.1–2 Spr.–Sum. 1979: 107.
101 "To be signed for the deaf." *Essence.* 11.6 Oct. 1980: 19.

Short Fiction

102 "Louisiana shade." *Southern Rev.* 21.3 July 1985: 672–681.

Mignon Holland Anderson

Short Fiction

103 *Mostly Womenfolk and a Man or Two: A Collection.* Chicago: Third World, 1976.

Textual Criticism

104 Kent, George E. *Black Books Bull.* 4.4 Wint. 1976: 52–53. Review of *Mostly Womenfolk and a Man or Two.*
105 Manning, Debra Lyn. *Black Collegian.* 7 May–June 1977: 62. Rev. of *Mostly Womenfolk and a Man or Two.*
106 Moore, Emily R. *Freedomways.* 17.1 1977: 48–49. Review of *Mostly Womenfolk and a Man or Two.*

Maya Angelou (1928–)

Autobiography

107 *All God's Children Need Traveling Shoes.* NY: Random, 1986.
108 "The bridge." *Essence.* 16.11 Mar. 1986: 66–68, 116–117, 121–122. Excerpt from *All God's Children Need Traveling Shoes.*
109 *Gather Together in My Name* [Excerpt]. In LONG: 663–670. Book was published in 1974.
110 *The Heart of a Woman.* NY: Random, 1981.
111 *The Heart of a Woman* [Excerpt]. *Essence.* 12.9 Jan. 1982: 76, 108, 111, 113.
112 "Maya's journey home." *Reader's Digest.* 121.725 Sept. 1982: 89–94. Excerpt from *I Know Why the Caged Bird Sings* (1970).
113 "The peckerwood dentist and Momma's incredible powers." In GILN: 2002–2007. Excerpt from *I Know Why the Caged Bird Sings.*
114 *Singin' and Swingin' and Gettin' Merry Like Christmas.* NY: Random, 1976.

Bibliography

115 Cameron, Dee Birch. "A Maya Angelou bibliography." *Bull. of Bibliography.* 36.1 Jan.–Mar. 1979: 50–52.

Essays

116 "Save the mothers." *Ebony.* 41.10 Aug. 1986: 38–39. Importance of mothers to the Black community.

117 "Shades and slashes of light." In EVAN: 3–5. About being an author.

118 "Why I moved back to the South." *Ebony.* 37.4 Feb. 1982: 130–134.

Poetry

119 *And Still I Rise: A Book of Poems.* NY: Random, 1978.

120 "Caged bird." *Ladies' Home J.* 100.7 July 1983: 40.

121 "The health-food diner." *Ladies' Home J.* 100.7 July 1983: 40.

122 "Insomniac." *Ladies' Home J.* 100.10 Oct. 1983: 192.

123 "My Arkansas." In STET: 266.

124 *Now Sheba Sings the Song.* NY: Dutton, 1987.

125 "On diverse deviations." In STET: 267.

126 "Phenomenal woman." In FISH: 287–288.

127 "Recovery." *Ladies' Home J.* 100.10 Oct. 1983: 192.

128 "Sepia fashion show." In STET: 267.

129 *Shaker, Why Don't You Sing?* NY: Random, 1983.

130 "Still I rise." In STET: 265–266.

131 "To a man." *Ebony.* 38.4 Feb. 1983: 50.

132 "Where we belong, a duet." *Ebony.* 38.4 Feb. 1983: 46.

133 "Woman me." In STET: 264.

Short Fiction

134 "The reunion." In BARA: 54–58.

Textual Criticism and Interviews

135 Arensberg, Liliane K. "Death as a metaphor of self in *I Know Why the Caged Bird Sings.*" *CLA J.* 20.2 Dec. 1976: 273–291.

136 Baker, Houston A., Jr. *N.Y. Times Book Rev.* May 11, 1986: 14. Rev. of *All God's Children Need Traveling Shoes.*

137 Baumgartner, Jill. "Irving, Angelou, and Faulkner: old, new and autobiographical." *Cresset.* 45.5 1982: 24–26. Rev. of *The Heart of a Woman.*

138 "The *Black Scholar* interviews: Maya Angelou." *Black Scholar.* 8.4 Jan.–Feb. 1977: 44–53.

139 Bloom, Lynn Z. "Maya Angelou." In DL38: 3–12. Includes biography and additional bibliography.

140 Blundell, Janet B. *Library J.* Apr. 1, 1983: 746–747. Rev. of *Shaker, Why Don't You Sing?*

141 Commire, Anne. "Maya Angelou." In CO49: 35–48. Biography and comments on work.

142 Cosgrave, Mary Silva. *Horn Book.* 52.1 Feb. 1976: 78. Rev. of *Oh Pray My Wings Are Gonna Fit Me Well* (1975).

143 Cudjoe, Selwyn R. "Maya Angelou and the autobiographical statement." In EVAN: 6–24.

144 Davis, Curt. *Encore Amer. and Worldwide News.* Nov. 8, 1976: 45. Rev. of *Singin' and Swingin' and Gettin' Merry Like Christmas.*

145 Davis, Curt. "Maya Angelou: and still she rises." *Encore Amer. and Worldwide News.* Sept. 12, 1977:28–32. Includes some biography.

146 Demetrakopoulos, Stephanie A. "The metaphysics of matrilinearism in women's autobiography: studies of Mead's *Blackberry Winter,* Hellman's *Pentimento,* Angelou's *I Know Why the Caged Bird Sings,* and Kingston's *The Woman Warrior.*" In JELI: 180–205.

147 Elliot, J.M. "Maya Angelou: in search of self." *Negro History Bull.* 40.3 May 1977: 694–695. An interview.

148 Elliot, Jeffrey. "Author Maya Angelou raps. . ." *Sepia.* 26.10 Oct. 1977: 22–27.

149 Fisher, M.F.K. *People Weekly.* Jan. 24, 1983: 63–64. Rev. of *Shaker, Why Don't You Sing?*

150 Gilbert, Sandra M. "A platoon of poets." *Poetry.* 128.5 Aug. 1976: 290–299. Rev. of *Oh Pray My Wings Are Gonna Fit Me Well.*

151 Hiers, John T. "Fatalism in Maya Angelou's *I Know Why the Caged Bird Sings.*" *Notes on Contemp. Lit.* 6.1 Jan. 1976: 5–7.

152 Ikerionwu, Maria K. Mootry. *Phylon.* 44.1 Mar. 1983: 86–87. Rev. of *The Heart of a Woman.*

153 Kinnamon, Keneth [sic]. "Call and response: intertextuality in two autobiographical works by Richard Wright and Maya Angelou." In WEIA: 121–134.

154 Kuehl, Linda. *Saturday Rev.* Oct. 30, 1976: 46. Rev. of *Singin' and Swingin' and Gettin' Merry Like Christmas.*

155 Mberi, A.S.K. *Freedomways.* 19.2 1979: 109–110. Rev. of *And Still I Rise.*

156 McCall, C. "Maya Angelou." *People Weekly.* Mar. 8, 1982: 92. Mostly biographical.

157 McDowell, Deborah E. "Traveling hopefully." *Women's Rev. of Books.* 4.1 Oct. 1986: 17. Rev. of *All God's Children Need Traveling Shoes.*

158 McMurry, Myra K. "Role playing as art in Maya Angelou's *Caged Bird.*" *South Atlantic Bull.* 41.2 May 1976: 106–111.

159 Miller, Adam David. *Black Scholar.* 13.4–5 Sum. 1982: 48–49. Rev. of *The Heart of a Woman.*

160 Neubauer, Carol E. "Displacement and autobiographical style in Maya Angelou's *The Heart of a Woman.*" *Black Amer. Lit. Forum.* 17.3 Fall 1983: 123–129.

161 Neubauer, Carol E. "An interview with Maya Angelou." *Massachusetts Rev.* 28.2 Sum. 1987: 286–292.

162 O'Connor, Karen. In OCON: 99–120. Some biography.

163 O'Neale, Sondra. "Reconstruction of the composite self: new images of Black women in Maya Angelou's continuing autobiography." In EVAN: 25–36.

164 Oliver, Stephanie Stokes. "Maya Angelou: the heart of a woman." *Essence.* 14.1 May 1983: 112–114, 116. An interview.

165 Paterson, Judith. "Interview: Maya Angelou — a passionate writer living fiercely with brains, guts, and joy." *Vogue.* 172.9 Sept. 1982: 416–417, 420, 422.

166 Seebohm, Caroline. "Talks with two singular women." *House and Garden.* 153.11 Nov. 1981: 128–130, 192. An interview.

167 Spigner, Nieda. *Freedomways.* 22.1 1982: 55–56. Rev. of *The Heart of a Woman.*

168 Stepto, Robert B. "The phenomenal woman and the severed daughter." *Parnassus.* 8.1 Fall–Wint. 1979: 312–320. Rev. of *And Still I Rise* and Audre Lorde's *The Black Unicorn.*

169 Thomas, Arthur E. In THOM: 1–15. An interview.

170 Wall, Cheryl. "Maya Angelou." In TODD: 58–67. On several works.

Denise Carreathers Armstrong (1950–)

Biography
171 Gite, Lloyd. "Taking care of business." *Essence.* 13.11 Mar. 1983: 32, 37. Armstrong's bookstore venture in Houston, TX.

Poetry
172 "A Black man's love song." *Black Books Bull.* 7.2 1981: 53.
173 "When a Black man smiles." *Black Books Bull.* 7.3 1981: 61.

Red Arobateau

Short Fiction
174 "Susie Q." In GRAH: 102–132.

Textual Criticism
175 Loewenstein, Andrea. *Gay Community News.* July 12, 1980: 2–3, 6. Rev. of *Bars Across Heaven* (1975 novel, self-published) and "Susie Q" in Book Supplement section.

Asante, Kariamu Welsh *see* Welsh, Kariamu

Toni Cade Bambara (1939–)

Essays
176 "Salvation is the issue." In EVAN: 41–47. On her writing.
177 "What it is I think I'm doing anyhow." In STER: 153–168.

Foreword
178 Moraga, Cherríe and Gloria Anzaldúa, Eds. *This Bridge Called My Back: Writings by Radical Women of Color.* Watertown, MA: Persephone, 1981. Bambara's foreword appears on pages vi–viii.

Novels
179 *The Salt Eaters.* NY: Random, 1980.

180 "Witchbird." *Essence.* 7.5 Sept. 1976: 52–54, 86, 88. Excerpt from *The Salt Eaters.*

181 "Witchbird." In WASH: 173–191. Excerpt from *The Salt Eaters.*

Short Fiction
182 "Baby's breath." *Essence.* 11.5 Sept. 1980: 90–91, 145–146, 148, 152.

183 "Christmas Eve at Johnson's Drugs N Goods." In LONG: 698–712. From *The Sea Birds Are Still Alive* (1977).

184 "The lesson." In BLIC: 159–163. From *Gorilla, My Love* (collection of short fiction, 1972).

185 "Luther on Sweet Auburn." *First World.* 2.4 1980: 54–55.

186 "Madame Bai and the taking of Stone Mountain." In BARA: 59–69.

187 "Maggie of the green bottles." In FISH: 196–201.

188 "The mama load." *Redbook.* 154.1 Nov. 1979: 33, 182, 184, 186, 188, 190, 192.

189 "Medley." In WASH: 255–274.

190 "My man Bovanne." In GILN: 2308–2312.

191 "Raymond's run." In HOFF: 117–126. Originally appeared in *Gorilla My Love.* Biographical headnote.

192 *The Sea Birds Are Still Alive: Collected Stories.* NY: Random, 1977.

193 "Wall of respect." *Obsidian.* 7.2–3. Sum.–Wint. 1981: 108–114.

Textual Criticism and Interviews
194 Burks, Ruth Elizabeth. "From baptism to resurrection: Toni Cade Bambara and the incongruity of language." In EVAN: 48–57.

195 Byerman, Keith E. "Women's blues: the fiction of Toni Cade Bambara and Alice Walker." In BYER: 104–170.

196 Deck, Alice A. In DL38: 12–22. Some biography and bibliography.

197 Dee, Ruby. *Freedomways.* 17.2 1977: 102–104. Rev. of *The Sea Birds Are Still Alive.*

198 El'zabar, Kai. *Black Books Bull.* 7.1 1980: 44–45. Rev. of *The Salt Eaters.*

199 Giddings, Paula. "'A call to wholeness' from a gifted storyteller." *Encore Amer. and Worldwide News.* 9.6 June 1980: 48–49. Edited transcript of interview of the author about *The Salt Eaters.*

200 Giddings, Paula. *Encore Amer. and Worldwide News.* 6.11 June 6, 1977: 44–46. Rev. of *The Sea Birds Are Still Alive.*

201 Guy-Sheftall, Beverly. "Commitment: Toni Cade Bambara speaks." In BELL: 230–250. An interview.

202 Hargrove, Nancy D. "Youth in Toni Cade Bambara's *Gorilla My Love.*" In PREN: 215–232.

203 Harris, Jessica. *Essence.* 8.2 June 1977: 31. Rev. of *The Sea Birds Are Still Alive.*

204 Harris, Norman. "A rainbow of possibilities." *Obsidian.* 7.1 Spr. 1981: 101–105. Rev. of *The Salt Eaters.*

205 Hull, Gloria T. "'What it is I think she's doing anyhow': a reading of

Toni Cade Bambara's *The Salt Eaters.*" In PRYS: 216–232. Different version of the essay from the one in SMIT: 124–142.

    206 Hull, Gloria T. "What it is I think she's doing anyhow: a reading of Toni Cade Bambara's *The Salt Eaters.*" In SMIT: 124–142.

    207 Jackson, Angela. *Black Scholar.* 13.6 Fall 1982: 52. Rev. of *The Salt Eaters.*

    208 Lardner, Susan. "Third eye open." *New Yorker.* May 5, 1980: 169. Rev. of *The Salt Eaters.*

    209 Macauley, Robi. *N.Y. Times Book Rev.* Mar. 27, 1977: 7. Rev. of *The Sea Birds Are Still Alive.*

    210 Mahone, Barbara D. "A handsome family quilt." *First World.* 1 May–June 1977: 40–42. Rev. of *The Sea Birds Are Still Alive.*

    211 O'Neale, Sondra. *Southern Exposure.* 9.2 Sum. 1981: 102–103. Rev. of *The Salt Eaters.*

    212 Rumens, Carol. "Heirs to the dream." *Times (London) Literary Supplement.* June 18, 1982: 676. Rev. of *The Salt Eaters.*

    213 Salaam, Kalamu ya. "Searching for the mother tongue: an interview." *First World.* 2.4 Sept. 1980: 48–52.

    214 Shipley, W. Maurice. *CLA J.* 26.1 Sept. 1982: 125–127. Rev. of *The Salt Eaters.*

    215 Tate, Claudia. "Toni Cade Bambara." In TATE: 12–38. On a number of works.

    216 Traylor, Eleanor W. "Music as theme: the jazz mode in the works of Toni Cade Bambara." In EVAN: 58–70.

    217 Utamu, Imani. *Black Books Bull.* 5 Fall 1977: 36–37. Rev. of *The Sea Birds Are Still Alive.*

    218 Ward, Jerry W., Jr. *New Orleans Rev.* 8.2 1981: 207–208. Rev. of *The Salt Eaters.*

    219 Washington, Mary Helen. "Blues women of the seventies." *Ms.* 6.1 July 1977: 36, 38. Rev. of *The Sea Birds Are Still Alive.*

    220 Willis, Susan. "Problematizing the individual: Toni Cade Bambara's stories for the revolution." In WILL: 129–158.

    221 Wilson, Judith. *Essence.* 11.5 Sept. 1980: 14, 16. Rev. of *The Salt Eaters.*

Barbara Banks (1948–)

Short Fiction
    222 *Dragonseeds.* NY: St. Martin's, 1977.
    223 "Miss Esther's land." In SKLA: 229–243.
    224 "Miss Esther's land." In SMIT: 179–196.

Carol Tillery Banks

Poetry
    225 "A difference." *Essence.* 15.10 Feb. 1985: 111.

226 "Even my pain's gonna be pretty." *Essence.* 12.5 Sept. 1981: 19.

227 *Hello to Me, with Love: Poems of Self-Discovery.* NY: Morrow, 1980.

228 "Inside." *Essence.* 17.12 Apr. 1987: 110.

229 "Point of view." *Essence.* 15.10 Feb. 1985: 111.

230 "So." *Essence.* 15.10 Feb. 1985: 147.

231 "Untitled [He came quietly]." *Essence.* 15.11 Mar. 1985: 137.

232 "Untitled [Learning to lift myself higher]." *Essence.* 14.6 Oct. 1983: 88.

Amina Baraka (Sylvia Jones)

Drama

233 *What Was the Relationship of the Lone Ranger to the Means of Production? A Play in One Act.* NY: Anti-Imperialist Cultural Union, 1978.

Editing

234 Baraka, Amiri and Amina Baraka, Eds. *Confirmation: An Anthology of African-American Women.* NY: Morrow, 1983.

Poetry

235 "Afroamerican child." *Steppingstone.* 1 1984: 13–15.

236 Baraka, Amiri and Amina Baraka. *The Music: Reflections on Jazz and Blues.* NY: Morrow, 1987. Has 15 poems by Amina Baraka related to Black music; the libretto for Amiri Baraka's jazz musical *Primitive World;* 35 poems by Amiri Baraka.

237 "For the lady in color." *Black Scholar.* 12.4 July–Aug. 1981: 54–55.

238 "Haiti." In BARA: 71.

239 "Hip songs (for Larry Neal)." *Black Scholar.* 12.4 July–Aug. 1981: 55.

240 "I wanna make freedom." In BARA: 72–73.

241 "Looking for the lyrics (for Jayne Cortez)." *Black Scholar.* 12.4 July–Aug. 1981: 54.

242 "Sometime woman." *Black Amer. Lit. Forum.* 16.3 Fall 1982: 105.

243 *Songs for the Masses.* Published by author, 1979. Published under the name "Sylvia Jones."

244 "Sortin-out." *Black Amer. Lit. Forum.* 16.3 Fall 1982: 106.

245 "Sortin-out." In BARA: 73–75.

246 "Soweto song." In BARA: 70.

Textual Criticism and Interviews

247 Berry, Jason. *N.Y. Times Book Rev.* July 5, 1987: 15. Rev. of *The Music: Reflections on Jazz and Blues.*

248 Buffalo, Audreen. "A revolutionary life together." *Essence.* 16.1 May 1985: 82–84, 86, 210, 214, 216, 220. Interview, including her husband, Amiri Baraka.

249 Sims-Wood, Janet. *J. of Negro Educ.* 53 Spr. 1984: 193–194. Rev. of *Confirmation.*

250 Whitehead, Kevin. *Down Beat.* 54.8 Aug. 1987: 56. Rev. of *The Music: Reflections on Jazz and Blues.*

S. Brandi Barnes

Poetry
251 *Blackberries in the China Cabinet.* Chicago: ENAAQ, 1984.
252 "Blackberries in the china cabinet." *Black Amer. Lit. Forum.* 19.3 Fall 1985: 103.
253 "A jazz festival." *Essence.* 18.5 Sept. 1987: 149.
254 "Mourning song." *Essence.* 18.6 Oct. 1987: 134.
255 "We got stuff." *Essence.* 18.5 Sept. 1987: 156.
256 "We got stuff for the sisterhood." *Black Amer. Lit. Forum.* 19.3 Fall 1985: 103.

Jonetta Rose Barras-Abney

Poetry
257 "Blossom." *Black Scholar.* 9.7 Apr. 1978: 36–37.
258 "Even the flies are dying." *Obsidian.* 6.1–2 Spr.–Sum. 1980: 167.
259 "Identity." *Obsidian.* 7.2–3 Sum.–Wint. 1981: 192.
260 "Peace." *Black Scholar.* 11.6 July–Aug. 1980: 84.
261 "Secondline for Susan." *Obsidian.* 7.2–3 Sum.–Wint. 1981: 192.
262 "Someone could get killed." *Obsidian.* 6.1–2 Spr.–Sum. 1980: 166.
263 "Untitled [In quiet glowing]." *Obsidian.* 7.2–3 Sum.–Wint. 1981: 193.
264 "The wake." *Black Scholar.* 11.6 July–Aug. 1980: 83–84.

Short Fiction
265 "Unabstract pictures from border guards." *Black Scholar.* 12.3 May–June 1981: 17–18.

Bates, Arthenia J. *see* Millican, Arthenia J. Bates

Gwendolyn B. Bennett (1902–1981)

Poetry
266 "Advice." In STET: 75.
267 "Fantasy." In STET: 72.
268 "Hatred." In STET: 73.
269 "Heritage." In STET: 77.
270 "Secret." In STET: 74–75.
271 "Song." In STET: 73–74.
272 "To a dark girl." In SIMC: 61.
273 "To a dark girl." In STET: 76.
274 "To usward." In STET: 76–77.

Textual Criticism

275 Daniel, Walter C. and Sandra Y. Govan. "Gwendolyn Bennett (1902–1981)." In DL51: 3–10. Biography and bibliography included.

276 Perry, Margaret. In PERM: 155–157. On several works.

Lorraine Bethel

Editing

277 Bethel, Lorraine and Barbara Smith, Eds. *Conditions: Five, the Black Women's Issue.* Brooklyn, NY: Conditions, 1979. The Autumn 1979 issue of the periodical *Conditions.*

Poetry

278 "What chou mean WE, white girl." *Conditions 5.* 2.2 Aut. 1979: 86–92.

Bessie Calhoun Bird (1906–)

Poetry

279 "Proof." In STET: 83–84.

Becky Birtha (1948–)

Essays

280 "Becoming visible: the first Black lesbian conference." *New Women's Times.* Jan. 7, 1981: 3–4.

281 "Is feminist criticism really feminist?" In CRUI: 148–151.

Poetry

282 "At twenty, I began to know." *Conditions 5.* 2.2 Aut. 1979: 97.

283 "Johnnieruth." In COOP: 15–20.

284 "Maria de las rosas." *Conditions 5.* 2.2 Aut. 1979: 98–99.

285 "Maria de las rosas." In SMIT: 177–178.

286 "Smallness, Sharon." *Sinister Wisdom.* 11 Fall 1979: 92.

287 "Sun-up, second of November." *Sinister Wisdom.* 11 Fall 1979: 92.

288 "The woman in Buffalo is given to waiting." In COOP: 13–14.

289 "The woman in Buffalo is given to waiting." *Iowa Rev.* 12.2-3 Spr.-Sum. 1981: 13–14.

Short Fiction

290 *For Nights Like This One: Stories of Loving Women.* E. Palo Alto, CA: Frog in the Well, 1983.

291 "For nights like this one." In CEDA: 99–106.

292 "Leftovers." *Sinister Wisdom.* 9 Spr. 1979: 45–47.

293 "A sense of loss." *Azalea.* Spr. 1978: 28–31.

294 "We used to be best friends." *Women.* 7.1 1980: 22–28.

Lou Blackdykewomon

Poetry
    295 "By the grace of God (the goddess isis)." *Common Lives / Lesbian Lives.* 1 Fall 1981: 37–41.

Julie Blackwomon (Julie Carter)

Poetry
    296 "Ghost story II." *Sinister Wisdom.* 11 Fall 1979: 93.
    297 "Johanna Barns." *Painted Bride Q.* 23 Sum. 1984: 21–23.
    298 "Revolutionary blues." *Dyke.* 5 Fall 1977: 22.

Short Fiction
    299 "Cat." In BULK: 159–165.
    300 "Kippy." In BULK: 77–84.

S. Diane Bogus (1946–)

Essay
    301 "To my mother's vision." In CRUW: 100–111. Bogus' inspiration to be a writer.

Miscellaneous
    302 *Sapphire's Sampler.* College Corner, OH: W.I.M., 1982. Poems, essays, book reviews, etc.
    303 *W.I.M. Poetry Test.* College Corner, OH: W.I.M., 1979. A workbook to test a poet's skills.

Poetry
    304 "California redwood." *Women's Rev. of Books.* 1.11 Aug. 1984: 9.
    305 *Her Poems.* College Corner, OH: W.I.M., 1980.
    306 *Lady Godiva.* California: Published by author, 1981. Broadside.
    307 "Mayree." *Black Amer. Lit. Forum.* 14.4 Wint. 1980: 175.
    308 [Poems]. California: Published by author, 1977. Five broadsides. Includes "Blind, cripple, and crazy," "Gabble gourmet," "Slavery," "Translation," "Woman, perception poem 1."
    309 "Sister wolf." *Women's Rev. of Books.* 1.11 Aug. 1984: 9.
    310 *Woman in the Moon.* Stanford, CT: Soap Box, 1977.

Short Fiction
    311 "Dignity be thine." *Sisters United.* July–Aug. 1980: 17–21.
    312 "A measure by June." *Azalea.* 1.3 Fall 1978: 11–21.

Textual Criticism

313 Birtha, Becky. "Celebrating themselves: four self-published Black lesbian authors." *Off Our Backs.* 15.7,8,9 July–Oct. 1985: various pagings. A three-part series on Stephanie Byrd, Doris Davenport, S. Diane Bogus, and Linda Brown.

Marita Bonner (Occomy) (1899-1971)

Essay

314 "On being young—a woman—and colored." In WASA: 168-173. Originally published Dec. 1925 by *Crisis* magazine, pages 63-65.

Summary of Play

315 Southgate, Robert L. In SOUT: 129-131. Summary of *The Purple Flower* (1928).

Textual Criticism

316 Flynn, Joyce. "Marita Bonner Occomy." In DL51: 222-228. Provides biography and additional bibliography.

317 Roses, Lorraine Elena and Ruth Elizabeth Randolph. "Marita Bonner: in search of other mothers' gardens." *Black Amer. Lit. Forum.* 21.1-2 Spr.-Sum. 1987: 165-183.

Sharon Bourke

Poetry

318 "Sopranosound, memory of John." In ADOF: 177.

Candy Dawson Boyd

Children's Stories

319 *Breadsticks and Blessing Places.* NY: Macmillan, 1985. Also published in 1985 by Puffin Books, NY, under the title *Forever Friends.*

320 *Charlie Pippin.* NY: Macmillan, 1987.

321 *The Circle of Gold.* NY: Scholastic, 1984.

Melba Joyce Boyd (1950-)

Poetry

322 "Beer drops." In STET: 285-286.

323 "Beer drops." *Obsidian.* 5.1-2 Spr.-Sum. 1979: 84.

324 *Cat Eyes and Dead Wood.* Highland Park, MI: Fallen Angel, 1978.

325 "The crowd wears sunglasses." *Black Scholar.* 12.5 Sept.-Oct. 1981: 34.

326 "Detroit Renaissance sin." *First World.* 2 Spr. 1978: 38.

327 "Gramma Wynn." *Obsidian.* 5.1-2 Spr.-Sum. 1979: 83.

328 "Like fine English china." *Black Scholar.* 18.4-5 July-Aug.-Sept.-Oct. 1987: 54.

329 "Silver lace." *Black Scholar.* 10.3-4 Nov.-Dec. 1978: 46.

330 *Song for Maya.* Highland Park, MI: Broadside, [1982?].

331 "Sundown sigh." In BELL: 357-358.

332 "Sunflowers and Saturdays." In STET: 281-282.

333 "Sunflowers and Saturdays." *Obsidian.* 5.1-2 Spr.-Sum. 1979: 85.

334 "Why?" In STET: 283-284.

335 "Why?" *Obsidian.* 5.1-2 Spr.-Sum. 1979: 86.

336 "Wild strawberries in the onion field (for Maya)." *Black Scholar.* 11.8 Nov.-Dec. 1980: 76-77.

Jill Witherspoon Boyer (1947-)

Poetry

337 "Again." *Essence.* 16.10 Feb. 1986: 133.

338 *Blacksongs, Series I: Four Poetry Broadsides by Black Women.* Detroit: Lotus, 1977. Includes Boyer's "Sun song," Louise Robinson's "Woman-song," Paulette C. White's "Lost your momma," and Naomi L. Madgett's "Woman with flower."

339 *Breaking Camp.* Detroit: Lotus, 1984. On divorce and self-affirmation.

340 "But I say." *Essence.* 14.8 Dec. 1983: 140.

341 "But I say." In SIMC: 101.

342 "Detroit City." In ADOF: 68-69.

343 "Dream farmer." In ADOF: 240.

344 "King lives." In ADOF: 199.

345 "When brothers forget." In ADOF: 241.

Short Fiction

346 "Blood sisters." *Essence.* 9.6 Oct. 1978: 92-93, 150.

Textual Criticism

347 Brown, Beth. *CLA J.* 29.2 Dec. 1985: 252. Rev. of *Breaking Camp.*

Linda Brown Bragg (1939-)

Interview

348 Smith, Virginia W. and Brian J. Benson. "An interview with Linda Brown Bragg." *CLA J.* 20.1 Sept. 1976: 75-87.

Poetry

349 "Dream." *Black Scholar.* 10.3-4 Nov.-Dec. 1978: 54.

350 "My sisters speak to me." *Black Scholar.* 10.3-4 Nov.-Dec. 1978: 55.

351 "Our Blackness did not come to us whole." In ADOF: 231-232.

352 "A poem about beauty, Blackness, poetry (and how to be all three)." In ADOF: 230–231.

353 *Rainbow Roun Mah Shoulder.* Chapel Hill, NC: Carolina Wren, 1984.

Joanne M. Braxton (Jody Braxton) (1950–)

Non-Fiction
354 *Black Grandmothers: Sources of Artistic Consciousness and Personal Strength.* Wellesley, MA: Wellesley College, Center for Research on Women, 1987.

Poetry
355 "Big old houses have passed away." *Nimrod.* 21–22.2–1 1977: 30.
356 "Conversion." *Chrysalis.* 2 1977: 128–129.
357 *Sometimes I think of Maryland.* Bronx, NY: Sunbury, 1977.
358 "Sometimes I think of Maryland." In ADOF: 56–57.
359 "We lay there ageless." *Essence.* 8.10 Feb. 1978: 54.

Textual Criticism
360 Hull, Gloria T. *Conditions 4.* 2.1 Wint. 1979: 142–145. Rev. of *Sometimes I Think of Maryland.*
361 Washington, Edward T. "Joanne M. Braxton." In DL41: 42–47. Includes biography and additional bibliography.

Brent, Linda *see* Jacobs, Harriet

Britton, Mariah *see* Howard, Mariah Britton

Gwendolyn E. Brooks (1917–)

Afterword
362 "'Afterword' to *Contending Forces.*" In WASA: 433–438. Brooks wrote the "Afterword" to a 1968 edition of Pauline Hopkins' novel *Contending Forces* (1900).

Collected Works
363 *Blacks.* Chicago: The David Company, 1987. New poetry and complete texts of *A Street in Bronzeville, Annie Allen, In the Mecca,* and *Maud Martha.*

Essays
364 "The field of the fever, the time of the tall-walkers." In EVAN: 75–78. Essay on blackness from *Report from Part One: An Autobiography* (1972).
365 "Requiem before revival." In BARA: 85–86. Defining blackness.

Novels

366 "The courtship and motherhood of Maud Martha." In WASA: 406–428. Excerpt from *Maud Martha* (autobiographical novel, 1953).

367 "The rise of Maud Martha." In WASA: 429–432. First chapter in a sequel to *Maud Martha.*

Poetry

368 "The Anniad." In STET: 102–111.

369 "Appendix to 'The Anniad,' leaves from a loose-leaf war diary." In STET: 111.

370 "An aspect of love, alive in the ice and fire." In LONG: 493–494. From *Riot* (1969).

371 "Ballad of Pearl May Lee." In BLIC: 212–213.

372 "The bean eaters." In GILN: 1854–1855.

373 "The bean eaters." In STET: 101.

374 "The birth in a narrow room." In STET: 102.

375 "Black love." *Ebony.* 36.10 Aug. 1981: 29.

376 "Black love." *Ebony.* 41.1 Nov. 1985: 158.

377 "A Black wedding song." In ADOF: 108.

378 "A Black wedding song." *Poetry Now.* 3.1 1976: 7.

379 "Boys. Black." In ADOF: 84–86.

380 "Bronzeville woman in a red hat." In FISH: 252–254.

381 "Bronzeville woman in a red hat." In GILN: 1856–1858.

382 "The *Chicago Defender* sends a man to Little Rock." In LONG: 489–491.

383 "The crazy woman." In GILN: 1856.

384 "Five men against the theme 'My name is red hot. Yo name ain doodley squat.'" In ADOF: 244–245.

385 "For Dudley Randall." *Black World.* 25.3 Jan. 1976: 91.

386 "Friend." In ADOF: 106.

387 "Jessie Mitchell's mother." In GILN: 1855–1856.

388 "Kitchenette building." In FISH: 251.

389 "Langston Hughes is merry glory." *Steppingstone.* Wint. 1984: 11.

390 "The last quatrain of the ballad of Emmett Till." In ADOF: 193.

391 "Life for my child is simple." In LONG: 491–492.

392 "The lovers of the poor." In BLIC: 332–334.

393 "Malcolm X." In ADOF: 181.

394 "Malcolm X." *Steppingstone.* Wint. 1983: 13.

395 "Martin Luther King, Jr." In ADOF: 196.

396 "Mentors." In LONG: 486.

397 "The mother." In FER2: 137–138.

398 "The mother." In GILN: 1853–1854.

399 "The mother." In LONG: 487–488.

400 "The mother." In STET: 100–101.

401 "The old marrieds." In FISH: 251–252.

402 "Paul Robeson." In ADOF: 209.

403 "Piano after war." In LONG: 485.

404 "The poetry of Gwendolyn Brooks." *Ebony.* 39.6 Apr. 1984: 78–80, 82.

Includes "To Black women," "When you have forgotten Sunday: the love story," "We real cool," "Malcolm X," "Speech to the young, Speech to the progress-toward," "Young Afrikans of the furious."

405 *Primer for Blacks.* Chicago: Black Position, 1980.

406 "Primer for Blacks." In BARA: 82–83.

407 "Queen of the blues." In GILN: 1858–1860.

408 "Riot." In GILN: 1861.

409 "A song in the front yard." *Harper's.* 269 Aug. 1984: 47.

410 "Takes time." In LONG: 492–493. From *In the Mecca* (1968).

411 "Telephone conversations." *Black Amer. Lit. Forum.* 17.4 Wint. 1983: 148.

412 *To Disembark.* Chicago: Third World, 1981.

413 "To those of my sisters who kept their naturals." In BARA: 84–85.

414 "We real cool." In LONG: 488.

415 "Weaponed woman." In SIMC: 88.

416 "What shall I give my children?" In FISH: 252.

417 "'When handed a lemon, make lemonade.'" *Poetry Now.* 3.1 1976: 7.

418 "When you have forgotten Sunday: the love story." *Ebony.* 36 Aug. 1981: 54. Excerpt from *A Street in Bronzeville* (1945).

419 "When you have forgotten Sunday: the love story." In DAHL: 333.

420 "The womanhood." In GILN: 1854. Excerpt (stanza 3).

Summary of Novel

421 Southgate, Robert L. In SOUT: 114–115. Summary of *Maud Martha.*

Textual Criticism and Interviews

422 Anderson, Kamili. "*Belles Lettres* interviews." *Belles Lettres.* 1.3 Jan.-Feb. 1986: 9–10.

423 Andrews, Larry R. "Ambivalent clothes imagery in Gwendolyn Brooks's 'The Sundays of Satin-legs Smith.'" *CLA J.* 24.2 Dec. 1980: 150–163.

424 Brown, Martha H. "*Great Lakes Review* interview: Gwendolyn Brooks." *Great Lakes Rev.* 6.1 Sum. 1979: 48–55.

425 Christian, Barbara. "Nuance and the novella: a study of Gwendolyn Brooks's *Maud Martha.*" In CHRF: 127–141.

426 Dash, Irene. "The literature of birth and abortion." *Regionalism and the Female Imagination.* 3 Spr. 1977: 8–13.

427 Davis, Marianna. In DAVI: 170–173, 175–176. On several works.

428 DeMontreville, Doris, Ed. "Gwendolyn Brooks." In DEMO: 59–61. Mostly biography.

429 Fuller, H.W. "*Primer for Blacks.*" *First World.* 2.4 1980: 43. A review.

430 Gayle, Addison, Jr. "Gwendolyn Brooks: poet of the whirlwind." In EVAN: 79–87.

431 Gould, Jean. "Gwendolyn Brooks." In GOUL: 176–209. On several works.

432 Greasley, Philip A. "Gwendolyn Brooks: the emerging poetic voice." *Great Lakes Rev.* 10.2 Fall 1984: 14–23.

433 Guy-Sheftall, Beverly. "The women of Bronzeville." In BELL: 157–170.

434 Hansell, William. "Essences, unifyings, and Black militancy: major themes in Gwendolyn Brooks's *Family Pictures* (1971) and *Beckonings* (1975)." *Black Amer. Lit. Forum.* 11.2 Sum. 1977: 63–66. Study of collections of her poetry.

435 Hansell, William. "The poet-militant and foreshadowings of a Black mystique: poems in the second period of Gwendolyn Brooks." *Concerning Poetry.* 10.2 Fall 1977: 37–45.

436 Hansell, William. "The uncommon commonplace in the early poems of Gwendolyn Brooks." *CLA J.* 30.3 Mar. 1987: 261–277.

437 Harris, Victoria F. "The voice of Gwendolyn Brooks." *Interpretations.* 11 1979: 56–66.

438 Hull, Gloria T. and Posey Gallagher. "Update on *Part One:* an interview with Gwendolyn Brooks." *CLA J.* 21.1 Sept. 1977: 19–40. *Report from Part One: The Autobiography of Gwendolyn Brooks* was published in 1972.

439 "Interview." *Triquarterly.* 60 Spr.–Sum. 1984: 405–410. Self-interview.

440 Israel, Charles. "Gwendolyn Brooks." In DL05: 100–106. Includes biography and additional bibliography.

441 Janssen, Ronald R. "Brooks's 'A song in the front yard.'" *Explicator.* 43.3 Spr. 1985: 42–43. On her poem.

442 Juhasz, Suzanne. "'A sweet inspiration . . . of my people': the poetry of Gwendolyn Brooks and Nikki Giovanni." In JUHA: 144–176.

443 Kent, George. *Black Books Bull.* 7.3 1981: 44–46. Rev. of *To Disembark.*

444 Kent, George. "Gwendolyn Brooks' poetic realism: a developmental survey." In EVAN: 88–105.

445 Kent, George. "Gwendolyn Brooks: portrait, in part, of the artist as a young girl and apprentice writer." *Callaloo.* 2 Oct. 1979: 74.

446 Kufrin, Joan. In KUFR 34–51. On several works.

447 Lattin, Patricia H. and Vernon E. Lattin. "Dual vision in Gwendolyn Brooks's *Maud Martha.*" *Critique.* 25.4 Sum. 1984: 180–187.

448 Lupack, Alan C. *Explicator.* 36.4 Sum. 1978: 2–3. On the poem 'Piano after war.'

449 Madhubuti, Haki R. *Say That the River Turns: The Impact of Gwendolyn Brooks.* Chicago: Third World, 1987.

450 Martin, Herbert W. *Great Lakes Rev.* 9–10.2–1 Fall 1983–Spr. 1984: 109–112.

451 Melhem, D.H. *Gwendolyn Brooks: Poetry and the Heroic Voice.* Lexington, KY: Univ. Pr. of Kentucky, 1987.

452 Melhem, D.H. "Gwendolyn Brooks: the heroic voice of prophecy." *Studies in Black Lit.* 8.1 Spr. 1977: 1–3.

453 Miller, R. Baxter. "'Define . . . the whirlwind': Gwendolyn Brooks' epic sign for a generation." In MILP: 160–173.

454 Miller, R. Baxter. "'Define . . . the whirlwind': *In the Mecca*—urban setting, shifting narrator and redemptive vision." *Obsidian.* 4 Spr. 1978: 19–31.

455 Miller, R. Baxter. *Langston Hughes and Gwendolyn Brooks: A Reference Guide.* Boston: G.K. Hall, 1978.

456 Mootry, Maria. "Brooks's 'A Bronzeville mother loiters in Mississippi, meanwhile a Mississippi mother burns bacon.'" *Explicator.* 42.4 Sum. 1984: 51–52.

457 Mootry, Maria. "'Chocolate Mabbie' and 'Pearl May Lee': Gwendolyn Brooks and the ballad tradition." *CLA J.* 30.3 March 1987: 278–293.

458 Mootry, Maria and Gary Smith, Eds. *A Life Distilled: Critical Essays on Gwendolyn Brooks.* Urbana: Univ. of Illinois, 1987.

459 Noble, Jeanne. In NOBL: 179–182. On several works.

460 Nykoruk, Barbara, Ed. "Gwendolyn Brooks." In AUTH: 63. Mostly biography.

461 Park, Clara C. *Nation.* Sept. 26, 1987: 308–312. Rev. of D.H. Melhem's *Gwendolyn Brooks: Poetry and the Heroic Voice* and Maria K. Mootry's and Gary Smith's *A Life Distilled: Gwendolyn Brooks.* Chronicles Brooks' literary career.

462 Park, Sue S. "A study in tension: Gwendolyn Brooks's 'The *Chicago Defender* sends a man to Little Rock.'" *Black Amer. Lit. Forum.* 11.1 Spr. 1977: 32–34.

463 Shaw, Harry B. *Gwendolyn Brooks.* Boston: G.K. Hall, 1980.

464 Shaw, Harry B. "Perceptions of men in the early works of Gwendolyn Brooks." In MILP: 136–159.

465 Sims, Barbara B. *Explicator.* 34.8 Apr. 1976: Item 58. On the poem "We real cool."

466 Smith, Gary. "Gwendolyn Brooks's *A Street in Bronzeville:* the Harlem Renaissance and the mythologies of Black women." In BLOO: 205–216.

467 Smith, Gary. "Gwendolyn Brooks's *A Street in Bronzeville:* the Harlem Renaissance and the mythologies of Black women." *Melus.* 10.3 Fall 1983: 33–46.

468 Spillers, Hortense J. "Gwendolyn the terrible: propositions on eleven poems." In GILS: 233–244.

469 Spillers, Hortense J. "'An order of constancy': notes on Brooks and the feminine." *Centennial Rev.* 29.2 Spr. 1985: 223–248.

470 Stern, Frederick C. "The 'populist' politics of Gwendolyn Brooks's poetry." *Midamerica, Yearbook of the Society for the Study of Midwestern Literature.* 12 1985: 111–119.

471 Stetson, Erlene. "*Songs After Sunset (1935–1936):* Gwendolyn Elizabeth Brooks." *CLA J.* 24.1 Sept. 1980: 87–96.

472 Struthers, Ann. "Gwendolyn Brooks' children." *Iowa English Bulletin: Yearbook.* 29.1 1979: 15–16.

473 Washington, Mary Helen. "Plain, Black, and decently wild: the heroic possibilities of Maud Martha." In ABEL: 270–286.

474 Washington, Mary Helen. "'Taming all that anger down': rage and silence in Gwendolyn Brooks' *Maud Martha.*" *Massachusetts Rev.* 24.2 Sum. 1983: 453–466.

475 Washington, Mary Helen. "'Taming all that anger down': rage and silence in Gwendolyn Brooks's *Maud Martha.*" In GATE: 249–262.

476 Washington, Mary Helen. "'Taming all that anger down': rage and silence in the writing of Gwendolyn Brooks." In WASA: 387–405.

477 Werner, Craig. "Gwendolyn Brooks: tradition in black and white." *Minority Voices.* 1.2 Fall 1977: 27–38.

478 Whitaker, Charles. "A poet for all ages." *Ebony.* 42.8 June 1987: 154, 156, 158, 160, 162. Mostly biography.

479 Williams, Gladys Margaret. "Gwendolyn Brooks's way with the sonnet." *CLA J.* 26.2 Dec. 1982: 215–240.

Beth Brown

Poetry
480 "Ancestors." *Obsidian*. 6.1–2 Spr.–Sum. 1980: 206.
481 "Blind music." *Black Scholar*. 11.5 May–June 1980: 72.
482 "Daily poems." *Obsidian*. 4.3 Wint. 1978: 84–88.
483 "For whom it is too late now." *Obsidian*. 4.3 Wint. 1978: 83.
484 "House arrest." *Obsidian*. 6.1–2 Spr.–Sum. 1980: 205.
485 *Lightyears: Poems, 1973–1976*. Detroit: Lotus, 1982.
486 "Sisters." *Black Scholar*. 11.5 May–June 1980: 73.
487 "Winter's end." *Obsidian*. 6.1–2 Spr.–Sum. 1980: 204.
488 "Woman without shadow." *Greenfield Rev*. 11.1–2 Sum.–Fall 1983: 119.

Short Fiction
489 "Sunshine and the troubadours." *Black Scholar*. 9.10 July–Aug. 1978: 11–17.

Linda Jean Brown

Essays
490 "Dark horse: a view of writing and publishing by dark lesbians." *Sinister Wisdom*. 13 Spr. 1980: 45–50. Part of an entire issue on lesbian writing and publishing.
491 *Kiwi*. Published by author, 1978.

Poetry
492 *To Be More Real*. NY: Published by author, 1976.

Short Fiction
493 "Jazz dancin wif mama." In CRUW: 57–60.
494 *Jazz Dancin wif Mama*. NY: Iridian, 1981.
495 "Osceola and Daly." *Sinister Wisdom*. 12 Wint. 1980: 22–26.
496 *The Rainbow River*. NY: Iridian, 1980.

Textual Criticism
497 Birtha, Becky. "Celebrating themselves: four self-published Black lesbian authors." *Off Our Backs*. 15.7,8,9 July–Oct. 1985: various pagings. A three-part series on Stephanie Byrd, Doris Davenport, S. Diane Bogus, and Linda Brown.

Wilmette Brown

Poetry
498 "Bushpaths." *Conditions 1*. 1.1 Apr. 1977: 30.

Mary Burrill (1879-1946)

Drama
    499 "Aftermath." In FRAN: 55-61.

Margaret T.G. Burroughs (1917-)

Poetry
    500 "Black pride." In STET: 118-120.
    501 "Everybody but me." In STET: 121-122.
    502 "Only in this way." In STET: 120-121.
    503 "To Soulfolk." In STET: 118.

Textual Criticism
    504 Dickerson, Mary Jane. "Margaret T.G. Burroughs." In DL41: 47-54. Biography and bibliography included.

Della Burt (1944-)

Poetry
    505 "A little girl's dream world." In STET: 162-163.
    506 "On the death of Lisa Lyman." In STET: 163.
    507 "Spirit flowers." In STET: 161-162.

Olivia Ward Bush-Banks (1869-1944)

Textual Criticism
    508 Guillaume, Bernice F. "Olivia Ward Bush: factors shaping the social and cultural outlook of a nineteenth-century writer." *Negro History Bull.* 43.2 Apr.-May-June 1980: 32-34.

Octavia E. Butler (1947-)

Bibliography
    509 Weixlmann, Joe. "An Octavia E. Butler bibliography." *Black Amer. Lit. Forum.* 18.11 Spr. 1984: 88-89. The bibliography provides an extensive list of criticisms of Ms. Butler's works in both general and in science fiction periodicals.

Novels
    510 *Clay's Ark.* NY: St. Martin's, 1984.
    511 *Dawn: Xenogenesis.* NY: Warner, 1987.
    512 *Kindred.* Garden City, NY: Doubleday, 1979.
    513 *Mind of My Mind.* NY: Avon, 1977.

514 *Patternmaster.* Garden City, NY: Doubleday, 1976.

515 *Survivor.* Garden City, NY: Doubleday, 1978.

516 *Wild Seed.* Garden City, NY: Doubleday, 1980.

517 *Wild Seed* [Excerpt]. *Essence.* 11.9 Jan. 1981: 86–87, 91, 93, 95, 99–100, 119, 121–122.

Short Fiction
518 "Bloodchild." In CARR: 258–277.

Textual Criticism
519 Beal, Frances M. "Black women and the science fiction genre." *Black Scholar.* 17.2 Mar.–Apr. 1986: 14–18. Interview.

520 Blagden, N. "Otherworldly women." *Life.* 7.8 July 1984: 112–117. Butler's picture appears on page 116 with a paragraph of commentary.

521 Fleming, Robert. *Encore Amer. and Worldwide News.* Sept. 17, 1979: 51. Rev. of *Kindred.*

522 Foster, Frances Smith. "Octavia Butler's Black female future fiction." *Extrapolation.* 23.1 Spr. 1982: 37–49.

523 Friend, Beverly. "Time travel as a feminist didactic in works by Phyllis Eisenstein, Marlys Millhiser, and Octavia Butler." *Extrapolation.* 23.1 Spr. 1982: 50–55.

524 Mixon, Veronica. "Futurist woman: Octavia Butler." *Essence.* 9.12 Apr. 1979: 12, 15. On her life and work.

525 O'Connor, Margaret Anne. "Octavia E. Butler." In DL33: 35–41. Includes biography and additional bibliography.

526 Salvaggio, Ruth, *et al. Suzy McKee Charnas, Octavia Butler and Joan Vinge.* Mercer Island, WA: Starmont House, 1985.

527 Shinn, Thelma J. "The wise witches: Black women mentors in the fiction of Octavia E. Butler." In PRYS: 203–215.

528 Terrell, Eve Ruth. *Black Books Bull.* 6.4 1980: 77. Review of *Kindred.*

529 Weinkauf, Mary S. "Octavia Estelle Butler." In SMTC: 109–110. Biography and bibliography.

530 Weinkauf, Mary S. "So much for the gentle sex." *Extrapolation.* 26.3 Fall 1985: 231–239. On Butler and other female science fiction writers.

531 Williams, Sherley Anne. "Sherley Anne Williams on Octavia E. Butler." *Ms.* 14.9 Mar. 1986: 70, 72, 74. General article.

532 Wilson, Judith. "Hallowed ground: sci-fi and genius." *Essence.* 9.11 Mar. 1979: 17. Rev. of *Survivor.*

Stephanie Byrd

Poetry
533 *A Distant Footstep on the Plain.* Published by author, 1981.

534 "I asked her to smile." *Sinister Wisdom.* 10 Sum. 1979: 87.

535 "A peck from a peck." *Sinister Wisdom.* 9 Spr. 1979: 44.

536 "Sham." *Sinister Wisdom.* 9 Spr. 1979: 44.

537 *Twenty-Five Years of Malcontent.* Boston: Good Gay Poets, 1976.

Textual Criticism

538 Birtha, Becky. "Celebrating themselves: four self-published Black lesbian authors." *Off Our Backs*. 15.7,8,9 July–Oct. 1985: various pagings. A three-part series on Stephanie Byrd, Doris Davenport, S. Diane Bogus, and Linda Brown.

Jeannette Caines

Children's Stories

539 *Chilly Stomach*. NY: Harper, 1986.
540 *Daddy*. NY: Harper, 1977.
541 *Just Us Women*. NY: Harper, 1982.
542 *Window Wishing*. NY: Harper, 1980.

Textual Criticism

543 Abdal-Haqq, Ismat. *Interracial Books for Children Bull.* 12.3 1981: 17. Rev. of *Window Wishing*.
544 Julian, Bea. *Encore Amer. and Worldwide News.* 9.9 Dec. 1981: 36. Rev. of *Window Wishing*.
545 Moore, Emily R. *Interracial Books for Children Bull.* 8.6–7 1977: 32. Rev. of *Daddy*.
546 Raymond, A. "Jeannette Caines: a proud author, with good reason." *Early Years*. 13.7 Mar. 1983: 24–25. Some biography.
547 Viorst, Judith. *N.Y. Times Book Rev.* Apr. 17, 1977: 50. Rev. of *Daddy*.

Annetta Elam Capdeville (1925–)

Poetry

548 *My Soul Sings: Lyrics*. Washington, DC: Published by author, 1978.

Carmen, Marilyn *see* Eshe, Aisha

Pandoura Carpenter

Poetry

549 *Deal with It!* Denver: She Wolf, 1979.

Vinette Carroll (1922–)

Biography

550 Harris, Jessica. "Broadway's new breed: Black producers on the Great White Way." *Essence*. 8.8 Dec. 1977: 72.

551 Peterson, Maurice. "Spotlight on Vinette Carroll." *Essence.* 7.11 Mar. 1976: 8.

Carter, Julie *see* Blackwomon, Julie

Barbara Chase-Riboud (1939-)

Novels

552 *Portrait of a Nude Woman as Cleopatra.* NY: Morrow, 1987. A "verse novel."

553 *Sally Hemings.* NY: Viking, 1979.

554 *Valide.* NY: Morrow, 1986.

Textual Criticism

555 Ahrold, Kyle. "Sally Hemings and Thomas Jefferson: the love story that belongs to us all." *Encore Amer. and Worldwide News.* July 2, 1979: 30–32, 34–36.

556 Brook, Valerie. *New Republic.* July 7, 1979: 38–39. Rev. of *Sally Hemings.*

557 Cleaver, Carole. *National Rev.* Dec. 21, 1979: 1638. Rev. of *Sally Hemings.*

558 Gillespie, Marcia. "The seraglio, the plantation—intrigue and survival." *Ms.* 15.3 Sept. 1986: 20–21. Rev. of *Valide.*

559 Levin, Martin. *N.Y. Times Book Rev.* Oct. 28, 1979: 14. Rev. of *Sally Hemings.*

560 McHenry, Susan. "*Sally Hemings:* a key to our national identity." *Ms.* 9.4 Oct. 1980: 35–40.

561 McMurran, K. "New Black novelist explores Thomas Jefferson's love affair with a beautiful slave." *People Weekly.* Oct. 8, 1979: 97–98.

562 Page, James A. *Black Scholar.* 11.4 Mar.-Apr. 1980: 86–87. Rev. of *Sally Hemings.*

563 Richardson, Marilyn. "Barbara Chase-Riboud." In DL33: 43–48. Includes biography and additional bibliography.

564 Smith, Wendy. *N.Y. Times Book Rev.* Aug. 10, 1986: 22. Rev. of *Valide.*

565 Wilson, Judith. "Barbara Chase-Riboud: sculpting our history." *Essence.* 10.8 Dec. 1979: 12–13.

Chesimard, Joanne *see* Shakur, Assata

Alice Childress (1920-)

Children's Plays

566 *Let's Hear It for the Queen.* NY: Coward, 1976.

Children's Stories
567 *Rainbow Jordan.* NY: Coward, 1980.

Drama
568 *Wedding Band.* In MOOR: 255–337. Play was written in 1973.
569 *Wedding Band.* In WILK: 69–133.
570 *Wine in the Wilderness.* In FER2: 443–474. Written in 1969.

Essays
571 "A candle in a gale wind." In EVAN: 111–116. On writing.
572 "Knowing the human condition." In MILL: 8–10.
573 "A woman playwright speaks her mind." In PATT: 75–79.

Novels
574 *A Short Walk.* NY: Coward, 1979.

Summary of Work
575 Southgate, Robert L. In SOUT: 81–82. Summary of *A Hero Ain't Nothin' But a Sandwich* (1973 children's story).

Textual Criticism and Interviews
576 Austin, Gayle. "Alice Childress: Black woman playwright as feminist critic." *Southern Q.* 25.3 Spr. 1987: 52–62.
577 Brown, Janet. In BROW: 56–70. On *Wine in the Wilderness.*
578 Brown-Guillory, Elizabeth. "Alice Childress: a pioneering spirit." *Sage.* 4.1 Spr. 1987: 66–68. Interview.
579 Brown-Guillory, Elizabeth. "Images of Blacks in plays by Black women." *Phylon.* 47.3 Sept. 1986: 230–237. On *Wine in the Wilderness.*
580 Commire, Anne. "Alice Childress." In CO48: 50–56. Biography and comments on work.
581 Curb, Rosemary. "Alice Childress." In DL07: 118–124. Has biography and bibliography.
582 Curb, Rosemary. "An unfashionable tragedy of American racism: Alice Childress's *Wedding Band.*" *Melus.* 7.4 Wint. 1980: 57–68.
583 Harris, Trudier. "Alice Childress." In DL38: 66–79. Has biography and bibliography.
584 Harris, Trudier. "Beyond the uniform: Alice Childress, *Like One of the Family.*" In HARS: 111–133.
585 Harris, Trudier. "'I wish I was a poet': the character as artist in Alice Childress's *Like One of the Family.*" *Black Amer. Lit. Forum.* 14.1 Spr. 1980: 24–30.
586 Hay, Samuel A. "Alice Childress's dramatic structure." In EVAN: 117–128.
587 Hill, E.R. "A hero for the movies." In STRE: 236–243. On *A Hero Ain't Nothin' but a Sandwich.*
588 Holliday, Polly. "I remember Alice Childress." *Southern Q.* 25.3 Spr. 1987: 63–65. Biographical article.
589 Holtze, Sally Holmes. In HOLT: 65–67. Mostly biographical.

590 Killens, John O. "The literary genius of Alice Childress." In EVAN: 129–133.

591 Richarson, Eni Carol. *Black Books Bull.* 7.3 1981: 65. Rev. of *Rainbow Jordan.*

592 Walker, Alice. "A walk through twentieth-century Black America." *Ms.* 8.6 Dec. 1979: 46, 48. Rev. of *A Short Walk.*

593 Wilson, Geraldine L. *Interracial Books for Children Bull.* 12.7–8 1981: 24–25. Rev. of *Rainbow Jordan.*

594 Wilson, Judith. *Essence.* 10.11 Mar. 1980: 18. Rev. of *A Short Walk.*

Robin Christian

Poetry
595 *Lady, These Are for You.* NY: Published by author, 1978.

Cheryl Clarke

Essays
596 "The failure to transform: homophobia in the Black community." In SMIT: 197–208.

597 "Lesbianism: an act of resistance." In MORA: 128–137.

Poetry
598 "Committed sex." *Conditions.* 13 1986: 110.

599 "Indira." *American Voice.* 3 Sum. 1986: 20–22.

600 "Journal entry: qualification." *Sinister Wisdom.* 28 1985: 10–12.

601 *Living as a Lesbian: Poetry.* Ithaca, NY: Firebrand, 1986.

602 "A mother's story." *Feminist Studies.* 9.3 Fall 1983: 523–525. From *Narratives.*

603 *Narratives: Poems in the Tradition of Black Women.* NY: Kitchen Table: Women of Color, 1982.

Short Fiction
604 "Women of summer." In SMIT: 230–254.

Textual Criticism
605 Clarke, Cheryl, *et al.* "*Narratives:* a dramatic event." *Heresies.* 17 1984: 74–75. Discussion of the 1982 performance version of Cheryl Clarke's book of poems.

606 Davies, Carole Boyce. "*Living as a Lesbian.*" *Off Our Backs.* 17.4 Apr. 1987: 17. Rev. of Clarke's book.

607 Hernton, Calvin. "The tradition." *Parnassus.* 12–13.2–1 Spr.–Sum.–Fall–Wint. 1985: 541–543. On her book *Narratives.* Article includes other poets.

608 Parkerson, Michelle. *Off Our Backs.* 13.4 Apr. 1983: 17. Rev. of *Narratives.*

Cleage, Pearl *see* Lomax, Pearl Cleage

Clemmons, Carole G. *see* Gregory, Carole Clemmons

Michelle Cliff

Editing
609 Cliff, Michelle, Ed. *The Winner Names the Age: A Collection of Writings by Lillian Smith.* NY: Norton, 1978. Lillian Smith (1897–1966) was an anti-racist activist.

Essays
610 "Anonymity and the denial of the self." *Sinister Wisdom.* 9 Spr. 1979: 62–71.

611 "Object into subject: some thoughts on the work of Black women artists." *Heresies.* 4.3 1982: 35–40. Includes commentary on authors.

612 "The resonance of interruption." *Chrysalis.* 8 Sum. 1979: 29–37. On women and creativity.

613 "Sister/outsider: some thoughts on Simone Weil." In ASCH: 310–325.

Novels
614 *Abeng.* Trumansburg, NY: The Crossing, 1984.

615 *No Telephone to Heaven.* NY: Dutton, 1987.

Poetry
616 "Against granite." *Heresies.* 2.4 Sum. 1979: 49.

617 *Claiming an Identity They Taught Me to Despise.* Watertown, MA: Persephone, 1980.

618 "A history of costume." *Conditions 4.* 2.1 Wint. 1979: 100–103. A prose poem.

619 "Obsolete geography." *Conditions 3.* 1.3 Spr. 1978: 44–49.

620 "Travel notes." In COOP: 32–35.

621 "Travel notes." *Iowa Rev.* 12.2–3 1981: 32–35.

Poetry and Prose
622 *The Land of Look Behind: Poetry and Prose by Michelle Cliff.* Ithaca, NY: Firebrand, 1985.

Textual Criticism and Interviews
623 Congo, Theresa. *Off Our Backs.* 11.2 Feb. 1981: 21. Rev. of *Claiming an Identity They Taught Me to Despise.*

624 Hodges, Beth. *Gay Community News.* Feb. 7, 1981: 8–9. Interview.

625 Sabrina. *Conditions.* 13 1986: 189–191. Rev. of *The Land of Look Behind.*

626 Smilowitz, Erika J. "Tales of the Caribbean." *Women's Rev. of Books.* 5.2 Nov. 1987: 13–14. Rev. of *No Telephone to Heaven.*

Carrie Williams Clifford (1882-1958)

Poetry
627 "The Black draftee from Dixie." In STET: 82-83.

Lucille Clifton (1936-)

Autobiography
628 *Generations: A Memoir.* NY: Random, 1976.
629 "Lucy." In FISH: 208-213. From *Generations.*

Children's Stories
630 *Amifika.* NY: Dutton, 1977.
631 *Everett Anderson's Friend.* NY: Holt, 1976.
632 *Everett Anderson's One-Two-Three.* NY: Holt, 1977.
633 *Everett Anderson's Nine Month Long.* NY: Holt, 1978.
634 *Everett Anderson's Goodbye.* NY: Holt, 1983.
635 *Everett Anderson's Goodbye* [Excerpt]. *Ms.* 13.12 June 1985: 83-84. In the column "Stories for Free Children."
636 *The Lucky Stone.* NY: Delacorte, 1979.
637 *My Friend Jacob.* NY: Dutton, 1980.
638 *Sonora Beautiful.* NY: Dutton, 1981.
639 *Three Wishes.* NY: Viking, 1976.

Editing
640 *Hoo-Doo 5.* DeRidder, LA: Energy Black South, 1976. Special woman's issue of the periodical, edited by Clifton, Anna Khalil, and Audre Lorde.

Essays
641 "A simple language." In EVAN: 137-138. On writing.
642 "So far." In HEYE: 34. Prose piece accompanying poems following in the anthology.
643 "We are the grapevine." *Essence.* 16.1 May 1985: 129. On the strength of women.

Poetry
644 "Admonitions." In GILN: 2255-2256.
645 "Africa." In ADOF: 2.
646 "Anna speaks of the childhood of Mary her daughter." In GILN: 2256-2257.
647 "The astrologer predicts at Mary's birth." In GILN: 2256.
648 "Confession." In HEYE: 40.
649 "Explanations." In HEYE: 38.

650 "For deLawd." In ADOF: 40–41.
651 "For her (if our grandchild be a girl)." In BARA: 87.
652 "For the blind." *Nimrod.* 21–22.2–1 1977: 54.
653 "Forgiving my father." In HEYE: 34–35.
654 "Friends come." In HEYE: 39.
655 "God send Easter." In ADOF: 224–225.
656 "Good times." In ADOF: 41–42.
657 "Holy night." In GILN: 2257.
658 "Holy night." In HEYE: 35–36.
659 "Homage to my hips." *Ms.* 9.6 Dec. 1980: 42.
660 "How is he coming then." In GILN: 2257.
661 "I once knew a man." In HEYE: 35.
662 "In Salem (to Jeanette)." *Mundus Artium.* 12–13 1980–1981: 184.
663 "In the inner city." In ADOF: 65.
664 "Island Mary." In GILN: 2258.
665 "Leanna's poem." *Essence.* 10.8 Dec. 1979: 22.
666 "Listen children." *Essence.* 14.6 Oct. 1983: 88.
667 "Listen children." In ADOF: 103.
668 "The lost baby poem." In STET: 247.
669 "Malcolm." In ADOF: 180.
670 "Mary's dream." In GILN: 2257.
671 "Miss Rosie." In ADOF: 40.
672 "Miss Rosie." In FER2: 434.
673 "Miss Rosie." In STET: 248.
674 "Morning mirror." In BARA: 88.
675 "My boys." *Essence.* 10.8 Dec. 1979: 22.
676 "My dream about being white." In BARA: 87.
677 "My dream about the cows." *Virginia Q. Rev.* 58.4 Aut. 1982: 687.
678 "My dream about the inevitability of the second coming." *Virginia Q. Rev.* 58.4 Aut. 1982: 688.
679 "My dream about time." *Virginia Q. Rev.* 58.4 Aut. 1982: 687.
680 "My mama moved among the days." In STET: 248.
681 "New bones." *Mundus Artium.* 12–13 1980–1981: 184.
682 "One village." *Nimrod.* 21–22.2–1 1977: 55.
683 "Perhaps." In HEYE: 38.
684 "The raising of Lazarus." In ADOF: 151.
685 "Sisters." *Essence.* 11.1 May 1980: 102.
686 "A song of Mary." In GILN: 2258.
687 "Testament." In HEYE: 36–37.
688 "There is a girl inside." *Amer. Poetry Rev.* 6.1 Jan.–Feb. 1977: 21.
689 "Those boys that ran together." In ADOF: 102.
690 "To Bobby Seale." In ADOF: 208.
691 "To Joan." In HEYE: 39–40.
692 *Two-Headed Woman.* Amherst: Univ. of Massachusetts, 1980.
693 "Untitled [I went to the valley]." In ADOF: 57–58.
694 "Untitled [In populated]." In HEYE: 41.
695 "Untitled [Incandescence]." In HEYE: 37.

696 "Untitled [Light that came]." In HEYE: 36.

697 "Untitled [Mother, i am]." In HEYE: 37–38.

698 "What I want to do (for Alice Smith who will understand completely)." *Nimrod.* 21–22.2–1 1977: 54.

Textual Criticism and Interviews

699 Abdal-Haqq, I. *Interracial Books for Children Bull.* 12.2 1981: 20. Rev. of *My Friend Jacob.*

700 Ahrold, Kyle. *Encore.* 7.13 July 10, 1978: 38–39. Rev. of *Amifika.*

701 Baughman, Ronald. In DL05: 132–136. Has biography and bibliography.

702 Beckles, Frances N. In BECK: 36–41. Mostly biography.

703 Commire, Anne. In CO20: 20–23. Some biography and bibliography.

704 Copeland, Hazel. *Black Books Bull.* 4.2 Sum. 1976: 63–64. Rev. of *Everett Anderson's Year.*

705 Dill, Barbara. *Wilson Library Bull.* 52.1 Sept. 1977: 78–79. Biographical article.

706 Edwards, Lynn. *Interracial Books for Children Bull.* 8.1 1977: 19–20. Rev. of *Three Wishes.*

707 Graham, Beryl. *Black Books Bull.* 7.1 1980: 55. Rev. of *The Lucky Stone.*

708 Grimes, Nikki. *Children's Book Rev. Service.* 6.4 Dec. 1977: 31. Rev. of *Amifika.*

709 Holtze, Sally Holmes. In HOLT: 72–73. Mostly biography.

710 *Interracial Books for Children Bull.* 10.5 1979: 17–18. Rev. of *Everett Anderson's Nine Month Long.*

711 *Interracial Books for Children Bull.* 11.1–2 1980: 28. Rev. of *The Lucky Stone.*

712 Johnson, Joyce. "The theme of celebration in Lucille Clifton's poetry." *Pacific Coast Philology.* 18.1–2 Nov. 1983: 70–76.

713 Lowe, Cynthia. *Black Books Bull.* 5.1 Spr. 1977: 61. Rev. of *Three Wishes.*

714 Madhubuti, Haki. "Lucille Clifton: warm water, greased legs, and dangerous poetry." In EVAN: 150–160.

715 McCluskey, Audrey T. "Tell the good news: a view of the works of Lucille Clifton." In EVAN: 139–149.

716 Peppers, Wallace R. "Lucille Clifton." In DL41: 55–60. Has biography and bibliography.

717 Scarupa, Harriet Jackson. "Lucille Clifton: making the world 'poem-up'." *Ms.* 5.4 Oct. 1976: 118, 120, 123.

718 Sutherland, Zena. *Bull. of the Center for Children's Books.* 32.8 Apr. 1979: 132. Rev. of *Everett Anderson's Nine Month Long.*

719 Sutherland, Zena. *Bull. of the Center for Children's Books.* 34.1 Sept. 1980: 4. Rev. of *My Friend Jacob.*

720 Ward, Jerry W. *New Orleans Rev.* 5.4 1977: 369–370. Rev. of *Generations.*

721 Wilson, Geraldine L. *Interracial Books for Children Bull.* 15.3 1984: 16. Rev. of *Everett Anderson's Goodbye.*

Michelle T. Clinton

Poetry

    722 "Debra." *Conditions 5.* 2.2 Aut. 1979: 121–122.

    723 "Debra." In SMIT: 13–14.

    724 "For strong women." *Conditions 5.* 2.2 Aut. 1979: 118–120.

    725 "For strong women." In SMIT: 325–327.

    726 *High Blood Pressure.* Los Angeles: West End, 1986.

Flyin' Thunda Cloud

Poetry

    727 *A Small Pain.* College Corner, OH: W.I.M., 1984.

Alice S. Cobb (1942–)

Poetry

    728 "Angela Davis." In STET: 147.

    729 "The searching." *Essence.* 15.5 Sept. 1984: 175.

    730 "The searching." In STET: 146–147.

    731 "To Erroll Garner." *Black Amer. Lit. Forum.* 13.4 Wint. 1979: 149.

    732 "Untitled [Up near Dragoon]." *Black Amer. Lit. Forum.* 13.4 Wint. 1979: 149.

    733 "A vision." *Black Amer. Lit. Forum.* 13.4 Wint. 1979: 149–150.

Cobb, Pamela *see* Sele, Baraka

Wanda Coleman (1946–)

Poetry

    734 "The African Queen meets her match." *Bachy.* 14 Spr.–Sum. 1979: 18.

    735 *Art in the Court of the Blue Fag.* Santa Barbara: Black Sparrow, 1977.

    736 "At vital statistics." *Partisan Rev.* 46.4 1979: 598.

    737 "Beneath the rubble." *Obsidian.* 6.1–2 Spr.–Sum. 1980: 229–233.

    738 "Casting call." *Michigan Q. Rev.* 25.3 Sum. 1986: 536.

    739 "Central Avenue soul train shuffle." *Bachy.* 11 Spr. 1978: 97.

    740 "El Hajj Malik el-Shabazz." *Black Amer. Lit. Forum.* 17.4 Wint. 1983: 175.

    741 "Emmett Till." *Callaloo.* 9.2 Spr. 1986: 295–299.

    742 "Ethiopian in the fuel supplies." *Black Amer. Lit. Forum.* 17.4 Wint. 1983: 176.

    743 "Flight of the California condor / Wind sistuh blooded eyes / Mind full of flesh." *Bachy.* 14 Spr.–Sum. 1979: 15.

744 "Flight of the condor." *Epoch.* 34.1 1984-1985: 43.

745 "Frustrations." *Bachy.* 11 Spr. 1978: 97.

746 "Growing up Black." *Epoch.* 32.1 Aug. 1982: 28-30.

747 "The head of my baby." *Bachy.* 14 Spr.-Sum. 1979: 19.

748 "High time lovers." *Poetry Now.* 6.4 1982: 39.

749 *Imagoes.* Santa Barbara, CA: Black Sparrow, 1983.

750 "In the kitchen my potatoes are polemical." *Massachusetts Rev.* 28.4 Wint. 1987: 705.

751 "Indian summer." *Essence.* 14.11 Mar. 1984: 140.

752 "Invitation to a gunfighter." *Michigan Q. Rev.* 25.3 Sum. 1986: 535.

753 "Jerry 1967." *Partisan Rev.* 46.4 1979: 601.

754 "Job hunter." *Thirteenth Moon.* 7.1-2 1983: 67.

755 "The lady with Bougainvillea in her eyes (for Kate Braverman)." *Bachy.* 11 Spr. 1978: 94.

756 "Last grave at Dimbaza." *Black Amer. Lit. Forum.* 13.1 Spr. 1979: 34.

757 "Lessons." *Partisan Rev.* 46.4 1979: 599.

758 "Luz." *Bachy.* 14 Spr.-Sum. 1979: 20.

759 *Mad Dog, Black Lady.* Santa Barbara, CA: Black Sparrow, 1979.

760 "Male order catalog." *Bachy.* 11 Spr. 1978: 93.

761 "Men lips." *Partisan Rev.* 46.4 1979: 597.

762 "My years." *Chomo-Uri.* 4.1 Sum. 1977: 24.

763 [Nine poems]. *Bachy.* 16 Wint. 1980: 62-68.

764 "On that stuff that ain't NEVAH been long enuff for no damn body, chain braids." *Black Amer. Lit. Forum.* 19.3 Fall 1985: 109.

765 "One war." *Greenfield Rev.* 7.3-4 Spr.-Sum. 1979: 293.

766 "The one who can." *Thirteenth Moon.* 6.1-2 1982: 18.

767 "Propaganda." *Epoch.* 34.1 1984-1985: 44-46.

768 "Queen of the sinking sand." *Partisan Rev.* 46.4 1979: 600.

769 "The silver satin Nigga' rides— (for Al and Pete who never see anymore)." *Bachy.* 11 Spr. 1978: 97.

770 "Sometimes I have a song for my mommy and daddy." *Bachy.* 11 Spr. 1978: 95.

771 "Somewhere there's an alley with my name on it." *Black Amer. Lit. Forum.* 13.1 Spr. 1979: 35.

772 "Stephen and Lady as seen thru windows." *Bachy.* 11 Spr. 1978: 94.

773 "Tomboy." *Tendril.* 13 Sum. 1982: 22.

774 "Under arrest." *Bachy.* 14 Spr.-Sum. 1979: 17.

775 "Under arrest (2)." *Bachy.* 14 Spr.-Sum. 1979: 18.

776 "The wait." *Thirteenth Moon.* 6.1-2 1982: 19.

777 "Walkin' papers blues (Urban blues / Jass Series)." *Thirteenth Moon.* 7.1-2 1983: 70.

778 "Worker (2)." *Thirteenth Moon.* 7.1-2 1983: 68-69.

Textual Criticism

779 Komunyakaa, Yusef. "A poet of apparent genius." *Obsidian.* 7.2-3 Sum.-Wint. 1981: 229-231. Rev. of *Mad Dog, Black Lady.*

Willie M. Coleman

Poetry
  780 "Among the things that use to be." In SMIT: 221–222.
  781 "Among the things that use to be." *Conditions 5.* 2.2 Aut. 1979: 59.

Eugenia W. Collier

Editing
  782 Long, Richard A. and Eugenia W. Collier, Eds. *Afro-American Writing: An Anthology of Prose and Poetry.* University Park: Pennsylvania State Univ., 1985. Second and enlarged edition. Originally published 1972.

Essay
  783 "The African presence in Afro-American literary criticism." *Obsidian.* 6.3 Wint. 1980: 30–35.

Poetry
  784 "Barbados." *Black World.* 25.5 Mar. 1986: 53.

June L. Collins

Poetry
  785 "My poem." *Essence.* 16.10 Feb. 1986: 138.
  786 "This woman." *Essence.* 16.8 Dec. 1985: 128.
  787 "Untitled [It's always after midnight]." *Essence.* 17.3 July 1986: 126.
  788 "Untitled [Roosevelt I love you]." *Essence.* 16.7 Nov. 1985: 12.

Kathleen Collins

Drama
  789 "The brothers." In MILA: 13–50.
  790 "The brothers." In WILK: 293–346.
  791 "In the midnight hour." In MILB: 35–83.

Brenda Connor-Bey

Poetry
  792 "The dancer." In BARA: 80–81.
  793 "Martha." In BARA: 78–79.
  794 "Pretending." In BARA: 76–78.

Afua Pam Cooper

Poetry

795 *Breakin Chains*. [No place of publication listed]: Weelahs Publications, 1983.

796 "Untitled 2." *Essence*. 15.10 Feb. 1985: 122.

J. California Cooper

Drama

797 "Loners." In OSTR: 17–27.

Short Fiction

798 *Homemade Love*. NY: St. Martin's, 1986.

799 *A Piece of Mine*. Navarro, CA: Wild Trees, 1984.

800 *Some Soul to Keep*. NY: St. Martin's, 1987.

801 "He was a man (but he done himself wrong)." *Essence*. 16.5 Sept. 1985: 86, 88, 146–148, 152.

Textual Criticism

802 Deck, A. *Choice*. 22.9 May 1985: 1330. Rev. of *A Piece of Mine*.

803 McMillan, Terri. *N.Y. Times Book Rev*. Nov. 8, 1987: 23. Rev. of *Some Soul to Keep*.

804 Schumacher, Michael. *Writer's Digest*. 67 Feb. 1987: 21. Rev. of *Homemade Love*.

Jayne Cortez (1936–)

Essay

805 "Black women writers visit Cuba." *Black Scholar*. 16.4 July–Aug. 1985: 61.

Poetry

806 "Assets." *Yardbird Reader*. 5 1976: 116.

807 "Big fine woman from Ruleville." *Essence*. 11.1 May 1980: 103.

808 "Big fine woman from Ruleville." In BARA: 94–95.

809 "Black feathered mules." *Black Scholar*. 12.5 Sept.–Oct. 1981: 32.

810 "Carolina Kingston." *Callaloo*. 5.2 1979: 70–71.

811 *Coagulations: New and Selected Poems*. NY: Thunder's Mouth, 1984.

812 "Cobra Club." *Callaloo*. 5.2 1979: 51.

813 "Comparative literature." *Black Scholar*. 18.4–5 July–Aug.–Sept.–Oct. 1987: 17.

814 "Do you think." *Heresies*. 1 Jan. 1977: 57.

815 *Firespitter*. NY: Bola, 1982.

816 "Firespitters." *Greenfield Rev*. 11.1–2 Sum.–Fall 1983: 15–16.

817 "For the brave young students in Soweto." In BARA: 95–97.

818 "For the brave young students in Soweto." *Nimrod.* 21–22.2–1 1977: 60.

819 "Global inequalities." *Black Scholar.* 18.4–5 July–Aug.–Sept.–Oct. 1987: 16–17.

820 "Grinding vibrato." In STET: 160–161.

821 "I am New York City." *Mundus Artium.* 12–13 1980–1981: 174–175.

822 "I see Chano Pozo." *Open Places.* 41 Spr. 1986: 34–36.

823 "I'm not saying." *Callaloo.* 5.2 1979: 118.

824 "If the drum is a woman." *Open Places.* 41 Spr. 1986: 32–33.

825 "In the morning." *Black Scholar.* 10.3–4 Nov.–Dec. 1978: 11–12.

826 "In the morning." In STET: 157–159.

827 "It came." *Black Scholar.* 12.5 Sept.–Oct. 1981: 31.

828 "Lynch fragment 2." *Yardbird Reader.* 5 1976: 113.

829 "Making it." *Yardbird Reader.* 5 1976: 111.

830 "Massive build up." *Black Scholar.* 18.4–5 July–Aug.–Sept.–Oct. 1987: 16.

831 "Mercenaries and minstrels." *Black Scholar.* 10.3–4 Nov.–Dec. 1978: 10.

832 *Merveilleux Coup de Foudre.* Paris, France: Handshake, 1982. Poetry of Jayne Cortez and Ted Joans, translated by I. Errus and S. Errus.

833 *Mouth on Paper.* NY: Bola, 1977.

834 "National security." *Yardbird Reader.* 5 1976: 111.

835 "Once upon a road." *Black Scholar.* 12.5 Sept.–Oct. 1981: 32.

836 "Opening act." *Essence.* 11.1 May 1980: 102.

837 "Orange chiffon." In STET: 153.

838 "Orisha." In STET: 151–152.

839 "Phraseology." In STET: 152.

840 "Phraseology." *Mundus Artium.* 12–13 1980–1981: 173.

841 "Rape." In BARA: 89–90.

842 "Rose solitude." *Yardbird Reader.* 5 1976: 114.

843 "Rose solitude (for Duke Ellington)." *Essence.* 8.11 Mar. 1978: 70.

844 "So many feathers." *Black Scholar.* 10.3–4 Nov.–Dec. 1978: 10–11.

845 "So many feathers." *Heresies 8.* 2.4 [Sum.] 1979: 40–41.

846 "So many feathers." In STET: 155–157.

847 "Stockpiling." *UNESCO Courier.* 35 Nov. 1982: 10–11.

848 "There it is." *Greenfield Rev.* 11.1–2 Sum.–Fall 1983: 13–14.

849 "There it is." In BARA: 90–92.

850 "Three day New York blues." *Yardbird Reader.* 5 1976: 112.

851 "Under the edge of February." In STET: 153–154.

852 "You know." *Callaloo.* 5.2 1979: 92–93.

853 "You know." In BARA: 92–94.

Textual Criticism and Interviews

854 Boyd, Melba Joyce. *Black Scholar.* 16.4 July–Aug. 1985: 65–66. Rev. of *Coagulations.*

855 Cannon, Steve. "The oral tradition and the phonograph record." *Yardbird Reader.* 5 1976: 93–95. On Cortez's recording of *Celebrations and Solitudes* (poetry).

856 Crouch, Stanley. "Big star calling." *Yardbird Reader.* 5 1976: 99. Cortez and the blues tradition.

857 Davis, Charles. "Jayne Cortez review." *Yardbird Reader.* 5 1976: 96–97. On her poetry.

858 DeVeaux, Alexis. "A poet's world: Jayne Cortez discusses her life and her work." *Essence.* 8.11 Mar. 1978: 77–79, 106, 109–110, 112, 114. A number of poems appear in the article.

859 Gillam, Deborah A. "Jayne Cortez." *Yardbird Reader.* 5 1976: 100–101. On her poetry.

860 Grosvenor, Verta Mae. "Jayne Cortez." *Yardbird Reader.* 5 1976: 106. On her poetry.

861 Kazi-Ferrouillet, Kuumba and Karima A. Belle. *Black Collegian.* 15.1 Sept.-Oct. 1984: 70. Rev. of *Coagulations.*

862 Melhem, D.H. "Interview with Jayne Cortez." *Greenfield Rev.* 11.1–2 Sum.-Fall 1983: 31–47.

863 Melhem, D.H. "Jayne Cortez: supersurrealism." *Greenfield Rev.* 11.1–2 Sum.-Fall 1983: 18–31. On a number of works.

864 Redmond, Eugene B. "Jayne Cortez: double clutch love poet." *Yardbird Reader.* 5 1976: 98. On her poetry.

865 Taylor, Clyde. "Jayne Cortez at the Rainbow Sign: Berkeley '75." *Yardbird Reader.* 5 1976: 107–109.

866 Thomas, Charles C. "The homeland and the poetry of Jayne Cortez." *Yardbird Reader.* 5 1976: 102–105.

867 Troupe, Quincy. "The poetry of Jayne Cortez as ritualized passage." *Yardbird Reader.* 5 1976: 91–92.

868 Woodson, Jon. "Jayne Cortez." In DL41: 69–74. Has biography and bibliography.

Mae V. Cowdery (1910–)

Poetry

869 "I sit and wait for beauty." In STET: 93–94.

Stella Crews (1950–)

Poetry

870 "Push pawn." *Black Scholar.* 12.5 Sept.-Oct. 1981: 15.

Kattie M. Cumbo (1938–)

Poetry

871 "Black sister." In STET: 135–136.

872 "Ceremony." In STET: 137–138.

873 "Domestics." In STET: 135.

874 "I'm a dreamer." In STET: 137.
875 "The morning after . . . love." In STET: 136.
876 "Nocturnal sounds." In STET: 134–135.

Nia Damali

Poetry
877 "Hello Mister. . ." *Black Amer. Lit. Forum.* 21.3 Fall 1987: 246.
878 "Your song." *Black Amer. Lit. Forum.* 21.3 Fall 1987: 245–246.

Daryl Cumber Dance

Editing
879 *Fifty Caribbean Writers: A Bio-Bibliographical Critical Sourcebook.* NY: Greenwood, 1986.

Folklore
880 *Folklore from Contemporary Jamaicans.* Knoxville: Univ. of Tennessee, 1985.
881 *Long Gone: The Mecklenburg Six and the Theme of Escape in Black Folklore.* Knoxville: Univ. of Tennessee, 1987.
882 *Shuckin' and Jivin': Folklore from Contemporary Black Americans.* Bloomington: Indiana UP, 1978.

Margaret Esse Danner (1915–1984)

Poetry
883 "And through the Caribbean Sea." In LONG: 554.
884 "At home in Dakar." In STET: 133–134.
885 "Dance of the Abakweta." In LONG: 550–551.
886 *The Down of a Thistle: Selected Poems, Prose Poems, and Songs.* Waukesha, WI: Country Beautiful, 1976.
887 "Gold is the shade esperanto." In LONG: 553.
888 "A grandson is a hoticeberg." In ADOF: 87–88.
889 "A grandson is a hoticeberg." In STET: 131–132.
890 "Passive resistance." In SIMC: 95.
891 "The rhetoric of Langston Hughes." In STET: 133.
892 "Visit of the Professor of Aesthetics." In LONG: 551–552.
893 "Women's lib." In BELL: 356.

Textual Criticism
894 Aldridge, June M. "Benin to Beale Street: African art in the poetry of Margaret Danner." *CLA J.* 31.2 Dec. 1987: 201–209.
895 Aldridge, June M. "Langston Hughes and Margaret Danner." *Langston Hughes Rev.* 3.2 Fall 1984: 7–9.

896 Mahone, Barbara. "A book to remember." *First World.* 2 Spr. 1978: 47. Rev. of *The Down of a Thistle.*

897 Stetson, Erlene. "Dialectic voices in the poetry of Margaret Esse Danner." In MILP: 93–103.

Doris Diosa Davenport

Essays
898 "Black lesbians in academia: visible invisibility." In CRUI: 9–11.

899 "The pathology of racism: a conversation with Third World Wimmin." In MORA: 85–90.

Poetry
900 *Eat Thunder and Drink Rain: Poems.* Los Angeles: Published by author, 1982.

901 "I have found." In CRUW: 40.

902 "I useta say i was a writer. . ." *Sinister Wisdom.* 31 1987: 38.

903 *It's Like This.* Los Angeles: Published by author, 1981.

904 "Teaching composition in California / With my Grandfather near death in Georgia." *Black Amer. Lit. Forum.* 18.1 Spr. 1984: 10.

905 "To the 'majority' from a 'minority'." In CRUW: 39.

Textual Criticism
906 Birtha, Becky. "Celebrating themselves: four self-published Black lesbian authors." *Off Our Backs.* 15.7,8,9 July–Oct. 1985: various pagings. A three-part series on Stephanie Byrd, Doris Davenport, S. Diane Bogus, and Linda Brown.

Gloria Davis

Poetry
907 "To Egypt." In SIMC: 71.

Thadious M. Davis (1944–)

Editing
908 Davis, Thadious M. and Trudier Harris, Eds. *Afro-American Fiction Writers After 1955.* Detroit: Gale, 1984. (*Dictionary of Literary Biography,* vol. 33).

909 Harris, Trudier and Thadious M. Davis, Eds. *Afro-American Poets Since 1955.* Detroit: Gale, 1985. (*Dictionary of Literary Biography,* vol. 41).

910 Davis, Thadious M. and Trudier Harris, Eds. *Afro-American Writers After 1955: Dramatists and Prose Writers.* Detroit: Gale, 1985. (*Dictionary of Literary Biography,* vol. 38).

911 Harris, Trudier and Thadious M. Davis, Eds. *Afro-American Writers*

Before the Harlem Renaissance. Detroit: Gale, 1986. (*Dictionary of Literary Biography,* vol. 50).

912 Harris, Trudier and Thadious M. Davis, Eds. *Afro-American Writers from the Harlem Renaissance to 1940.* Detroit: Gale, 1987. (*Dictionary of Literary Biography,* vol. 51).

Essays

913 "Black writers on *Adventures of Huckleberry Finn* one hundred years later." *Mark Twain J.* 22.2 Fall 1984: 2-3. The Foreword, special issue.

914 "Crying in the wilderness: legal, racial, and moral codes in *Go Down, Moses.*" *Mississippi College Law Rev.* 4 Spr. 1984: 299-318. On one of Faulkner's novels. Part of "The Law and Southern Literature: a Symposium, Part 1."

915 "Other family and Luster in *The Sound and the Fury.*" *CLA J.* 20.2 Dec. 1976: 245-261.

916 "Wright, Faulkner, and Mississippi as racial memory." *Callaloo.* 9.3 Sum. 1986: 469-480.

Non-Fiction

917 *Faulkner's "Negro": Art and the Southern Context.* Baton Rouge: Louisiana State Univ., 1983.

Poetry

918 "Asante sana, te te." In STET: 280.

919 "Asante, te te." *Black Amer. Lit. Forum.* 13.3 Fall 1979: 100.

920 "Cloistered in high school." *Black Amer. Lit. Forum.* 17.4 Wint. 1983: 148.

921 "Double take at Relais de l'Espadon." *Black Amer. Lit. Forum.* 13.3 Fall 1979: 100-101.

922 "Double take at Relais de l'Espadon." In STET 277-278.

923 "Emergence: for Gerry, a neo-New Yorker." *Black Amer. Lit. Forum.* 13.3 Fall 1979: 101.

924 "For Alice Faye Jackson, from *The Vanishing Black Family in Memoriam* (January 1986)." *Black Amer. Lit. Forum.* 20.3 Fall 1986: 301.

925 "For Flo Hyman, Captain of the Olympic Volleyball Team (1984)." *Black Amer. Lit. Forum.* 20.3 Fall 1986: 299.

926 "For papa (and Marcus Garvey)." *Obsidian.* 4.1 Spr. 1978: 91.

927 "For us: in love and hope." *Black Scholar.* 8.6 Apr. 1977: 12.

928 "Funeral sequence." *Black Scholar.* 8.6 Apr. 1977: 12.

929 "A greeting on Tabaski." *Black Amer. Lit. Forum.* 13.3 Fall 1979: 100.

930 "Honeysuckle was the saddest odor of all, I think." In STET: 279-280.

931 "Honeysuckle was the saddest odor of all, I think." *Obsidian.* 4.1 Spr. 1978: 93.

932 "In Mordiop's room: Rue Mohamed V, Dakar." *Black Amer. Lit. Forum.* 13.3 Fall 1979: 100.

933 "It's all the same." In STET: 276.

934 "New World griot." *Black Amer. Lit. Forum.* 17.4 Wint. 1983: 149.

935 "Nomzamo." *Black Amer. Lit. Forum.* 20.3 Fall 1986: 302.

936 "Ramona Johnson Africa MOVE survivor." *Black Amer. Lit. Forum.* 20.3 Fall 1986: 300-301.

937 "Remembering Fannie Lou Hamer." In STET: 277.
938 "Reunion." *Black Amer. Lit. Forum.* 17.4 Wint. 1983: 149.
939 "Strong women survive hurricane season." *Obsidian.* 4.1 Spr. 1978: 92.
940 "Unfinished kinship." *Black Scholar.* 8.6 Apr. 1977: 13.

Thulani Davis (Thulani Nkabinde) (1949–)

Poetry
941 "Accra 8/75." In BRUA: 187.
942 *All the Renegade Ghosts Rise.* Washington: Anemone, 1978.
943 "Cicatrix." *J. of New Jersey Poets.* 1.1 Spr. 1976: 38.
944 "He didn't give up / he was taken." *Nimrod.* 21–22.2–1 1977: 290.
945 "Forest green." In BRUA: 184–185.
946 "[Fragment]." *Heresies 14.* 4.2 1982: 13.
947 "In the tenth month birth comes easy." *Chrysalis.* 7 1979: 83.
948 "Like fire spreadin / the joylessness." In BRUA: 184.
949 "Missing ms." In BRUA: 187.
950 "Not when the moon." *Yardbird Reader.* 5 1976: 26.
951 "Parable." *Yardbird Reader.* 5 1976: 24.
952 *Playing the Changes.* Middletown, CT: Wesleyan Univ., 1985.
953 "Rogue and Jar." *Nimrod.* 21–22.2–1 1977: 288.
954 "She got so drunk she didn't know herself." *Yardbird Reader.* 5 1976: 28.
955 "Song for the Nkazi or the final ironies." In BRUA: 185–186.
956 "Song to some other man." *Obsidian.* 3.2 Sum. 1977: 57.
957 "He was taken." *Obsidian.* 3.2 Sum. 1977: 56.

Textual Criticism
958 Hernton, Calvin. "The tradition." *Parnassus.* 12–13.2–1
Spr.–Sum.–Fall–Wint. 1985: 530–537. Criticism on Davis's *Playing the Changes.*
Article includes other poets.

Ruby Dee

Poetry
959 "For Marvin Gaye." *Essence.* 18.2 June 1987: 111.

Betty DeRamus

Short Fiction
960 "Anderson's ordeal." *Obsidian.* 6.1–2 Spr.–Sum. 1980: 98–103.
961 "The neighborhood." In BELL: 371–374.
962 "A time for burning." *Obsidian.* 3.2 Sum. 1977: 28–33.
963 "Waiting for Beale." *Essence.* 7.1 May 1976: 72–73.

Toi Derricotte (1941–)

Essays

964 "The Black notebooks." In LIFS: 281–285. About her family's experiences as one of the first Black families in Upper Montclair, New Jersey.

Non-Fiction

965 Derricotte, Toi and Madeline Tiger Bass. *Creative Writing: A Manual for Teachers.* Trenton, NJ: New Jersey State Council on the Arts, 1985.

Poetry

966 "The anesthesia is taking effect." *Black Amer. Lit. Forum.* 17.4 Wint. 1983: 155.

967 "Beau monde." *Black Amer. Lit Forum.* 17.4 Wint. 1983: 155.

968 "Black letter." *Open Places.* 33 Spr. 1982: 48.

969 "Boxes." In WETH: 17.

970 "Couplets." *U.S. 1 Worksheets.* 9 Spr. 1977: 6.

971 "The creation." *Open Places.* 33 Spr. 1982: 52–53.

972 "The cruel mother." *Feminist Studies.* 11.1 Spr. 1985: 105.

973 "The damned." In SMIT: 6–7.

974 "The distrust of logic." *Northwest Rev.* 22.1–2 1984: 34.

975 "Doll poem." In WETH: 18.

976 *The Empress of the Death House.* Detroit: Lotus, 1978.

977 "The face as it might be of love." In WETH: 19.

978 "For a godchild, Regina, on the occasion of her first love." *Conditions 5.* 2.2 1979: 109–111.

979 "For a godchild, Regina, on the occasion of her first love." In SMIT: 3–5.

980 "For a new child." *Feminist Studies.* 11.1 Spr. 1985: 106.

981 "For Sandra Maria Esteves." *Thirteenth Moon.* 5.1–2 1980: 19.

982 "Gynecology." *Thirteenth Moon.* 6.1–2 1982: 44–45.

983 "Hester's song." In SMIT: 8–9.

984 "The house is the enemy." *Black Amer. Lit. Forum.* 17.4 Wint. 1983: 155.

985 "In knowledge of young boys." *Chrysalis.* 9 Fall 1979: 105.

986 "Intimations of mortality." *U.S. 1 Worksheets.* 9 Spr. 1977: 6.

987 "Justice." *Conditions 10.* 3.4 1984: 12.

988 "The key." *Chrysalis.* 9 Fall 1979: 104.

989 "Last will of one who lived alone." *Gravida.* 12 1977: 55.

990 "The mirror." *Open Places.* 33 Spr. 1982: 47.

991 "Morning coffee: 1945." *Conditions 10.* 3.4 1984: 11.

992 "Morning ride." *Hanging Loose.* 29 Wint. 1976–1977: 3.

993 *Natural Birth.* Trumansburg, NY: The Crossing, 1983. A prose poem on the birth of her son.

994 *"Natural Birth* [Selections]." In COOP: 63–68.

995 *"Natural Birth* [Selections]." *Iowa Rev.* 12.2–3 Spr.–Sum. 1981: 63–68.

996 "The night she dreamed she was mad." *Black Amer. Lit. Forum.* 17.4 Wint. 1983: 155.

997 "Poem for my father." *Open Places.* 33 Spr. 1982: 49–51.

998 "The sculpture at night." *Black Amer. Lit. Forum.* 17.4 Wint. 1983: 155.

999 "Sleeping with Mr. Death." *J. of New Jersey Poets.* 1.2 Aut. 1976: 12.

1000 "The story of a very broken lady." *J. of New Jersey Poets.* 1.2 Aut. 1976: 10.

1001 "The testimony of Sister Maureen." In DALE: 59–61.

1002 "This woman will not bear children." In WETH: 20.

1003 "To a woman who went free." *Chrysalis.* 9 Fall 1979: 103.

Textual Criticism

1004 Hernton, Calvin. "The tradition." *Parnassus.* 12–13.2–1 Spr.-Sum.-Fall-Wint. 1985: 519–524. On *Natural Birth.* Article includes other poets.

Alexis DeVeaux (1948–)

Children's Poetry

1005 *Don't Explain* [Selections]. *Essence.* 12.2 June 1981: 72, 120, 122, 125–126, 128, 133, 136, 138, 141.

1006 *Don't Explain: A Song of Billie Holiday.* NY: Harper, 1980. A poem in story form for children.

Children's Stories

1007 *An Enchanted Hair Tale.* NY: Harper, 1987.

Drama

1008 "The tapestry." In WILK: 135–195.

Essays

1009 "Sister love." *Essence.* 14.6 Oct. 1983: 83–84, 150, 155. On feminism.

Poetry

1010 "And do you love me." *Open Places.* 34 Aut.-Wint. 1982: 42–43.

1011 "...And then she said." In BARA: 98–99.

1012 *Blue Heat: A Portfolio of Poems and Drawings.* Brooklyn, NY: Diva, 1985.

1013 "French doors: a vignette." *Open Places.* 34 Aut.-Wint. 1982: 40–41.

1014 "Madeleine's dreads." In COOP: 62.

1015 "Madeleine's dreads." *Iowa Rev.* 12.2–3 Spr.-Sum. 1981: 62.

1016 "The sisters." *Conditions 5.* 2.2 Aut. 1979: 31–33.

1017 "The sisters." In SMIT: 10–12.

1018 "The woman who lives in the botanical gardens." In BARA: 101–102.

1019 "The woman who lives in the botanical gardens." *Open Places.* 34 Aut.-Wint. 1982: 44–45.

Short Fiction

1020 "Remember him a outlaw." In WASH: 109–120.

1021 "The riddles of Egypt Brownstone." *Essence.* 9.4 Aug. 1978: 64–65, 96, 97–98.

1022 "The riddles of Egypt Brownstone." In WASH: 19–29.

1023 "The riddles of Egypt Brownstone." *Nimrod.* 21–22.2–1 1977: 67–77.

Textual Criticism

1024 Clarke, Cheryl. *Conditions.* 13 1986: 154–158. Rev. of *Blue Heat.*

1025 Jordan, June. *Ms.* 8.12 June 1980: 32–33. Rev. of *Don't Explain.*

1026 Ramsey, Priscilla R. "Alexis DeVeaux." In DL38: 92–97. Includes biography and additional bibliography.

1027 Wilson, Geraldine L. *Interracial Books for Children Bull.* 12.7–8 1981: 18–19. Rev. of *Don't Explain.*

Schavi Mali Diara (1948–)

Poetry

1028 "African woman." *Black Amer. Lit. Forum.* 16.2 Sum. 1982: 71.

1029 "Lament for the sixties." *Black Books Bull.* 7.2 1981: 50.

1030 "Most likely to succeed." *Black Amer. Lit. Forum.* 16.2 Sum. 1982: 71.

1031 "Struggling and surviving." *Black Amer. Lit. Forum.* 16.2 Sum. 1982: 71.

1032 "To a special friend." *Black Amer. Lit. Forum.* 16.2 Sum. 1982: 71.

Michelle Dionetti

Children's Stories

1033 *The Day Eli Went Looking for Bear.* Reading, MA: Addison-Wesley, 1980.

1034 *Thalia Brown and the Blue Bug.* Reading, MA: Addison-Wesley, 1979.

Textual Criticism

1035 Terrell, Eve Ruth. *Black Books Bull.* 6.4 1980: 87. Rev. of *Thalia Brown and the Blue Bug.*

Rita Dove (1952–)

Novels

1036 "The first suite." *Black Amer. Lit. Forum.* 20.3 Fall 1986: 241–250. From a novel in progress.

Poetry

1037 "The abduction." *Virginia Q. Rev.* 56.2 Spr. 1980: 276.

1038 "Adolescence-II." In VEND: 404.

1039 "The Afghani nomad coat (Part V)." *Northwest Rev.* 22.1-2 1984: 134-135.

1040 "Agosta the winged man and Rasha the black dove." *Poetry.* 139.2 Nov. 1981: 64-65.

1041 "Anniversary." *Callaloo.* 9.1 Wint. 1986: 46.

1042 "Anti-father." *Massachusetts Rev.* 23.2 Sum. 1982: 253.

1043 "The ants of Argos." *Nation.* Dec. 19, 1981: 664.

1044 "Aurora Borealis." *Ohio Rev.* 28 1982: 77.

1045 "Beauty and the beast." *North Amer. Rev.* 264.4 Wint. 1979: 47.

1046 "The bird Frau." *Ohio Rev.* 19.2 Spr.-Sum. 1978: 18.

1047 "Canary." *Triquarterly.* 67 Fall 1986: 114-115.

1048 "Champagne." In SMTD: 156.

1049 "Champagne." *Ohio Rev.* 20.2 Spr.-Sum. 1979: 36.

1050 "La Chapelle. 92nd Division. Ted." *Southern Rev.* 21.3 July 1985: 849-850.

1051 "The charm." *Ohio Rev.* 28 1982: 78.

1052 "Company." *Callaloo.* 9.1 Wint. 1986: 50.

1053 "Compendium." *Ohio Rev.* 28 1982: 75.

1054 "Courtship." *Ohio Rev.* 28 1982: 71-72.

1055 "Courtship, diligence." *New England Rev.* 7.1 Aut. 1984: 61.

1056 "David Walker (1785-1830)." *Missouri Rev.* 2.2-3 Spr. 1979: 56.

1057 "Definition in the face of unnamed fury." *Ohio Rev.* 28 1982: 76.

1058 "The distinguished lecturer spouts a few obscenities." *Poetry Now.* 7.2 1983: 13-14.

1059 "Dog days, Jerusalem." *Southern Rev.* 21.3 July 1985: 853.

1060 "Dusting." In SMTD: 153-154.

1061 "Dusting." In VEND: 405-406.

1062 "Dusting." *Poetry.* 139.2 Nov. 1981: 66-67.

1063 "Eastern European eclogues." *Ontario Rev.* 17 Aut.-Wint. 1982: 25.

1064 "The event." *Ohio Rev.* 28 1982: 67.

1065 "Fifth grade autobiography." *Southern Rev.* 21.3 July 1985: 852-853.

1066 "The fish in the stone." In VEND: 406-407.

1067 "Five elephants." *Nation.* Mar. 1, 1980: 253.

1068 "Flirtation." *Poetry.* 141.1 Oct. 1982: 10.

1069 "Genie's prayer under the kitchen sink." *Triquarterly.* 67 Fall 1986: 114-115.

1070 "Geometry." In VEND: 404.

1071 "Geometry." *Poetry Now.* 6.1 1981: 24.

1072 "The gorge." *Southern Rev.* 21.3 July 1985: 850-852.

1073 "Gospel." *Georgia Rev.* 38.3 Aut. 1984: 618-619.

1074 "Gospel." *Western J. of Black Studies.* 11.3 Fall 1987: 131.

1075 "Headdress." *Callaloo.* 9.1 Wint. 1986: 47.

1076 "The hill has something to say." *Georgia Rev.* 35.3 Aut. 1981: 554-555.

1077 "The house on Bishop Street." *Callaloo.* 9.1 Wint. 1986: 45.

1078 "The house slave." *Virginia Q. Rev.* 56.2 Spr. 1980: 275.

1079 "Jiving." *Ohio Rev.* 28 1982: 69.

1080 "Kentucky, 1833." *Paris Rev.* 68 Wint. 1976: 165.

1081 "The left-handed cellist." *New Orleans Rev.* 9.1 Spr.–Sum. 1982: 88.

1082 "Lines muttered in sleep." *Poetry Now.* 6.4 1982: 19.

1083 "Lucille, post-operative years." *Georgia Rev.* 40.4 Wint. 1986: 937.

1084 "Magic." *Nimrod.* 27.1 Aut.–Wint. 1983: 68.

1085 "Motherhood." *Callaloo.* 9.1 Wint. 1986: 44.

1086 *Museum: Poems.* Pittsburgh: Carnegie-Mellon Univ., 1983.

1087 "Nexus." *Poetry Now.* 6.1 1981: 24.

1088 "Nightmare." *Callaloo.* 9.1 Wint. 1986: 49.

1089 "November for beginners." *Poetry.* 139.2 Nov. 1981: 63.

1090 "Ö." In SMTD: 155.

1091 "Ö." In VEND: 405.

1092 "Ö." *Ohio Rev.* 23 1979: 37.

1093 "Ö." *Ohio Rev.* 30 1983: 59.

1094 "One volume missing." *Callaloo.* 9.1 Wint. 1986: 39.

1095 *The Only Dark Spot in the Sky: Poems.* Tempe, AZ: Porch, 1980.

1096 "The oriental ballerina (Georgianna Magdalena Hord, 1896–1979)." *New England Rev.* 7.1 Aut. 1984: 62-63.

1097 "Parsley." In VEND: 407-409.

1098 "Planning the perfect evening." *Antaeus.* 24 Wint. 1976: 79.

1099 "Planning the perfect evening." In SMTD: 156-157.

1100 "Pomade." *Poetry.* 144.6 Sept. 1984: 324-325.

1101 "Primer for the nuclear age." *Poetry.* 145.1 Oct. 1984: 49.

1102 "Promises." *Callaloo.* 9.1 Wint. 1986: 43.

1103 "Quaker Oats." *Ploughshares.* 10.1 1984: 50.

1104 "Receiving the stigmata." *Georgia Rev.* 36.3 Aut. 1982: 496.

1105 "Recovery." *Callaloo.* 9.1 Wint. 1986: 48.

1106 "Refrain." *Ohio Rev.* 28 1982: 73.

1107 "Roast possum." *Callaloo.* 9.1 Wint. 1986: 41-42.

1108 "Robert Schumann, or: Musical genius begins with affliction." *Georgia Rev.* 32.3 Aut. 1978: 643.

1109 "Small town." *Georgia Rev.* 33.4 Wint. 1979: 805.

1110 "Small town." *Poetry Now.* 6.1 1981: 24.

1111 "Straw hat." *Callaloo.* 9.1 Wint. 1986: 37.

1112 "The stroke." *Ohio Rev.* 28 1982: 79.

1113 "Sunday greens." *Nimrod.* 27.1 Aut.–Wint. 1983: 68-69.

1114 "Sunday greens." *Western J. of Black Studies.* 11.3 Fall 1987: 130.

1115 "Taking in wash." In PESE: 72.

1116 "Taking in wash." *Ploughshares.* 8.2-3 1982: 85.

1117 *Ten Poems.* Lisbon, IA: Penumbra, 1977. The Manila Series: No. 4.

1118 "This life." *Callaloo.* 9.1 Wint. 1986: 63.

1119 *Thomas and Beulah: Poems.* Pittsburgh: Carnegie-Mellon Univ., 1986.

1120 "Three days of a forest, a river, free." *Massachusetts Rev.* 23.2 Sum. 1982: 254.

1121 "Tou Wan speaks to her husband, Liu Sheng." *Poetry Now.* 6.4 1982: 35.

1122 "Under the viaduct." *Callaloo.* 9.1 Wint. 1986: 38.

1123 "Variation on gaining a son." *Callaloo.* 9.1 Wint. 1986: 40.

1124 "Variation on guilt." *Ohio Rev.* 28 1982: 74.

1125 "Variation on pain." *Ohio Rev.* 28 1982: 68.

1126 "The wake." *Poetry.* 144.6 Sept. 1984: 325-326.

1127 "Watching *Last Year at Marienbad* at Roger Haggerty's house in Auburn, Alabama." *Telescope.* 3.3 Aut. 1984: 44-45.

1128 *The Yellow House on the Corner: Poems.* Pittsburgh: Carnegie-Mellon Univ., 1980.

1129 "The zeppelin factory." *Ohio Rev.* 28 1982: 70.

Short Fiction

1130 "Bach, or The shape of space." *Nimrod.* 30.2 Spr.-Sum. 1987: 82-86.

1131 *Fifth Sunday: Stories.* Lexington: Univ. of Kentucky, 1985. Callaloo Fiction Series.

Textual Criticism and Interviews

1132 Hernton, Calvin. "The tradition." *Parnassus.* 12-13.2-1 Spr.-Sum.-Fall-Wint. 1985: 543-549. On her *Museum.* Article includes other poets.

1133 Lozano, Rafael. "Doce poetas jóvenes de los Estados Unidos [Twelve young poets of the U.S.]." *Revista Nacional de Cultura.* 39.237 1978: 100-119.

1134 McGraw, Erin. *North Amer. Rev.* 271.1 Mar. 1986: 72-73. Rev. of *Fifth Sunday.*

1135 Rampersad, Arnold. "The poetry of Rita Dove." *Callaloo.* 9 Wint. 1986: 52-60.

1136 Rubin, Stan Sanvel and Earl G. Ingersoll, Eds. "A conversation with Rita Dove." *Black Amer. Lit. Forum.* 20.3 Fall 1986: 227-240.

1137 Shoptaw, John. *Black Amer. Lit. Forum.* 21.3 Fall 1987: 335-341. Rev. of *Thomas and Beulah.*

1138 Smith, Dave. "Some recent American poetry: come all ye fair and tender ladies." *Amer. Poetry Rev.* 11.1 1982: 36-46. Rev. of *The Yellow House on the Corner.*

1139 Stitt, Peter. *Georgia Rev.* 40.4 Wint. 1986: 1031-1033. Rev. of *Thomas and Beulah.*

1140 Vendler, Helen H. "In the zoo of the new." *N.Y. Rev. of Books.* Oct. 23, 1986: 47-52. Rev. of *Thomas and Beulah.*

Shirley Graham DuBois (1908-1977)

Biography

1141 *DuBois: A Pictorial Biography.* Chicago: Johnson, 1978. On her husband, W.E.B. DuBois.

Textual Criticism

1142 Banfield, Beryle. *Interracial Books for Children Bull.* 10.5 1979: 16-17. Rev. of *DuBois: A Pictorial Biography.*

1143 Commire, Anne. In CO24: 105-108. Some biography and bibliography.

1144 Davis, Thadious M. "Shirley Graham." In MAIN: 167–169. Bibliography included.

1145 Howink, Eda. In HOWI: 137–141. Mostly biographical.

1146 Perkins, Kathy A. "The unknown career of Shirley Graham." *Freedomways*. 25.1 1985: 6–17.

1147 Peterson, Bernard L., Jr. "Shirley Graham DuBois: composer and playwright." *Crisis*. 84.5 May 1977: 177–179. Mostly biographical.

Alice M. Dunbar-Nelson (1875–1935)

Autobiography

1148 Dunbar-Nelson, Alice. *Give Us Each Day: The Diary of Alice Dunbar-Nelson*. Gloria T. Hull, Ed. NY: Norton, 1984.

Bibliography

1149 Williams, Ora. "Works by and about Alice Ruth (Moore) Dunbar-Nelson: a bibliography." *CLA J.* 19.3 Mar. 1976: 322–326.

Collected Works

1150 Williams, R. Ora, Ed. *An Alice Dunbar-Nelson Reader*. Washington, D.C.: Univ. Pr. of America, 1979.

Poetry

1151 "I sit and sew." In GILN: 1337.
1152 "I sit and sew." In STET: 65–66.
1153 "Music." In STET: 67.
1154 "Snow in October." In STET: 66.
1155 "Sonnet." In STET: 65.

Textual Criticism

1156 Cliff, Michelle. *Black Scholar*. 16.5 Sept.–Oct. 1985: 56. Rev. of *Give Us Each Day*.

1157 Hull, Gloria T. "Alice Dunbar-Nelson: a personal and literary perspective." In ASCH: 105–111.

1158 Hull, Gloria T. "Alice Dunbar-Nelson: a regional approach." In HOFM: 64–68.

1159 Hull, Gloria T. "Researching Alice Dunbar-Nelson: a personal and literary perspective." *Feminist Studies*. 6.2 Sum. 1980: 314–320.

1160 Hull, Gloria T. "Researching Alice Dunbar-Nelson: a personal and literary perspective." In HULL: 189–195.

1161 Staples, Brent. "She was hard to impress." *N.Y. Times Book Rev.* Apr. 14, 1985: 20. Rev. of *Give Us Each Day*.

1162 Whitlow, Roger. "Alice Dunbar-Nelson, New Orleans writer." In TOTH: 119–120.

Easton, Y.W. *see* Yvonne

Leatrice W. Emeruwa

Poetry

1163 *Black Girl, Black Girl.* Beachwood, OH: Sharaqua, 1976.

1164 "East 105th and Euclid Street peddler's song." *Pigiron.* 7 May 1980: 63.

1165 *Ev'ry Shut Eye Ain't Sleep: Ev'ry Goodby Ain't Gon'.* Beachwood, OH: Sharaqua, 1977.

1166 "For what-sa-name." *Pigiron.* 7 May 1980: 78.

1167 "Rage." *Pigiron.* 7 May 1980: 77.

Aisha Eshe (Marilyn Carmen) (1941–)

Poetry

1168 "The bad tit." *Heresies.* 6.1 1987: 64.

1169 "Birthday party." *Obsidian.* 7.2–3 Sum.–Wint. 1981: 211.

1170 "Black folks." *Black Books Bull.* 7.3 1981: 61.

1171 "Black poet tryin' ta rest fore school start nex' month." *San Fernando Poetry J.* 4.2 1983: 66–68.

1172 "Camp Rielly with Crystall." *Obsidian.* 7.2–3 Sum.–Wint. 1981: 213.

1173 "Campsite memory." *Obsidian.* 7.2–3 Sum.–Wint. 1981: 213.

1174 "Daydream." *San Fernando Poetry J.* 5.3 1983: 77.

1175 "For my mother." *Obsidian.* 7.2–3 Sum.–Wint. 1981: 210.

1176 "Geneva." *Obsidian.* 7.2–3 Sum.–Wint. 1981: 209.

1177 "Harrisburg Hospital 1980." *Black Amer. Lit. Forum.* 14.4 Wint. 1980: 175.

1178 "He can go home, I guess we pulled the wrong nigga this time." *Black Amer. Lit. Forum.* 18.1 Spr. 1984: 28.

1179 "I cry when I return." *Black Books Bull.* 7.3 1981: 61.

1180 "Imaginative thinking." *Carousel Q.* 2.3 Wint. 1977: 12.

1181 "Invisible black face." *Obsidian.* 5.1–2 Spr.–Sum. 1979: 78.

1182 "Kiss." *Obsidian.* 7.2–3 Sum.–Wint. 1981: 211.

1183 "A meal." *Heresies.* 6.1 1987: 65.

1184 "Melting pot to America." *Obsidian.* 7.2–3 Sum.–Wint. 1981: 212.

1185 "Mother." *Amelia.* 1.2 Oct. 1984: 62.

1186 "Nationalist life marriage." *San Fernando Poetry J.* 4.2 1983: 31.

1187 "Signs." *Obsidian.* 7.2–3 Sum.–Wint. 1981: 212.

1188 "Starved." *Heresies.* 6.1 1987: 65.

1189 "Sunday dinner (Everytime. . .)." *Heresies.* 6.1 1987: 65.

1190 "Sunday dinner (For you)." *Heresies.* 6.1. 1987: 64.

1191 "Terror tales." *Heresies.* 5.2 1985: 74.

1192 "Therapy." *Helicon Nine.* 14–15 1986: 143.

1193 "Time stopped." *Heresies.* 6.1 1987: 65.

1194 "A vision from beneath the skin." *Obsidian.* 5.1–2 Spr.–Sum. 1979: 77.

1195 "Was it you I dreamed about (Charles)." *San Fernando Poetry J.* 4.2 1983: 30.

Mari Evans (1923-)

Children's Poetry
1196 *Singing Black.* Chicago: Third World, 1976.

Children's Stories
1197 *Jim Flying High.* Garden City, NY: Doubleday, 1979.

Editing
1198 *Black Women Writers (1950-1980): A Critical Evaluation.* Garden City, NY: Doubleday, 1984.

Essays
1199 "My father's passage." In EVAN: 165-169. Essay on writing.
1200 "The nature and methodology of colonization and its relationship to creativity (a systems approach to Black literature)." *Black Books Bull.* 6.3 Aug. 1979: 10-17.
1201 "Political writing as device." *First World.* 2.3 1979: 34-39.

Poetry
1202 ". . . And the old women gathered (the gospel singers)." In STET: 146.
1203 "Black jam for Dr. Negro." In LONG: 591-592.
1204 "Blues in B flat." *Callaloo.* 5.2 1979: 47.
1205 "Cellblock blues." *Black Scholar.* 10.3-4 Nov.-Dec. 1978: 47.
1206 "Conceptuality." In LONG: 597.
1207 "Curving stonesteps in the sun." *Nimrod.* 21-22.2-1 1977: 80.
1208 "Daufuskie (four movements)." In STET: 142.
1209 "Early in the morning." In BARA: 108-109.
1210 "The Friday ladies of the pay envelope." In FISH: 260.
1211 "A good assassination should be quiet." In FISH: 261.
1212 "How sudden dies the blooming." *Black Scholar.* 18.4-5 July-Aug.-Sept.-Oct. 1987: 22.
1213 "How will you call me, brother." In STET: 144-145.
1214 "I am a Black woman." In ADOF: 225-226.
1215 "I am a Black woman." In BARA: 105-106.
1216 "I am a Black woman." In FISH: 259-260.
1217 "Jake." In STET: 143.
1218 "Janis." In STET: 144.
1219 "Langston." In ADOF: 205.
1220 "A man without food." *Black Scholar.* 18.4-5 July-Aug.-Sept.-Oct. 1987: 22.
1221 "Maria Pina and the B & G Grill." *Callaloo.* 5.2 1979: 49.

1222 "Nicodemus (1879-1970)." *Amer. Poetry Rev.* 6.1 Jan.–Feb. 1977: 22.

1223 "Nicodemus quartette." *Great Lakes Rev.* 6.1 Sum. 1979: 75–78.

1224 "The nigger who is now hunting you." *Black Scholar.* 8.7 May 1977: 35.

1225 *Nightstar: 1973–1978.* Los Angeles: Univ. of California Center for Afro-American Studies, 1981.

1226 "On the death of Boochie by starvation." *Callaloo.* 5.2 1979: 46.

1227 "On the death of Boochie by starvation." *First World.* 2 Spr. 1978: 11.

1228 "One more black belt gone." *Callaloo.* 5.2 1979: 50.

1229 "The people gather." In STET: 143.

1230 "The rebel." In KONE: 150.

1231 "The rebel." In SIMC: 87.

1232 "Remembering Willie." *Black Scholar.* 10.3–4 Nov.–Dec. 1978: 47.

1233 "Remembering Willie." *Nimrod.* 21–22.2–1 1977: 81.

1234 "The seven twenty-five trolley." In BELL: 338.

1235 "Speak the truth to the people." In BARA: 107–108.

1236 "Status symbol." In LONG: 590–591.

1237 "Street lady." *Callaloo.* 5.2 1979: 48.

1238 "Street lady." *First World.* 2 Spr. 1978: 11.

1239 "To mother and Steve." *Ebony.* 36.10 Aug. 1981: 54. Excerpt from *I Am a Black Woman* (1970).

1240 "Uhuru." In ADOF: 240.

1241 "Vive noir!" In KONE: 203–206.

1242 "Vive noir!" In LONG: 592–595.

1243 "Where have you gone." In BARA: 106.

1244 *Whisper.* Berkeley, CA: Univ. of California Center for Afro-American Studies, 1979.

1245 "Who can be born Black." In ADOF: 225.

1246 "The writers." In LONG: 596–597.

Textual Criticism

1247 Commire, Anne. In CO10: 39–40. Has biography and bibliography.

1248 Dorsey, David. "The art of Mari Evans." In EVAN: 170–189.

1249 Dorsey, David. *CLA J.* 25.1 Sept. 1981: 106–107. Rev. of *Nightstar.*

1250 Edwards, Solomon. "Affirmation in the works of Mari Evans." In EVAN: 190–200.

1251 Gilbert, Gwen. *Black Books Bull.* 6.4 1980: 87. Rev. of *Jim Flying High.*

1252 Peppers, Wallace R. In DL41: 117–123. Has biography and bibliography.

1253 Simson, Rennie. *New Directions for Women.* 14 May–June 1985: 18. Rev. of *Black Women Writers (1950–1980).*

1254 Williams, David. *CAAS Newsletter.* 6 May 1982: 1–4. Rev. of *Nightstar.*

1255 Zhana. *New Statesman.* May 3, 1985: 29–30. Rev. of *Black Women Writers.*

Audrey Ewart

Essay
   1256 "Silence, culture, and slow awakening." *Conditions 5.* 2.2 Aut. 1979: 79–80.

Poetry
   1257 "Beneath my hands." In CRUW: 44.
   1258 "A vessel to continue the line." In CRUW: 43–44.

Sarah Webster Fabio (1928-1979)

Essays
   1259 "Blowing the whistle on some jive." *Black Scholar.* 10.8–9 May–June 1979: 56–58. On Black male-female relationships.

Poetry
   1260 "All day we've longed for night." In STET: 141.
   1261 "Back into the garden." In STET: 139.
   1262 "A butts' end remark rebuff." *Black Scholar.* 9.1 Sept. 1977: 24–25.
   1263 "Chromo." In ADOF: 228–229.
   1264 "To turn from love." In STET: 140.

Ruth Farmer

Poetry
   1265 "The dream." *Conditions 5.* 2.2 Aut. 1979: 96.

Fatisha

Poetry
   1266 "Reflective whimpers in the banging silence." *Essence.* 8.10 Feb. 1978: 55.

Jessie Redmon Fauset (1882-1961)

Bibliography
   1267 Perry, Margaret. "Jessie Fauset." In PERH: 77–82. Annotated bibliography.
   1268 Sims, Janet L. "Jessie Redmon Fauset (1885-1961): a selected annotated bibliography." *Black Amer. Lit. Forum.* 14.4 Wint. 1980: 147–152.

Biography
1269 Sicherman, Barbara and Carol H. Green. In SICH: 225–227.

Poetry
1270 "Oriflamme." In STET: 64.
1271 "Touché." In STET: 63–64.

Summary of Novel
1272 Southgate, Robert L. In SOUT: 56–58. Summary of her 1933 novel *Comedy American Style.*

Textual Criticism
1273 Bell, Bernard W. "Jessie Redmon Fauset (1882–1961)." In BELA: 107–109. Comments on various works.

1274 Davis, Marianna W. In DAVI: 115, 159–161. Comments on various works.

1275 Feeney, Joseph J. "Jessie Fauset of *The Crisis:* novelist, feminist, centenarian." *Crisis.* 90.6 June–July 1983: 20, 22.

1276 Feeney, Joseph J. "A sardonic, unconventional Jessie Fauset: the double structure and double vision of her novels." *CLA J.* 22.4 June 1979: 365–382.

1277 Johnson, Abby Arthur. "Literary midwife: Jessie Redmon Fauset and the Harlem Renaissance." *Phylon.* 39.2 Sum. 1978: 143–153.

1278 Lupton, Mary Jane. "Bad blood in Jersey: Jessie Fauset's *The Chinaberry Tree* (1931)." *CLA J.* 27.4 June 1984: 383–392.

1279 Lupton, Mary Jane. "Clothes and closure in three novels by Black women." *Black Amer. Lit. Forum.* 20.4 Wint. 1986: 409–421. On her *Comedy American Style* (1933) [and on other authors].

1280 McDowell, Deborah E. "The neglected dimension of Jessie Redmon Fauset." *Afro-Americans in New York Life and History.* 5.2 July 1981: 33–49.

1281 McDowell, Deborah E. "The neglected dimension of Jessie Redmon Fauset." In PRYS: 86–104.

1282 Noble, Jeanne. In NOBL: 119, 155, 159–162, 163, 165, 174, 175, 176. On various works.

1283 Perry, Margaret. In PERM: 94–99. On various works.

1284 Singh, Amritjit. In SING: 61–64, 72–76, 92–93, 95–98. On a number of works.

1285 Sylvander, Carolyn Wedin. *Jessie Redmon Fauset: Black American Writer.* Boston: G.K. Hall, 1980.

1286 Sylvander, Carolyn Wedin. "Jessie Redmon Fauset." In DL51: 76–86. Includes biography and additional bibliography.

1287 Sylvander, Carolyn Wedin. "Jessie Redmon Fauset." In MAIN: 18–20. Includes biography and some bibliography.

Naomi F. Faust

Poetry
1288 *All Beautiful Things: Poems.* Detroit: Lotus, 1983.
1289 "Danny takes the bus." In SIMC: 102–103.

Muriel Feelings (1938–)

Textual Criticism
1290 Commire, Anne. In CO16: 104–105. Biography and bibliography.
1291 DeMontreville, Doris and Elizabeth D. Crawford. In DEMO: 129–131. Mostly biographical.

Julia Fields (1938–)

Poetry
1292 "Aardvark." In ADOF: 182.
1293 "August heat." *Callaloo.* 4 Oct. 1978: 37–45.
1294 "Harlem in January." In ADOF: 65–66.
1295 "High on the hog." In ADOF: 130–132.
1296 "Jass." *Southern Exposure.* 6.3 Fall 1978: 49. From *East of Moonlight* (1973).
1297 "Mr. Tut's house: a recollection." *First World.* 2 1979: 38–39.
1298 "A poem for heroes." In ADOF: 190–191.
1299 *Slow Coins: Minted by Julia Fields.* Washington, DC: Three Continents, 1981.
1300 *A Summoning, a Shining.* Scotland Neck, NC: [no publisher listed], 1976.
1301 "Thoughts is what you asked for." *Callaloo.* 4 Oct. 1978: 52.

Textual Criticism
1302 Broussard, Mercedese. "Blake's bard." *Callaloo.* 1 Dec. 1976: 60–62. Rev. of *A Summoning, a Shining.*
1303 Burger, Mary Williams. "Julia Fields." In DL41: 123–131. Has biography and bibliography.

Nikky Finney

Essay
1304 "Doing write at last." *Essence.* 16.9 Jan. 1986: 128. On Black women writers.

Poetry
1305 "Automatic natural." *Essence.* 17.12 Apr. 1987: 120.

1306 "Chariots." *Essence.* 17.4 Aut. 1986: 144.
1307 *On Wings Made of Gauze.* NY: Morrow, 1985.
1308 "Uncles." *Essence.* Nov. 1984: 138.

Yvonne A. Flowers

Poetry
  1309 "Books (to Yolie, Audre, and Buster)." *Chrysalis.* 10 1980: 107.
  1310 "The nightmare is." *Conditions 5.* 2.2 Aut. 1979: 112.

Forten, Charlotte L. *see* Grimké, Charlotte Forten

Carol Freeman (1941–)

Poetry
  1311 "Do not think." In ADOF: 241–242.

Stephany Inua Fuller (1948–)

Biography
  1312 Fauntleroy, Mark. "*Essence* women." *Essence.* 9.6 Oct. 1978: 7. Fuller self-published a poem in 1976, "Of thee I sing."

Ruth M. Garnett

Poetry
  1313 "Rites after victory." *Black Scholar.* 11.8 Nov.–Dec. 1980: 79–80.
  1314 "Trump." *Steppingstone.* Premier issue. Sum. 1982: 19–21.

Gayles, Gloria *see* Wade-Gayles, Gloria

Lethonia Gee

Poetry
  1315 "By glistening, dancing seas." *Essence.* 15.10 Feb. 1985: 29.

Joan Gibbs

Editing

1316 Gibbs, Joan and Sara Bennett, Eds. *Top Ranking: A Collection of Articles on Racism and Classism in the Lesbian Community.* NY: February 3, 1980.

Poetry

1317 *Between a Rock and a Hard Place.* NY: February 3, 1979.

1318 "Internal geography—part one." In COOP: 99–100.

1319 "Internal geography—part one." *Iowa Rev.* 12.2-3 Spr.-Sum. 1981: 99–100.

1320 "Poetry." *Lesbian Feminist.* June 1977: 17. Includes "Poem for Black dykes," "Personal statement," and "Another poem for the victory of women."

Michele Gibbs

Poetry

1321 *Sketches from Home.* Detroit: Broadside, 1983.

P.J. Gibson

Drama

1322 "Brown silk and magenta sunsets." In WILK: 425–505. Written in 1985.

1323 *Long Time Since Yesterday: A Drama in Two Acts.* NY: S. French, 1986.

Nikki Giovanni (1943-)

Biography

1324 Stokes, Stephanie J. "'My house,' Nikki Giovanni." *Essence.* 12.4 Aug. 1981: 84–86, 88.

Children's Poetry

1325 *Vacation Time: Poems for Children.* NY: Morrow, 1980.

Essays

1326 "An answer to some questions on how I write: in three parts." In EVAN: 205–210.

1327 "Celebrating the human species." *Encore.* Dec. 18, 1978: 20.

1328 "My own style." *Essence.* 16.1 May 1985: 60, 62.

Poetry

1329 "Adulthood." In BLIC: 341–342.

1330 "A certain peace." In ADOF: 119–120.

1331 "Communication." *Ebony.* 38.4 Feb. 1983: 48.

1332 *Cotton Candy on a Rainy Day.* NY: Morrow, 1978.

1333 "Cotton candy on a rainy day." *Paintbrush.* 11 Spr. 1979: 13.

1334 "Dreams." In ADOF: 224.

1335 "I don't know James Tate." *Little Balkans Rev.*4.2 Wint. 1983–1984: 7.

1336 "I wrote a good omelet." *Essence.* 14.6 Oct. 1983: 88.

1337 "Introspection." *Encore.* Dec. 18, 1978: 26.

1338 "Knoxville, Tennessee." In ADOF: 50.

1339 "Knoxville, Tennessee." In STET: 237.

1340 "Legacies." In FISH: 266.

1341 "Mothers." In ADOF: 32–33.

1342 "Mothers." *Phantasm.* 3.1 1978: [21].

1343 "Mother's habits." In STET: 236–237.

1344 "Nikki-Rosa." In STET: 233–234.

1345 "Nikki-Rosa." In BLIC: 115.

1346 "Poem for Aretha." In HOFF: 42–45.

1347 "Revolutionary dreams." In ADOF: 223.

1348 "Scrapbooks." In ADOF: 146–148.

1349 "They clapped." *Essence.* 16.1 May 1985: 226.

1350 "They clapped." In FISH: 265–266.

1351 *Those Who Ride the Night Winds.* NY: Morrow, 1983.

1352 "Twelve gates to the city." In KONE: 200–201.

1353 "Untitled [One ounce of truth benefits]." In ADOF: 148–149.

1354 "Woman poem." In STET: 234–236.

1355 "The women gather." In BELL: 340–341.

1356 "You are there." *Mademoiselle.* 84.10 Oct. 1978: 228.

Textual Criticism and Interviews

1357 *Black Books Bull.* 7.2 1981: 59. Rev. of *Vacation Time.*

1358 Bonner, Carrington. "An interview with Nikki Giovanni." *Black Amer. Lit. Forum.* 18.1 Spr. 1984: 29–30.

1359 Commire, Anne. In CO15: 120–121. Biography and some bibliography.

1360 Elder, Arlene. "A *Melus* interview: Nikki Giovanni." *Melus.* 9.3 Wint. 1982: 61–75.

1361 Fannin, Alice. "Black poetry: three for the children." *Children's Lit. Assoc. Q.* 6.2 Sum. 1981: 35. Rev. of *Spin a Soft Black Song* (1971).

1362 Giddings, Paula. "Nikki Giovanni: taking a chance on feeling." In EVAN: 211–217.

1363 Gould, Jean. "Nikki Giovanni." In GOUL: 330–340. On various works.

1364 Harris, William J. "Sweet soft essence of possibility: the poetry of Nikki Giovanni." In EVAN: 218–228.

1365 Holtze, Sally Holmes. In HOLT: 133–134. Mostly biography.

1366 Juhasz, Suzanne. "'A sweet inspiration . . . of my people': the poetry of Gwendolyn Brooks and Nikki Giovanni." In JUHA: 144–176.

1367 Kelley, Patricia. *Off Our Backs.* 13.6 June 1983: 18. Rev. of *Those Who Ride the Night Winds.*

1368 Kennedy, X.J. *N.Y. Times Book Rev.* Nov. 9, 1980: 62. Rev. of *Vacation Time.*

1369 McDowell, Margaret B. "Groundwork for a more comprehensive criticism of Nikki Giovanni." In WEIA: 135-160.

1370 Mitchell, Mozella G. "Nikki Giovanni." In DL41: 135-151. Includes biography and additional bibliography.

1371 Noble, Jeanne. In NOBL: 197-198. On various works.

1372 Styron, Rose. "A pocketful of rhyme." *Book World (Washington Post).* Mar. 8, 1981: 10-11. Rev. of *Vacation Time.*

1373 Sutherland, Zena. *Bull. of the Center for Children's Books.* 34.2 Oct. 1980: 31. Rev. of *Vacation Time.*

1374 Thomas, Arthur E. "Nikki Giovanni." In THOM: 73-88. Interview.

Frankcina Glass

Novel
1375 *Marvin and Tige.* NY: St. Martin's, 1977.

Textual Criticism
1376 "Writer's dream comes true." *Ebony.* 33 May 1978: 156. On her life and her novel.

Marita Golden (1950–)

Autobiography
1377 *Migrations of the Heart: A Personal Odyssey.* NY: Anchor, 1983.

1378 "My father, my mother, myself." *Essence.* 14.1 May 1983: 72-74, 130, 132, 134.

Novel
1379 *A Woman's Place.* Garden City, NY: Doubleday, 1986.

1380 *A Woman's Place* [Excerpt]. *Essence.* 17.4 Aug. 1986: 88.

Textual Criticism
1381 Aschenbrenner, Joyce. *Western J. of Black Studies.* 11.4 Wint. 1987: 204. Rev. of *A Woman's Place.*

1382 Bovoso, Carole. *Ms.* 11.12 June 1983: 37. Rev. of *Migrations of the Heart.*

1383 Guy-Sheftall, Beverly. *Black Southerner.* 1 June 1984: 8. Rev. of *Migrations of the Heart.*

1384 Hill, Christine M. *Library J.* Feb. 1, 1983: 202. Rev. of *Migrations of the Heart.*

1385 McWhorter, Diane. *N.Y. Times Book Rev.* May 1, 1983: 16. Rev. of *Migrations of the Heart.*

Jewelle Gomez (1948–)

Essays
1386 "Black women heroes: here's reality, where's the fiction?" *Black Scholar.* 17.2 Mar.–Apr. 1986: 8–13.
1387 "A cultural legacy denied and discovered: Black lesbians in fiction by women." In SMIT: 110–123.

Poetry
1388 "Flamingoes and bears: a parable." *Conditions.* 9 Spr. 1983: 56.
1389 "For Toi." *Essence.* 16.10 Feb. 1986: 136.
1390 "Golden song." *Essence.* 8.10 Feb. 1978: 26.
1391 *The Lipstick Papers.* NY: Grace, 1980.
1392 "Pomegranate." *Conditions.* 9 Spr. 1983: 57.

Short Fiction
1393 "No day too long." In BULK: 219–225.

Gordon, Vivian V. *see* Satiafa

Hattie Gossett

Poetry
1394 "Billie lives! Billie lives!" In MORA: 109–112. Prose poem.
1395 "Billie lives! Billie lives!" *Sinister Wisdom.* 18 1981: 57–60.
1396 "Dakar / Samba." *Conditions 8.* 3.2 Spr. 1982: 22–27.
1397 "Intro and ten takes, a satire." *Heresies.* 3.4 1981: 15–18. Prose poem.
1398 "Is it true what they say about colored pussy?" *Heresies.* 4.3 1982: 40.
1399 "My soul looks back in wonder." *Essence.* 12.4 Aug. 1981: 21.
1400 "On the question of fans / the slave quarters are never air-conditioned." *Conditions 8.* 3.2 Spr. 1982: 19–21.
1401 "On the question of fans / the slave quarters are never air-conditioned." In SKLA: 52–54.
1402 "Who told you anybody wants to hear from you? You aint [sic] nothing but a Black woman!" In MORA: 175–176. Prose poem.
1403 "Yo daddy! — an 80's version of the dozens." *Heresies.* 3.4 1981: 19. Prose poem.

Jaki Shelton Green

Poetry
1404 "Eva I." *Essence.* 17.11 Mar. 1987: 122.

Eloise Greenfield (1929–)

Children's Biography

1405 Greenfield, Eloise and Alesia Revis. *Alesia.* NY: Philomel, 1981.

1406 Greenfield, Eloise and Lessie Jones Little. *Childtimes: A Three-Generation Memoir.* NY: Crowell, 1979.

1407 *Mary McLeod Bethune.* NY: Crowell, 1977.

Children's Poetry

1408 *Daydreamers.* NY: Dial, 1980.

1409 *Honey, I Love: And Other Love Poems.* NY: Crowell, 1978.

Children's Stories

1410 *Africa Dream.* NY: John Day, 1977.

1411 *Darlene.* NY: Methuen, 1980.

1412 *First Pink Light.* NY: Crowell, 1976.

1413 *Grandmama's Joy.* NY: Philomel, 1980.

1414 Little, Lessie Jones and Eloise Greenfield. *I Can Do It By Myself.* NY: Crowell, 1978.

1415 *Talk About a Family.* Philadelphia: Lippincott, 1978.

Essays

1416 "African American literature: a new challenge." *Interracial Books for Children Bull.* 17.2 1986: 4–5. On the scarcity of good books for children by Black American authors.

1417 "Writing for children — a joy and a responsibility." In MACC: 19–22. Speech given at the American Library Association meeting in Chicago, June 1978.

1418 "Writing for children — a joy and a responsibility." *Interracial Books for Children Bull.* 10.3 1979: 3–4.

Textual Criticism

1419 Ahrold, Kyle. *Encore Amer. and Worldwide News.* July 10, 1978: 38. Revs. of *Africa Dream* and *Honey, I Love.*

1420 Banfield, Beryle. *Interracial Books for Children Bull.* 9.4–5 1978: 30–31. Rev. of *I Can Do It by Myself.*

1421 Banfield, Beryle. *Interracial Books for Children Bull.* 9.2 1978: 19. Rev. of *Honey, I Love.*

1422 Banfield, Beryle. *Interracial Books for Children Bull.* 11.8 1980: 16–17. Revs. of *Grandmama's Joy* and *Talk About a Family.*

1423 Barras, Jonetta Rose. *Freedomways.* 22.2 1982: 117–119. Rev. of *Alesia.*

1424 Bashira, Damali. *Black Books Bull.* 4.1 Spr. 1976: 58. Rev. of *She Come Bringing Me That Little Baby Girl* (1974).

1425 Burns, Mary M. *Horn Book.* 55.6 Dec. 1979: 676. Rev. of *Childtimes.*

1426 Byrd, C. Maxine. *Black Scholar.* 9.7 Apr. 1978: 57. Rev. of *Mary McLeod Bethune.*

1427 Commire, Anne. In CO19: 141–143. Biography and bibliography.

1428 Dresher, Caryl-Robin. *Interracial Books for Children Bull.* 13.4–5 1982: 7. Rev. of *Alesia.*

1429 Edwards, Lynn. *Interracial Books for Children Bull.* 7.7 1976: 16. Rev. of *First Pink Light.*

1430 Elswit, Sharon. *School Library J.* 24.9 May 1978: 55. Rev. of *Honey, I Love.*

1431 Graham, Beryl. *Black Books Bull.* 7.2 1981: 56. Rev. of *Childtimes.*

1432 Graham, Beryl. *Black Books Bull.* 7.2 1981: 57. Rev. of *Grandmama's Joy.*

1433 Graham, Beryl. *Negro History Bull.* 41.5 Sept.–Oct. 1978: 894. Rev. of *Mary McLeod Bethune.*

1434 Haviland, Virginia. *Horn Book.* 52.1 Feb. 1976: 44. Rev. of *Me and Neesie* (1975).

1435 Heins, Ethel L. *Horn Book.* 57.5 Oct. 1981: 547. Rev. of *Daydreamers.*

1436 Holtze, Sally Holmes. In HOLT: 137–139. Biography and bibliography.

1437 Humes, Linda. *Interracial Books for Children Bull.* 8.4–5 1977: 32. Rev. of *Mary McLeod Bethune.*

1438 Kiah, R.B. "Profile: Eloise Greenfield." *Language Arts.* 57 Sept. 1980: 653–659. Some criticism.

1439 Lewis, Marjorie. *School Library J.* 24.7 Mar. 1978: 118–119. Rev. of *Africa Dream.*

1440 McDonnell, Christine. *School Library J.* 24.9 May 1978: 67–68. Rev. of *Talk About a Family.*

1441 Monette, Elizabeth. *Children's Book Rev. Service.* 9.5 Jan. 1981: 31. Rev. of *Darlene.*

1442 Olamina, Soyini. *Black Books Bull.* 4.4 Wint. 1976: 73. Rev. of *First Pink Light.*

1443 Perry, Thelma D. *Negro History Bull.* 41.1 Jan.–Feb. 1978: 801. Rev. of *Africa Dream.*

1444 Pettyjohn, Leila Davenport. *Children's Book Rev. Service.* 9.11 June 1981: 92. Rev. of *Daydreamers.*

1445 Singer, Marilyn R. *School Library J.* 26.4 Dec. 1979: 85. Rev. of *Childtimes.*

1446 Spigner, Nieda. *Freedomways.* 22.2 1982: 114–115. Rev. of *Daydreamers.*

1447 Sutherland, Zena. *Bull. of the Center for Children's Books.* 31.6 Feb. 1978: 93. Rev. of *Africa Dream.*

1448 Sutherland, Zena. *Bull. of the Center for Children's Books.* 31.2 Oct. 1977: 32. Rev. of *Good News* (reissued in 1977, former title *Bubbles,* originally published 1972).

1449 Sutherland, Zena. *Bull. of the Center for Children's Books.* 31.11 July–Aug. 1978: 177. Rev. of *Honey, I Love.*

1450 Sutherland, Zena. *Bull. of the Center for Children's Books.* 29.6 Feb. 1976: 96–97. Rev. of *Me and Neesie.*

1451 Sutherland, Zena. *Bull. of the Center for Children's Books.* 29.5 Jan. 1976: 77. Rev. of *Paul Robeson* (1975).

1452 Turner, Glennette Tilley. *Encore Amer. and Worldwide News.* 9.9 Dec.: 1981: 38–39. Rev. of *Grandmama's Joy.*

1453 Watson, Emily Strauss. *Interracial Books for Children Bull.* 12.2 1981: 22. Rev. of *Darlene.*

1454 Wilms, Denise M. *Booklist.* Aug. 15, 1981: 105. Rev. of *Daydreamers.*

1455 Wilson, Geraldine L. *Encore Amer. and Worldwide News.* 9.9 Dec. 1981: 38. Rev. of *Daydreamers.*

1456 Wilson, Geraldine L. *Interracial Books for Children Bull.* 11.5 1980: 14–15. Rev. of *Childtimes.*

1457 Wilson, Judith. *Essence.* 10.1 May 1979: 17. Rev. of *Talk About a Family.*

Carole Clemmons Gregory (1945–)

Essays

1458 "On becoming a feminist writer." *Heresies.* 4.3 1982: 51–52.

1459 "Wild beauties." *Heresies.* 5.2 1985: 75–76. Shaping of Gregory's identity by the relationship with her mother.

Poetry

1460 "A freedom song for the Black woman." In STET: 188–190.

1461 "The Greater Friendship Baptist Church." In STET: 190–191.

1462 "A letter from home." *Obsidian.* 7.2–3 Sum.–Wint. 1981: 219.

1463 "Lotus women." *Obsidian.* 7.2–3 Sum.–Wint. 1981: 220.

1464 "Love from my father." In ADOF: 31–32.

1465 "Love letter." *Conditions 5.* 2.2 Aug. 1979: 64.

1466 "Love letter." In STET: 185.

1467 "Revelation." *Conditions 5.* 2.2 Aug. 1979: 61–63.

1468 "Revelation." In STET: 185–188.

1469 "Singing exercise in the U.S. Army." *Obsidian.* 7.2–3 Sum.–Wint. 1981: 219.

1470 "A vacation." *Obsidian.* 7.2–3 Sum.–Wint. 1981: 221.

1471 "'Writers and lovers'." *Obsidian.* 7.2–3 Sum.–Wint. 1981: 220.

Lois Elaine Griffith

Poetry

1472 "Chica." *Conditions.* 6 1980: 106.

1473 "Chica." *Essence.* 11.11 Mar. 1981: 22.

1474 "Fire wind's song to Sundae (Loba)." In DALE: 77.

1475 "For all the homesick sunshine girls in spring." In DALE: 76.

1476 "Howard Beach." *Conditions.* 6 1980: 108.

Short Fiction

1477 "Places." In COOP: 137–149.

1478 "Prince Harlem." In BARA: 110–119.

Nikki Grimes (1950–)

Children's Poetry
1479 *Something on My Mind.* NY: Dial, 1978.

Children's Stories
1480 *Growin'.* NY: Dial, 1977.

Poetry
1481 "Definition." In BARA: 121.
1482 "For Gwendolyn Brooks on Mother's Day." *Greenfield Rev.* 7.3–4 Spr.-Sum. 1979: 14.
1483 "Fragments: mousetrap." In BARA: 120–121.
1484 "Niks: 1." *Greenfield Rev.* 7.3–4 Spr.-Sum. 1979: 14.
1485 "Niks: 2." *Greenfield Rev.* 7.3–4 Spr.-Sum. 1979: 15.
1486 "Quiet." *Black Forum.* 1.2 Wint. 1976–1977: 49.
1487 "Somewhere green." *Black Forum.* 1.2 Wint. 1976–1977: 28.
1488 "The takers." In BARA: 121–123.
1489 "We the poets." *Black Forum.* 1.2 Wint. 1976–1977: 41.
1490 "Who raps for the dead lecturer (in seance)." *Greenfield Rev.* 7.3–4 Spr.-Sum. 1979: 17.
1491 "The women in my life." *Greenfield Rev.* 7.3–4 Spr.-Sum. 1979: 16.

Textual Criticism
1492 Banfield, Beryle. *Interracial Books for Children Bull.* 9.8 1978: 17–18. Rev. of *Growin'.*
1493 Banfield, Beryle. *Interracial Books for Children Bull.* 9.4–5 1978: 31. Rev. of *Something on My Mind.*
1494 Harris, Jessica. *Essence.* 9.2 June 1978: 12. Rev. of *Growin'.*

Angelina Weld Grimké (1880–1958)

Bibliography
1495 Perry, Margaret. "Angelina Weld Grimké." In PERH: 86–87. Includes criticism.

Poetry
1496 "At April." In STET: 61.
1497 "For the candle light." In STET: 63.
1498 "A Mona Lisa." In STET: 60.
1499 "To keep the memory of Charlotte Forten Grimké." In STET: 61–62.

Summary of Play
1500 Southgate, Robert L. In SOUT: 134–138. Summary of *Rachel* (1920).

Textual Criticism

1501 Greene, Michael. "Angelina Weld Grimké." In DL50: 149–155. Includes biography and additional bibliography.

1502 Hull, Gloria. "Under the days: the buried life and poetry of Angelina Weld Grimké." *Conditions 5.* 2.2 1979: 17–25.

1503 Hull, Gloria. "Under the days: the buried life and poetry of Angelina Weld Grimké." In SMIT: 73–82.

1504 Miller, Jeanne-Marie A. "Angelina Weld Grimké." In DL54: 129–136. Includes biography and additional bibliography.

1505 Miller, Jeanne-Marie A. "Angelina Weld Grimké: playwright and poet." *CLA J.* 21.4 June 1978: 513–524.

Charlotte Forten Grimké (1837–1914)

Poetry

1506 "A parting hymn." In STET: 22–23.
1507 "Poem." In STET: 23.
1508 "To W.L.G. on reading his 'Chosen queen'." In STET: 24.

Textual Criticism

1509 Braxton, Joanne M. *Charlotte Forten Grimké (1837–1914).* Wellesley, MA: Wellesley College Center for Research on Women, 1985. Working Paper No. 153. Essay on Grimké's use of the diary.

1510 Harris, Trudier. "Charlotte L. Forten." In DL50: 130–139. Has biography and bibliography.

Grosvenor, Verta Mae *see* Smart-Grosvenor, Verta Mae

Rosa Guy (1925–)

Children's Stories

1511 *And I Heard a Bird Sing.* NY: Delacorte, 1987.
1512 *The Disappearance.* NY: Delacorte, 1979.
1513 *Edith Jackson.* NY: Viking, 1978.
1514 *Mirror of Her Own.* NY: Delacorte, 1981.
1515 *Mother Crocodile: An Uncle Amadou Tale from Senegal.* NY: Delacorte, 1981. Original story, *Maman-Caiman,* is by Birago Diop, and was translated and adapted by Guy.
1516 *My Love, My Love,* or *The Peasant Girl.* NY: Holt, Rinehart & Winston, 1985.
1517 *New Guys Around the Block.* NY: Delacorte, 1983.
1518 *Paris, Pee Wee, and Big Dog.* NY: Delacorte, 1984.
1519 *Ruby.* NY: Viking, 1976.

Essay
1520 "Young adult books: I am a storyteller." *Horn Book.* 61.2 Mar.–Apr. 1985: 220–221.

Novel
1521 *A Measure of Time.* NY: Holt, Rinehart & Winston, 1983.

Summary of Novel
1522 Southgate, Robert L. In SOUT: 39–40. Summary of *Bird at My Window* (1966).

Textual Criticism
1523 Banfield, Beryle. *Interracial Books for Children Bull.* 9.6 1978: 15. Rev. of *Edith Jackson.*
1524 Brown, Beth. *Black Scholar.* 16.1 Jan.–Feb. 1985: 54–55. Rev. of *A Measure of Time.*
1525 Clark, Terri. *Off Our Backs.* 9.10 Nov. 1979: 21. Rev. of *Ruby.*
1526 Commire, Anne. In CO14: 77. Some biography and bibliography.
1527 Dee, Ruby. *Freedomways.* 16.2 1976: 118–120. Rev. of *Ruby.*
1528 Fritz, Jean. *N.Y. Times Book Rev.* Dec. 2, 1979: 40. Rev. of *The Disappearance.*
1529 Holtze, Sally Holmes. In HOLT: 140–141. Some biography and bibliography.
1530 Isaacs, Susan. *N.Y. Times Book Rev.* Oct. 9, 1983: 14. Rev. of *A Measure of Time.*
1531 Lanes, Selma G. *N.Y. Times Book Rev.* Aug. 28, 1983: 22. Rev. of *New Guys Around the Block.*
1532 Lanes, Selma G. *N.Y. Times Book Rev.* July 2, 1978: 11. Rev. of *Edith Jackson.*
1533 Lawrence, Leota S. "Rosa Guy." In DL33: 101–106. Includes biography and additional bibliography.
1534 Omowale, Jadi Z. *Black Books Bull.* 7.3 1981: 67, 72. Rev. of *Mirror of Her Own.*
1535 Roebuck, Marcia V. *Encore Amer. and Worldwide News.* 9.9 Dec. 1981: 36. Rev. of *Mother Crocodile.*
1536 Rogers, Judy. *Interracial Books for Children Bull.* 16.8 1985: 16. Rev. of *Paris, Pee Wee, and Big Dog.*
1537 Walker, Alice. *Black Scholar.* 8.3 Dec. 1976: 51–52. Rev. of *Ruby.*
1538 Williams, Regina. *Interracial Books for Children Bull.* 8.2 1977: 14–15. Rev. of *Ruby.*
1539 Wilson, Judith. *Essence.* 10.1 May 1979: 17. Rev. of *Edith Jackson.*
1540 Wilson, Judith. *Freedomways.* 23.4 1983: 281–282. Rev. of *A Measure of Time.*
1541 Wilson, Judith. "Rosa Guy: writing with bold vision." *Essence.* 10.6 Oct. 1979: 14, 20.

Jo Ann Hall-Evans (1934–)

Poetry
1542 "Cape coast castle revisited." In STET: 191.
1543 "Hope." *Essence.* 17.12 Apr. 1987: 131.
1544 "Seduction." In STET: 192.

Virginia Hamilton (1936–)

Bibliography
1545 Roginski, Jim. In ROGI: 136.

Children's Stories
1546 *Arilla Sundown.* NY: Greenwillow, 1976.
1547 *Dustland.* NY: Greenwillow, 1980.
1548 *The Gathering.* NY: Greenwillow, 1981.
1549 *Jahdu.* NY: Greenwillow, 1980.
1550 *Junius Over Far.* NY: Harper, 1985.
1551 *Justice and Her Brothers.* NY: Greenwillow, 1978.
1552 *A Little Love.* NY: Philomel, 1984.
1553 *The Magical Adventures of Pretty Pearl.* NY: Harper, 1983.
1554 *The Mystery of Drear House: Book Two of the Dies Drear Chronicle.* NY: Greenwillow, 1987.
1555 *The People Could Fly: American Black Folktales.* NY: Knopf, 1985.
1556 *Planet of Junior Brown.* NY: Dell, 1978.
1557 "Sheema's journey." *Seventeen.* 43 Apr. 1984: 202–203.
1558 *Sweet Whispers, Brother Rush.* NY: Philomel, 1982.
1559 *A White Romance.* NY: Philomel, 1987.
1560 *Willie Bea and the Time the Martians Landed.* NY: Avon, 1982.
1561 *Zeely.* NY: Dell, 1978.

Essays
1562 "Changing woman, working." In HEAR: 54-61. On writing.
1563 *Illusion and Reality.* Washington, D.C.: Library of Congress, 1976. An 18-page lecture, Nov. 17, 1975, for National Children's Book Week.
1564 "Illusion and reality." In HAVI: 115-131. On writing for children.

Summary of Children's Story
1565 Southgate, Robert L. In SOUT: 86-87. Summary of *The House of Dies Drear* (1968).

Textual Criticism and Interviews
1566 Apseloff, Marilyn. "A conversation with Virginia Hamilton." *Children's Lit. in Ed.* 14.4 Wint. 1983: 204-213.
1567 Apseloff, Marilyn. *Virginia Hamilton: Ohio Explorer in the World of Imagination.* Columbus: State Library of Ohio, 1979.

1568 Ball, Jane. "Virginia Hamilton." In DL33: 107–110. Has biography and bibliography.

1569 Blouin, Rose. *Black Books Bull.* 7.2 1981: 58–59. Rev. of *Dustland.*

1570 Burns, Mary M. *Horn Book.* 61.5 Sept.–Oct. 1985: 563–564. Rev. of *Junius Over Far.*

1571 Cook, Martha E. "Virginia Hamilton." In MAIN: 232–234. Biography and bibliography.

1572 Dressel, Janice Hartwick. "The legacy of Ralph Ellison in Virginia Hamilton's *Justice* trilogy." *English J.* 73.7 Nov. 1984: 42–48.

1573 Fritz, Jean. *N.Y. Times Book Rev.* Dec. 17, 1978: 27. Rev. of *Justice and Her Brothers.*

1574 Fritz, Jean. *N.Y. Times Book Rev.* May 4, 1980: 26. Rev. of *Dustland.*

1575 Kaye, M. *N.Y. Times Book Rev.* Mar. 18, 1984: 31. Rev. of *Willie Bea and the Time the Martians Landed.*

1576 Langton, Jane. *N.Y. Times Book Rev.* Oct. 31, 1976: 39. Rev. of *Arilla Sundown.*

1577 Milton, Joyce. *N.Y. Times Book Rev.* Sept. 27, 1981: 36. Rev. of *The Gathering.*

1578 Montreville, Doris de. In DEMO: 162–164. Biography and bibliography.

1579 Moss, Anita. "Frontiers of gender in children's literature: Virginia Hamilton's *Arilla Sundown.*" *Children's Lit. Assoc. Q.* 8.4 Wint. 1983: 25–27.

1580 Muse, Daphne. *Interracial Books for Children Bull.* 17.3–4 1986: 34. Rev. of *Junius Over Far.*

1581 Orgel, D. *N.Y. Times Book Rev.* Apr. 7, 1985: 20. Rev. of *Junius Over Far.*

1582 Paterson, Katerine. *N.Y. Times Book Rev.* Nov. 14, 1982: 41. Rev. of *Sweet Whispers, Brother Rush.*

1583 Porte, Barbara Ann. *N.Y. Times Book Rev.* Sept. 4, 1983: 14. Rev. of *The Magical Adventures of Pretty Pearl.*

1584 Rees, David. "Long ride through a painted desert." In REES: 168–184.

1585 Scarupa, Harriet Jackson. "Virginia Hamilton: teller of tales." *Essence.* 6.10 Jan. 1976: 58–59, 62, 94.

1586 Southerland, Ellease. *N.Y. Times Book Rev.* Nov. 8, 1987: 36. Rev. of *A White Romance.*

1587 Spigner, Nieda. *Freedomways.* 25.1 1985: 57. Rev. of *Willie Bea and the Time the Martians Landed.*

1588 Townsend, John R. "Virginia Hamilton." In TOWN: 97–110. On various works.

1589 Wagner, Judith. "More vivid than daylight." In AUTN: 3–5. Interview. Originally published in the *Cincinnati Enquirer,* Jan. 5, 1975.

1590 Wilson, Geraldine L. *Interracial Books for Children Bull.* 16.4 1985: 19. Rev. of *A Little Love.*

1591 Wilson, Geraldine L. *Interracial Books for Children Bull.* 15.5 1984: 17–18. Rev. of *The Magical Adventures of Pretty Pearl.*

1592 Wilson, Geraldine L. *Interracial Books for Children Bull.* 14.1–2 1983: 32. Rev. of *Sweet Whispers, Brother Rush.*

Hanna *see* Loftin, Elouise

Lorraine Hansberry (1930–1965)

Bibliography
1593 Kaiser, Ernest and Robert Nemiroff. "A Lorraine Hansberry bibliography." *Freedomways.* 19.4 Fall 1979: 285–304.

Biography
1594 Carter, Steven R. "Commitment amid complexity: Lorraine Hansberry's life in action." *Melus.* 7.3 Fall 1980: 39–53. Biographical and intellectual life of Hansberry, with chronology.

1595 Collins, David and Evelyn Witter. "Lorraine Hansberry." In COLL: 43–53. Juvenile literature.

1596 Sicherman, Barbara and Carol H. Green. In SICH: 310–312.

Drama
1597 Nemiroff, Robert, Ed. *Lorraine Hansberry: The Collected Last Plays: Les Blancs, The Drinking Gourd, What Use Are Flowers.* NY: New American Library, 1983.

1598 "Toussaint, excerpt from Act I of a work in progress." In WILK: 41–67.

Essays
1599 "In defense of the equality of men." In GILN: 2058–2067.

1600 "The Negro writer and his roots: toward a new romanticism." *Black Scholar.* 12.2 Mar.–Apr. 1981: 2–12.

Novel
1601 "The Buck Williams Tennessee Memorial Association." *Southern Exposure.* 12.5 Sept.–Oct. 1984: 28. Excerpt from her uncompleted novel, *All the Dark and Beautiful Warriors.*

Poetry
1602 "Ocomogosiay!" *Black Collegian.* 14.4 Mar.–Apr. 1984: 48. Written in 1951.

1603 "Three hundred years later." *Black Collegian.* 14.4 Mar.–Apr. 1984: 48. Written in 1949.

1604 "To Ghana off the top of my head, March 1957." *Black Collegian.* 14.4 Mar.–Apr. 1984: 48.

Textual Criticism
1605 Adams, Michael. "Lorraine Hansberry." In DL07: 247–254. Includes biography and additional bibliography.

1606 Baldwin, James. "Lorraine Hansberry at the summit." *Freedomways.* 19.4 Fall 1979: 269–272.

1607 Barthelemy, Anthony. "Mother, sister, wife: a dramatic perspective." *Southern Rev.* 21.3 July 1985: 770–789. On *A Raisin in the Sun.*

1608 Bennett, Lerone, Jr. and Margaret G. Burroughs. "A Lorraine Hansberry rap." *Freedomways.* 19.4 Fall 1979: 226–233. Transcript of a discussion of the life and works of Hansberry.

1609 Bigsby, C.W.E. "Black drama: the public voice." In BIGS: 214–225.

1610 Bigsby, C.W.E. "In BIGC: 381–387. On several works.

1611 Bond, Jean Carey. "Lorraine Hansberry: to reclaim her memory." *Freedomways.* 19.4 Fall 1979: 183–185. Editorial introducing the *Freedomways* special issue on Hansberry.

1612 Bray, Rosemary L. "Work in progress: the definitive Lorraine Hansberry." *Ms.* 15.8 Feb. 1987: 31. On Margaret B. Wilkerson's research on Hansberry.

1613 Breitinger, Eckard. "Lorraine Hansberry: *A Raisin in the Sun.*" In GRAB: 153–168.

1614 Carter, Steven R. "Images of men in Lorraine Hansberry's writing." *Black Amer. Lit. Forum.* 19.4 Wint. 1985: 160–162.

1615 Carter, Steven R. "The John Brown Theatre: Lorraine Hansberry's cultural views and dramatic goals." *Freedomways.* 19.4 Fall 1979: 186–191.

1616 Carter, Steven R. "Lorraine Hansberry." In DL38: 120–134. Includes biography and additional bibliography.

1617 Cheney, Anne. *Lorraine Hansberry.* Boston: Twayne, 1984. First full-length study of Hansberry.

1618 Elder, Lonne, III. "Lorraine Hansberry: social consciousness and the will." *Freedomways.* 19.4 Fall 1979: 213–218.

1619 Friedman, Sharon. "Feminism as theme in twentieth century American women's drama." *American Studies.* 25.1 Spr. 1984: 69–89. On several works.

1620 Giovanni, Nikki. "An emotional view of Lorraine Hansberry." *Freedomways.* 19.4 Fall 1979: 281–282. A memoir.

1621 Gresham, Jewell Handy. "Lorraine Hansberry as prose stylist." *Freedomways.* 19.4 Fall 1979: 192–204.

1622 Hairston, Loyle. "Lorraine Hansberry — portrait of an angry young writer." *Crisis.* 86.4 Apr. 1979: 123–124, 126, 128.

1623 Haley, Alex. "The once and future vision." *Freedomways.* 19.4 Fall 1979: 277–280.

1624 Keyssar, Helene. "Locating the rainbow: gestures of drama and political acts." In KEYS: 207–218.

1625 Keyssar, Helene. "Sounding the rumble of dreams deferred: Lorraine Hansberry's *A Raisin in the Sun.*" In KEYS: 113–146.

1626 Killens, John Oliver. "Lorraine Hansberry: on time!" *Freedomways.* 19.4 Fall 1979: 273–276.

1627 King, Woodie, Jr. "Lorraine Hansberry's children: Black artists and *A Raisin in the Sun.*" *Freedomways.* 19.4 Fall 1979: 219–221.

1628 Mayfield, Julian. "Lorraine Hansberry: a woman for all seasons." *Freedomways.* 19.4 Fall 1979: 263–268.

1629 McGovern, Edyth M. "Lorraine Hansberry." In MAIN: 236–239. Includes biography and some bibliography.

1630 Miller, Jordan Y. In FREN: 256–258. On several works.

1631 Mootry, Maria K. *The Crisis of Feminist Criticism: A Case Study of Lorraine Hansberry's Feminine Triads in "Raisin" and "Sign."* Urbana: Univ. of Illinois, 1982 (?). Afro Scholar Working Papers, vol. 16.

1632 Nellhaus, A. "His faith and love kept Hansberry's legacy to share." In AUTN: 211. On her husband.

1633 Noble, Jeanne. In NOBL: 182–184. On several works.

1634 Olauson, Judith. In OLAU: 89–92, 102–108. On several works.

1635 Powell, Bertie J. "The Black experience in Margaret Walker's *Jubilee* and Lorraine Hansberry's *The Drinking Gourd*." *CLA J.* 21.2 Dec. 1977: 304–311.

1636 Rich, Adrienne. "The problem with Lorraine Hansberry." *Freedomways*. 19.4 Fall 1979: 247–255.

1637 Riley, Clayton. "Lorraine Hansberry: a melody in a different key." *Freedomways*. 19.4 Fall 1979: 205–212.

1638 Royals, Demetria Brendan. "The me Lorraine Hansberry knew." *Freedomways*. 19.4 Fall 1979: 261–262.

1639 Salaam, Kalamu ya. "What use is writing? Re-reading Lorraine Hansberry." *Black Collegian*. 14.4 Mar.–Apr. 1984: 45–46.

1640 Scanlan, Tom. In SCAN: 195–201. On several works.

1641 Ward, Douglas Turner. "Lorraine Hansberry and the passion of Walter Lee." *Freedomways*. 19.4 Fall 1979: 223–225.

1642 Wilkerson, Margaret B. "The dark vision of Lorraine Hansberry: excerpts from a literary biography." *Massachusetts Rev.* 28.4 Wint. 1987: 642–650.

1643 Wilkerson, Margaret B. "Lorraine Hansberry: the complete feminist." *Freedomways*. 19.4 Fall 1979: 235–245.

1644 Wilkerson, Margaret B. "The sighted eyes and feeling heart of Lorraine Hansberry." *Black Amer. Lit. Forum.* 17.1 Spr. 1983: 8–13. Revised version of essay appearing in BOCK: 91–104.

1645 Wilkerson, Margaret B. "The sighted eyes and feeling heart of Lorraine Hansberry." In BOCK: 91–104. On various works.

1646 Wright, Sarah E. "Lorraine Hansberry on film." *Freedomways*. 19.4 Fall 1979: 283–284.

Frances E.W. Harper (1825–1911)

Biography
1647 Ammons, Elizabeth. "Frances Ellen Watkins Harper (1825–1911)." *Legacy.* 2.2 Fall 1985: 61–66.

Novel
1648 "Iola." In WASA: 87–108. Excerpt from novel *Iola Leroy* (1892).

Poetry
1649 "An appeal to my countrywomen." In STET: 31–32.

1650 "Aunt Chloe's politics." In GILN: 832.
1651 "Bury me in a free land." In LONG: 105–106.
1652 "The crocuses." In STET: 33–34.
1653 "A double standard." In STET: 26–27.
1654 "Learning to read." In GILN: 832–834.
1655 "Learning to read." In STET: 29–30.
1656 "The mission of the flowers." In STET: 34–36.
1657 "She's free!" In STET: 32–33.
1658 "The slave auction." In LONG: 103.
1659 "The slave mother." In LONG: 104.
1660 "Vashti." In GILN: 830–832.
1661 "Vashti." In STET: 27–29.

Short Fiction
1662 "The two offers." In KOPM: 117–129. First story published in the U.S. by an Afro-American.

Textual Criticism
1663 Bell, Bernard W. "Frances Ellen Watkins Harper (1825–1911)." In BELA: 57–60. On various works.

1664 Campbell, Jane. "Female paradigms in Frances Harper's *Iola Leroy* and Pauline Hopkins's *Contending Forces*." In CAMP: 18–41.

1665 Carby, Hazel V. "'Of lasting service for the race': the work of Frances E.W. Harper." In CARB: 62–94.

1666 Christian, Barbara. "'Shadows uplifted'." In NEWT: 181–215. On *Iola Leroy, Shadows Uplifted,* first novel published by an Afro-American woman.

1667 Christian, Barbara. "The uses of history: Frances Harper's *Iola Leroy, Shadows Uplifted.*" In CHRF: 165–170. A paper given at the National Women's Studies Association Conference, 1983, University of Wisconsin.

1668 Davis, Marianna W. In DAVI: 154–156, 157, 165, 166. On several works.

1669 Graham, Maryemma. "Frances Ellen Watkins Harper." In DL50: 164–173. Biography and bibliography.

1670 Hill, Patricia Liggins. "'Let me make the songs for the people': a study of Frances Watkins Harper's poetry." *Black Amer. Lit. Forum.* 15.2 Sum. 1981: 60–65.

1671 Lewis, Vashti. "The near-white female in Frances Ellen Harper's *Iola Leroy.*" *Phylon.* 45.4 Dec. 1984: 314–322.

1672 Washington, Mary Helen. "Uplifting the women and the race: the forerunners—Harper and Hopkins." In WASA: 73–86.

Deloris Harrison (1938–)

Short Fiction
1673 "Clarissa's problem." *Essence.* 8.6 Oct. 1977: 50, 52, 134, 136.

Summary of Novel
   1674 Southgate, Robert L. In SOUT: 101–102. Summary of *Journey All Alone* (1971).

Textual Criticism
   1675 Commire, Anne. "Deloris Harrison." In CO09: 97–98. Includes biography and bibliography.

Safiya Henderson (1950–)

Poetry
   1676 "Letter to my father . . . a solidarity long overdue." *Essence.* 10.2 June 1979: 12.
   1677 "A memoir to workers . . . no compensation." *Black Scholar.* 8.5 Mar. 1977: 49–50.
   1678 "Portrait of a woman artist." In BARA: 131–134.

Frenchy Hodges (1940–)

Short Fiction
   1679 "Requiem for Willie Lee." In WASH: 97–108.
   1680 "Requiem for Willie Lee." *Ms.* 8.4 Oct. 1979: 61–62, 75, 77–78.

Bell Hooks (Gloria Watkins)

Essay
   1681 "Reflections of a 'good' daughter." *Sage.* 1.2 Fall 1984: 28–29.

Non-Fiction
   1682 *Ain't I a Woman: Black Women and Feminism.* Boston: South End, 1981.
   1683 *Feminist Theory from Margin to Center.* Boston: South End, 1984.

Poetry
   1684 *And There We Wept: Poems.* Los Angeles: Golemics, 1978.

Textual Criticism
   1685 Clarke, Cheryl. *Off Our Backs.* 12.4 Apr. 1982: 7. Rev. of *Ain't I a Woman.*
   1686 Guy-Sheftall, Beverly. *Phylon.* 44 Mar. 1983: 84–85. Rev. of *Ain't I a Woman.*

Akua Lezli Hope (1957–)

Poetry

1687 "August (for Baron)." In BARA: 142–143.

1688 "Djamila." *Conditions 3.* 1.3 Spr. 1978: 43.

1689 "Getting to know, or Stepping out in an entirely different way." In COOP: 189.

1690 "Getting to know, or Stepping out in an entirely different way." *Iowa Rev.* 12.2–3 Spr.–Sum. 1981: 189.

1691 "Gowanus Canal (because you said look again)." In COOP: 190.

1692 "Gowanus Canal (because you said look again)." *Iowa Rev.* 12.2–3 Spr.–Sum. 1981: 190.

1693 "Lament." In BARA: 141–142.

1694 "Leaving is a little death." *Black Amer. Lit. Forum.* 20.3 Fall 1986: 262–263.

1695 *Lovecycles.* [New York?]: Center for New Images, 1976.

1696 "No one comes home to lonely women." In DALE: 102.

1697 "One." In BARA: 143–144.

1698 "Revoltillo Bacalao." *Black Scholar.* 12.1 Jan.–Feb. 1981: 92.

1699 "Survival is its own revenge." *Black Scholar.* 12.1 Jan.–Feb. 1981: 93.

1700 "To Sister for Mother." In DALE: 103.

1701 "Untitled [Collect images like flowers]." *Conditions 3.* 1.3 Spr. 1978: 42.

Lea Hopkins

Biography

1702 Ebert, Alan. "Lea Hopkins, just different." *Essence.* 10.12 Apr. 1980: 88–89, 122, 124, 127–128, 130, 134.

Poetry

1703 "Hallelujah lady." *Helicon Nine.* 14–15 1986: 166–167.

1704 "The mammy." *Helicon Nine.* 14–15 1986: 167.

1705 *Womyn I Have Known You.* Overland Park, KS: Published by author, 1978.

1706 "The yipper." *Helicon Nine.* 14–15 1986: 166.

Poetry and Prose

1707 *I'm Not Crazy, Just Different.* Overland Park, KS: Published by author, 1977.

Pauline E. Hopkins (1859–1930)

Novel

1708 "Sappho." In WASA: 109–129. Excerpt from novel *Contending Forces* (1900).

Short Fiction

1709 "Bro'r Abr'm Jimson's wedding." In WASA: 130-149. Originally published in 1901.

Textual Criticism

1710 Campbell, Jane. "Female paradigms in Frances Harper's *Iola Leroy* and Pauline Hopkins's *Contending Forces.*" In CAMP: 18-41.

1711 Carby, Hazel V. "'All the fire and romance': the magazine fiction of Pauline Hopkins." In CARB: 145-162.

1712 *Crisis.* 86.5 May 1979: 177. Rev. of *Contending Forces.*

1713 Lamping, Marilyn. "Pauline Elizabeth Hopkins." In MAIN: 325-327. Biography and bibliography.

1714 "'Of what use is fiction?': Pauline Elizabeth Hopkins." In CARB: 121-144.

1715 Tate, Claudia. "Pauline Hopkins: our literary foremother." In PRYS: 53-66.

1716 Washington, Mary Helen. "Uplifting the women and the race: the forerunners — Harper and Hopkins." In WASA: 73-86.

House, Gloria Larry *see* Kgositsile, Aneb

Diane Houston (1954-)

Drama

1717 "The fishermen." In OSTR: 73-103.

Mariah Britton Howard

Poetry

1718 "Mabel." *Black Forum.* 1.1 Jan. 1976: 13.

1719 "Reports." In BARA: 145.

1720 "Solution 9 'to touch you'." In BARA: 147-149.

1721 "A using." In BARA: 145-147.

1722 "A wellness has spoken." *Essence.* 14.6 Oct. 1983: 89.

1723 *With Fire.* NY: Meta, 1982.

Textual Criticism

1724 Jordan, June. *Freedomways.* 23.1 1983: 50. Rev. of *With Fire.*

Gloria T. Hull

Editing

1725 *Give Us Each Day: The Diary of Alice Dunbar-Nelson.* NY: Norton, 1984.

1726 Hull, Gloria T. and Patricia Bell Scott and Barbara Smith, Eds. *All the Women Are White, All the Blacks Are Men, But Some of Us Are Brave: Black Women's Studies.* Old Westbury, NY: Feminist, 1982.

Essays

1727 "Afro-American women poets: a bio-critical survey." In GILS: 165–182.

1728 "The Black woman writer and the diaspora." *Black Scholar.* 17.2 Mar.–Apr. 1986: 2–4. Closing address from the Black Women Writers and the Diaspora Conference, E. Lansing, MI, Oct. 1985.

1729 "Black women poets from Wheatley to Walker." In BELL: 69–86.

1730 "The 'bridge' between Black studies and women's studies: Black women's studies." *Women's Studies Q.* 10.2 Sum. 1982: 12–13.

1731 "'Keeping Black women at the center': a conversation between Gloria T. Hull and Barbara Smith." *Off Our Backs.* 12.5 May 1982: 22–23.

1732 "Notes on a Marxist interpretation of Black American literature." *Black Amer. Lit. Forum.* 12.4 1978: 148–153.

1733 "Researching Alice Dunbar-Nelson: a personal and literary perspective." In HULL: 189–195.

1734 "Rewriting Afro-American literature: a case for Black women writers." *Radical Teacher.* 6 Dec. 1977: 10–14.

Non-Fiction

1735 *Color, Sex, and Poetry: Three Women Writers of the Harlem Renaissance.* Bloomington: Indiana Univ., 1987. Biographical and critical study of Alice M. Dunbar-Nelson, Angelina Weld Grimké, and Georgia Douglas Camp Johnson.

Poetry

1736 "Blues snatch." *Obsidian.* 7.2–3 Sum.–Wint. 1981: 191.

1737 "For Audre." In SMIT: lvii–lviii.

1738 "Movin' and steppin'." *Obsidian.* 7.2–3 Sum.–Wint. 1981: 188–189.

1739 "Pictures my mother left me, growing up." *Frontiers.* 9.3 1987: 80–82.

1740 "Poem (for Audre)." *Conditions 5.* 2.2 Aut. 1979: [4].

1741 "Poem for Audre Lorde." *Callaloo.* 5.2 1979: 79–80.

1742 "Poem for Nenia." *Chrysalis.* 11 1980: 106.

1743 "The prison and the park." *Obsidian.* 7.2–3 Sum.–Wint. 1981: 189–190.

Textual Criticism and Interviews

1744 Bovoso, Carole. *Essence.* 13.1 May 1982: 24. Rev. of *All the Women Are White*. . . .

1745 Dickerson, Dolores Pawley. *J. of Negro Educ.* 51 Sum. 1982: 361–363. Rev. of *All the Women Are White*. . . .

1746 Guy-Sheftall, Beverly. *Phylon.* 43.3 Sept. 1982: 280–281. Rev. of *All the Women Are White*. . . .

1747 Jenkins, Verdia. *Afro-Americans in New York Life and History.* 6 July 1982: 63–64. Rev. of *All the Women Are White*. . . .

1748 Nussbaum, Felicity. *Black Amer. Lit. Forum.* 19.4 Wint. 1985: 167–169. Rev. of *Give Us Each Day.*

1749 Thomas, June. "Public-private diary: finding Black women's history." *Off Our Backs.* 15.5 May 1985: 20–22. Interview, on *Give Us Each Day.*

Lee Hunkins (1930–)

Drama
1750 "Revival." In OSTR: 105–109.

Jacquelyn Furgus Hunter

Poetry
1751 "Mis' Lou." In BELL: 328–330.

Kristin Hunter (1931–)

Children's Stories
1752 *Lou in the Limelight.* NY: Scribner, 1981. Sequel to *The Soul Brothers and Sister Lou* (1968).

Novel
1753 *The Lakestown Rebellion.* NY: Scribner, 1978.

Poetry
1754 *Africa Speaks to the West.* [Pittsburgh]: Three Rivers, 1976. Broadside.

Short Fiction
1755 "Bleeding berries." *Callaloo.* 2.2 1979: 25–35.
1756 "Debut." In DAHL: 20–26.

Summary of Children's Story
1757 Southgate, Robert L. In SOUT: 149–151. Summary of *The Soul Brothers and Sister Lou* (1968).

Textual Criticism
1758 Commire, Anne. In CO12: 105–107. Mostly biography.
1759 Dee, Ruby. *Freedomways.* 22.4 1982: 264–265. Rev. of *Lou in the Limelight.*
1760 Early, Gerald. "Working girl blues: mothers, daughters, and the image of Billie Holiday in Kristin Hunter's *God Bless the Child.*" *Black Amer. Lit. Forum.* 20.4 Wint. 1986: 423–442.
1761 Harris, Trudier. "The maid as southern and northern mammy: Charles W. Chesnutt, *The Marrow of Tradition* (1901), Kristin Hunter, *God Bless the Child* (1964), Toni Morrison, *The Bluest Eye* (1970)." In HARS: 35–69.
1762 Kaye, Marilyn. *N.Y. Times Book Rev.* Feb. 21, 1982: 35. Rev. of *Lou in the Limelight.*

1763 Montreville, Doris de and Elizabeth D. Crawford. In DEMO: 187–189. Biography and bibliography.

1764 O'Neale, Sondra. "Kristin Hunter." In DL33: 119–124. Biography and bibliography.

1765 Osborne, Gwendolyn E. *Crisis.* 83.6 June–July 1976: 214. Rev. of *The Survivors* (novel, 1975).

1766 Polak, Maralyn L. "Kristin Hunter: a writer and a fighter." In AUTN: 236–237.

1767 Stimpfle, N. *"Soul Brothers and Sister Lou." English J.* 66.3 Mar. 1977: 61.

Zora Neale Hurston (1891–1960)

Autobiography
1768 *Dust Tracks on a Road: An Autobiography* [Excerpt]. In FORK: 587–597. Originally written in 1942.

Bibliography
1769 Dance, Daryl C. "Zora Neale Hurston." In DUKE: 321–351. Bibliographical essay.

1770 Newson, Adele S. *Zora Neale Hurston: A Reference Guide.* Boston: G.K. Hall, 1987. Annotated.

1771 Perry, Margaret. "Zora Neale Hurston." In PERH: 100–107. Commentary included.

1772 Pettis, Joyce. "Zora Neale Hurston." In MAIN: 363–366. Includes biographical information.

Biography
1773 Sicherman, Barbara and Carol Green. "Zora Neale Hurston." In SICH: 361–363.

Essays
1774 "Folklore field notes from Zora Neale Hurston." *Black Scholar.* 7.7 Apr. 1976: 39–46. Introduction by Robert Hemenway.

1775 "How it feels to be colored me." In GILN: 1649–1653.

Folklore
1776 *Mules and Men* [Excerpt]. In FORK: 582–587. The work, written in 1935, consists of folk tales and voodoo practices in the South.

Novels
1777 "His over-the-creek girl." In WASA: 255–279. Excerpt from *Jonah's Gourd Vine* (1934).

1778 "Janie Crawford." In WASA: 280–293. Excerpt from *Their Eyes Were Watching God* (1937).

Selections
1779 Walker, Alice, Ed. *I Love Myself When I Am Laughing . . . And Then*

Again When I Am Looking Mean and Impressive: A Zora Neale Hurston Reader. Old Westbury, NY: Feminist, 1979. Has autobiography, essays, short fiction, excerpts from novels. Introduction was written by Mary Helen Washington, "Zora Neale Hurston: a woman half in shadow," pages 7–25.

Short Fiction

1780 "The gilded six-bits." *Helicon Nine.* 17–18 1987: 51–59.

1781 "The gilded six-bits." In FORK: 90–99.

1782 *Spunk: The Selected Stories of Zora Neale Hurston.* Berkeley, CA: Turtle Island Foundation, 1985.

1783 "Sweat." In GILN: 1639–1649.

1784 "Sweat." In LONG: 392–402.

Summary of Novel

1785 Southgate, Robert L. In SOUT: 163–165. Summary of *Their Eyes Were Watching God* (1937).

Textual Criticism

1786 Bell, Bernard W. "Zora Neale Hurston." In BELA: 119–128. On several works.

1787 Bernstein, Dennis and Connie Blitt. "Zora Neale Hurston: genius of the South." *Helicon Nine.* 17–18 1987: 49–50.

1788 Bethel, Lorraine. "'This infinity of conscious pain': Zora Neale Hurston and the Black female literary tradition." In HULL: 176–188.

1789 Bloom, Harold, Ed. *Zora Neale Hurston.* NY: Chelsea House, 1986.

1790 Bloom, Harold, Ed. *Zora Neale Hurston's* Their Eyes Were Watching God. NY: Chelsea House, 1987.

1791 Boyd, Melba Joyce. *Black Scholar.* 11.8 Nov.–Dec. 1980: 82–83. Rev. of *I Love Myself When I Am Laughing. . . .*

1792 Brown, Lloyd W. "Zora Neale Hurston and the nature of female perception." *Obsidian.* 4.3 Wint. 1978: 39–45.

1793 Burke, Virginia M. "Zora Neale Hurston and Fannie Hurst as they saw each other." *CLA J.* 20.4 June 1977: 435–447.

1794 Cantarow, Ellen. "Sex, race and criticism: thoughts of a white feminist on Kate Chopin and Zora Neale Hurston." *Radical Teacher.* 9 Sept. 1978: 30–33.

1795 Carr, Glynis. "Storytelling as 'Bildung' in Zora Neale Hurston's *Their Eyes Were Watching God.*" *CLA J.* 31.2 Dec. 1987: 189–200.

1796 Cooke, Michael G. "Solitude: the beginnings of self-realization in Zora Neale Hurston." In COOK: 71–109.

1797 Crabtree, Claire. "The confluence of folklore, feminism and Black self-determination in Zora Neale Hurston's *Their Eyes Were Watching God.*" *Southern Literary J.* 17.2 Spr. 1985: 54–66.

1798 Davis, Marianna W. In DAVI: 162–165. On several works.

1799 Ferguson, SallyAnn. "Folkloric men and female growth in *Their Eyes Were Watching God.*" *Black Amer. Lit. Forum.* 21.1-2 Spr.–Sum. 1987: 185–197.

1800 Fleming, Robert. "Long-awaited anthology, a 'mean and impressive'

Zora Neale Hurston." *Encore Amer. and Worldwide News.* Dec. 17, 1979: 46–47. Rev. of *I Love Myself*. . . .

1801 Gates, Henry Louis, Jr. "'A Negro way of saying'." *N.Y. Times Book Rev.* Apr. 21, 1985: 1. Revs. of her *Dust Tracks on a Road* (Robert Hemenway, Ed.) and *Moses, Man of the Mountain* (Blyden Jackson, "Introduction").

1802 Gates, Henry Louis, Jr. "Soul of a Black woman." *N.Y. Times Book Rev.* Feb. 19, 1978: 13. Rev. of Hemenway's *Zora Neale Hurston: A Literary Biography.*

1803 Hausman, R. *English J.* 65 Jan. 1976: 61–62. On *Their Eyes Were Watching God.*

1804 Hemenway, Robert, Ed. *Zora Neale Hurston: A Literary Biography.* Urbana: Univ. of Illinois, 1977. Foreword by Alice Walker, "Zora Neale Hurston — a cautionary tale and a partisan view," pages xi–xviii.

1805 Hine, Darlene Clark. "To be gifted, female, and Black." *Southwest Rev.* 67.4 Aut. 1982: 357–369.

1806 Holloway, Karla F.C. *The Character of the Word: The Texts of Zora Neale Hurston.* Westport, CT: Greenwood, 1987. Bibliography on pages 119–123.

1807 Holt, Elvin. "Zora Neale Hurston." In FLOR: 259–269. Biography and bibliography.

1808 Howard, Lillie P. "Marriage: Zora Neale Hurston's system of values." *CLA J.* 21.2 Dec. 1977: 256–268.

1809 Howard, Lillie P. "Nanny and Janie, will the twain ever meet? (A look at Zora Neale Hurston's *Their Eyes Were Watching God*)." *J. of Black Studies.* 12.4 June 1982: 403–414.

1810 Howard, Lillie P. *Zora Neale Hurston.* Boston: G.K. Hall, 1980.

1811 Howard, Lillie P. "Zora Neale Hurston." In DL51: 133–145. Includes biography and additional bibliography.

1812 Howard, Lillie P. "Zora Neale Hurston: just being herself." *Essence.* 11.7 Nov. 1980: 101, 156, 160–161, 164, 166. Biography and general criticism.

1813 Johnson, Barbara. "Metaphor, metonymy and voice in *Their Eyes Were Watching God.*" In GATE: 205–219.

1814 Johnson, Barbara. "Thresholds of difference: structures of address in Zora Neale Hurston." *Critical Inquiry.* 12.1 Aut. 1985: 278–289.

1815 Kennedy, Randall. "Looking for Zora." *N.Y. Times Book Rev.* Dec. 30, 1979: 8. Rev. of *I Love Myself*. . . .

1816 Kitch, Sally L. "Gender and language: dialect, silence and the disruption of discourse." *Women's Studies.* 14.1 1987: 65–78. On *Their Eyes Were Watching God.*

1817 Kubitschek, Missy Dehn. "'Tuh de horizon and back': the female quest in *Their Eyes Were Watching God.*" *Black Amer. Lit. Forum.* 17.3 Fall 1983: 109–115.

1818 Lewis, Vashti Crutcher. "The declining significance of the mulatto female as major character in the novels of Zora Neale Hurston." *CLA J.* 28.2 Dec. 1984: 127–149.

1819 Love, Theresa R. "Zora Neale Hurston's America." *Papers on Language and Lit.* 12.4 Fall 1976: 422–437. Hurston's use of dialect and folk tales.

1820 Lupton, Mary Jane. "Zora Neale Hurston and the survival of the female." *Southern Literary J.* 15.1 Fall 1982: 45–54.

1821 Marks, Donald R. "Sex, violence, and organic consciousness in Zora Neale Hurston's *Their Eyes Were Watching God." Black Amer. Lit. Forum.* 19.4 Wint. 1985: 152–157.

1822 McCredie, Wendy J. "Authority and authorization in *Their Eyes Were Watching God." Black Amer. Lit. Forum.* 16.1 Spr. 1982: 25–28.

1823 Meese, Elizabeth A. "Orality and textuality in Zora Neale Hurston's *Their Eyes Were Watching God."* In MEES: 41–53.

1824 Mikell, Gwendolyn. "The anthropological imagination of Zora Neale Hurston." *Western J. of Black Studies.* 7.1 Spr. 1983: 27–35.

1825 Mikell, Gwendolyn. "When horses talk: reflections on Zora Neale Hurston's Haitian anthropology." *Phylon.* 43.3 Fall 1982: 218–230.

1826 Noble, Jeanne. In NOBL: 164–170. On various works.

1827 Olney, J. *"Zora Neale Hurston: A Literary Biography." New Republic.* Feb. 11, 1978: 26. Rev. of Hemenway's book.

1828 Perry, Margaret. In PERM: 121–124. On several works.

1829 Pinckney, Darryl. "In sorrow's kitchen." *N. Y. Rev. of Books.* Dec. 21, 1978: 55–57. Rev. of Hemenway's *Zora Neale Hurston: A Literary Biography* and several Hurston publications.

1830 Pondrom, Cyrena N. "The role of myth in Hurston's *Their Eyes Were Watching God." Amer. Lit.* 58.2 May 1986: 181–202.

1831 Pryse, Marjorie. "Zora Neale Hurston, Alice Walker, and the 'ancient power' of Black women." In PRYS: 1–24. On the influence of Black women fiction writers on women's literary criticism.

1832 Rambeau, James. "The fiction of Zora Neale Hurston." *Markham Rev.* 5 Sum. 1976: 61–64.

1833 Reich, Alice. "Phoeby's hungry listening." *Women's Studies.* 13.1–2 1986: 163–169. On *Their Eyes Were Watching God.*

1834 Reilly, John M. "Zora Neale Hurston." In FREN: 288–290. On several works.

1835 Rushing, Andrea Benton. "Jumping at the sun." *Callaloo.* 3.1–3 1980: 228–230. Rev. of *I Love Myself When I Am Laughing. . . .*

1836 Sadoff, Dianne F. "Black matrilineage: the case of Alice Walker and Zora Neale Hurston." *Signs.* 11.1 Aut. 1985: 4–26.

1837 Sheffey, Ruthe T., Ed. *Rainbow Round Her Shoulder: The Zora Neale Hurston Symposium Papers.* Baltimore: Morgan St. U., 1983. Symposium took place 1981.

1838 Sheffey, Ruthe T. "Zora Neale Hurston's *Moses, Man of the Mountain:* a fictionalized manifesto of the imperatives of Black leadership." *CLA J.* 29.2 Dec. 1985: 206–220.

1839 Smith, Barbara. "Sexual politics and the fiction of Zora Neale Hurston." *Radical Teacher.* 8 May 1978: 26–30.

1840 Southerland, Ellease. "The influence of voodoo on the fiction of Zora Neale Hurston." In BELL: 171–183.

1841 Spillers, Hortense J. "A hateful passion, a lost love." *Feminist Studies.* 9.2 Sum. 1983: 293–323. On Toni Morrison's *Sula,* Margaret Walker's *Jubilee,* and Hurston's *Their Eyes Were Watching God.*

1842 Stetson, Erlene. *"Their Eyes Were Watching God:* a woman's story." *Regionalism and the Female Imagination.* 4.1 1978: 30.

1843 Wall, Cheryl A. "Zora Neale Hurston: changing her own words." In FLEI: 371–393.

1844 Washington, Mary Helen. "I love the way Janie Crawford left her husbands: Zora Neale Hurston's emergent female hero." In WASA: 237–254.

1845 Weidman, B.S. *Commonweal.* Oct. 4, 1985: 535–536. Revs. of *Dust Tracks on a Road,* second edition, and of *Moses, Man of the Mountain,* reprint of the original 1939 edition.

1846 Wideman, John. "Defining the Black voice in fiction." *Black Amer. Lit. Forum.* 11.3 Fall 1977: 79–82.

1847 Willis, Miriam DeCosta. "Folklore and the creative artist: Lydia Cabrera and Zora Neale Hurston." *CLA J.* 27.1 Sept. 1983: 81–90.

1848 Willis, Susan. "Wandering: Zora Neale Hurston's search for self and method." In WILL: 26–52.

1849 Wilson, Margaret F. "Zora Neale Hurston, author and folklorist." *Negro History Bull.* 45.4 Oct.–Nov.–Dec. 1982: 109–110.

1850 Wolff, Marie Tai. "Listening and living: reading and experience in *Their Eyes Were Watching God.*" *Black Amer. Lit. Forum.* 16.1 Spr. 1982: 29–33.

Lateifa-Ramona L. Hyman

Poetry

1851 "Paraphernalia for a suicide: a revelation of life." In BARA: 150–151.

1852 "Respiration (for Queen Mother Moore)." *Black Books Bull.* 7.3 1981: 61.

1853 "Silhouettes from the street." *Obsidian.* 6.1–2 Spr.–Sum. 1980: 228.

Adrienne Ingrum

Poetry

1854 "Friday the 13th candlelight march." In BARA: 158–161.

1855 "Loomit." In BARA: 152–158.

Rashidah Ismaili

Poetry

1856 "Dialogue." In BARA: 164–165.

1857 "Epilogue." *Essence.* 9.3 July 1978: 16.

1858 "Murderous intent with a deadly weapon." In BARA: 162–163.

1859 "Preparations 2." *Poetry East.* 15 Aut. 1984: 29–30.

1860 "Reminiscence." *Essence.* 9.3 July 1978: 16.

1861 "Struggle of class." In BARA: 166–167.

Angela Jackson (1951-)

Biography
1862 "Women to watch." *Ebony.* 37.10 Aug. 1982: 56.

Novel
1863 "From *Treemont Stone.*" *Triquarterly.* 60 Spr. 1984: 154-170. Excerpt from novel.

Poetry
1864 "Arachnia: her side of the story." *Thirteenth Moon.* 8.1-2 1984: 64-65.

1865 "Blackmen: who make morning." In ADOF: 245-246.

1866 "The bloom amid alabaster still." *Obsidian.* 5.3 Wint. 1979: 90.

1867 "Divination." *Obsidian.* 5.3 Wint. 1979: 88-89.

1868 "Doubting Thomas." *Callaloo.* 5.2 Feb. 1979: 85.

1869 "Fannie." *Black Amer. Lit. Forum.* 19.3 Fall 1985: 101.

1870 "Gathering after those years long ago: five women circa: the last twenties." *Black Scholar.* 11.6 July-Aug. 1980: 78-79.

1871 "George, after all, means farmer." *Callaloo.* 5.2 Feb. 1979: 86.

1872 "The house of the spider." *Open Places.* 37 Spr.-Sum. 1984: 4.

1873 "In her solitude: the inca divining spider." *Open Places.* 37 Spr.-Sum. 1984: 7.

1874 "In search of the bop in the absence of antiphonals." *Black Scholar.* 11.6 July-Aug. 1980: 78.

1875 "In search of the bop in the absence of antiphonals." *Essence.* 11.9 Jan. 1981: 17.

1876 "Invocation." *Obsidian.* 5.3 Wint. 1979: 87.

1877 "The itsy bitsy spider climbs and analyzes." *Open Places.* 37 Spr.-Sum. 1984: 6.

1878 "The leaves listen to Aretha sing." *Primavera.* 6-7 1981: 68.

1879 *The Man with the White Liver.* NY: Contact II, 1987. Originally published in the periodical *Contact/II,* Fall 1985.

1880 "Monroe, Louisiana." *Callaloo.* 5.2 Feb. 1979: 84.

1881 "One kitchen." *Obsidian.* 5.3 Wint. 1979: 88.

1882 "Rain." *Yellow Silk.* 13 Wint. 1984: 22.

1883 "The ritual calendar of yes." *Black Scholar.* 12.5 Sept.-Oct. 1981: 59.

1884 "Rosaries." *Steppingstone.* 1 1984: 29.

1885 "Solo for an alto." *Black Collegian.* 10.5 Apr.-May 1980: 121.

1886 *Solo in the Boxcar Third Floor E.* Chicago: OBAhouse, 1985.

1887 "Solo in the boxcar third floor E." *Black Collegian.* 10.5 Apr.-May 1980: 121.

1888 "Spider divine." *Open Places.* 37 Spr.-Sum. 1984: 5.

1889 "The spider speaks on the need for solidarity." *Open Places.* 37 Spr.-Sum. 1984: 8-9.

1890 "The spider's mantra." *Open Places.* 37 Spr.-Sum. 1984: 3.

1891 "Untitled [Who would trade it]." *Obsidian.* 5.3 Wint. 1979: 91.

1892 "The war chant of the architect (Toni Cade Bambara)." *Black Amer. Lit. Forum.* 19.3 Fall 1985: 100.

1893 "Wares for the man wherever the song is." *Obsidian.* 5.3 Wint. 1979: 92.

1894 "Why I must make language." *Open Places.* 37 Spr.–Sum. 1984: 10–11.

1895 "Woman in moonlight washes blues from dreams." *Yellow Silk.* 11 Sum. 1984: 37.

1896 "Woman walk/n down a Mississippi road." *Essence.* 15.10 Feb. 1985: 121.

1897 "Woman watches ocean on a reef through a glass-bottomed boat." *Black Scholar.* 12.5 Sept.–Oct. 1981: 60.

Short Fiction

1898 "Advanced technology." *Storyquarterly.* 9 1979: 110–111.

1899 "Dreamer." *First World.* 1 Jan. 1977: 54–57.

1900 "Prologue." *Storyquarterly.* 9 1979: 105–106.

1901 "Some money for carfare." *Storyquarterly.* 9 1979: 108–109.

1902 "Witchdoctor." *Chicago Rev.* 28 Wint. 1977: 76–82.

Textual Criticism

1903 Smith, D.L. "Angela Jackson." In DL41: 176–183. Biography and bibliography included.

Cherry Jackson

Drama

1904 "In the master's house there are many mansions." In OSTR: 111–121.

Elaine Jackson

Drama

1905 "Paper dolls." In WILK: 347–423.

Textual Criticism

1906 *Encore Amer. and Worldwide News.* Jan. 5, 1976: 26–27. On *Toe Jam* (1971 play).

Mae Jackson (1946–)

Poetry

1907 "For the count." In BARA: 168–169.

1908 "I remember." In ADOF: 183.

1909 "My last feeling this way poem." In BARA: 170–173.

1910 "On learning." In BARA: 169–170.

1911 "On learning." *Nimrod.* 21–22.2–1 1977: 96.

1912 "A poem for all the mens [sic] in the world." In BARA: 169.

Short Fiction

1913 "Cleaning out the closet." *Black Scholar.* 8.5 Mar. 1977: 31–35.

1914 "Cleaning out the closet." In BELL: 345–351.

1915 "I could rest forever." *Essence.* 8.12 Apr. 1978: 88–89, 102, 107.

1916 "These ain't all my tears." *Essence.* 11.6 Oct. 1980: 94–95, 120, 123–124, 172.

1917 "Who's gonna tell Wilma?" *Essence.* 10.5 Sept. 1979: 88–89, 124, 150, 152, 154.

Patti-Gayle Jackson

Poetry

1918 "Orbit." *Essence.* 11.1 May 1980: 103.

1919 "These loves: revolution." *Obsidian.* 7.1 Spr. 1981: 44.

1920 "This Black girl fall." *Essence.* 10.11 Mar. 1980: 19.

1921 "What do you dream of." *Black Amer. Lit. Forum.* 15.1 Spr. 1981: 30.

Sandra J. Jackson-Opoku

Poetry

1922 "Age of womanhood." *Essence.* 14.10 Feb. 1984: 146.

1923 "Blackbirds." *Black World.* 25.5 Mar. 1976: 53.

1924 "Conversation with a sister I do not know." *Black Books Bull.* 7.3 1981: 63.

1925 "Swamp fever." *Black Books Bull.* 7.3 1981: 63.

1926 "Well, after all what is there to say." *Essence.* 14.6 Oct. 1983: 89.

Short Fiction

1927 "One mother of a mountain." *Heresies.* 5.2 1985: 56–63.

Harriet Jacobs

Autobiography

1928 "The perils of a slave woman's life." In WASA: 16–70. Excerpt from *Incidents in the Life of a Slave Girl* (1861).

Textual Criticism

1929 Aponte, Wayne L. *Nation.* Sept. 12, 1987: 242. Rev. of *Incidents in the Life of a Slave Girl* (the new edition edited by Jean Fagan Yellin).

1930 Braxton, Joanne M. "Harriet Jacobs' *Incidents in the Life of a Slave Girl:* the redefinition of the slave narrative genre." *Massachusetts Rev.* 27.2 Sum. 1986: 379–387.

1931 Doherty, Thomas. "Harriet Jacobs' narrative strategies: *Incidents in the Life of a Slave Girl.*" *Southern Literary J.* 19.1 Fall 1986: 79–91.

1932 Gates, Henry Louis, Jr. "To be raped, bred or abused." *N.Y. Times*

Book Rev. Nov. 22, 1987: 12. Rev. of *Incidents in the Life of a Slave Girl* (new edition).

1933 Gwin, Minrose C. "Green-eyed monsters of the slavocracy: jealous mistresses in two slave narratives." In PRYS: 39–52. On Harriet Jacobs' *Incidents in the Life of a Slave Girl* (1861) and Elizabeth Keckley's *Behind the Scenes: Thirty Years a Slave and Four Years in the White House* (1868).

1934 Smith, Valerie. "Form and ideology in three slave narratives." In SMTV: 9–43. On the *Narrative of the Life of Frederick Douglass, an American Slave, Written by Himself* (1854), *The Interesting Narrative of the Life of Olaudah Equiano, or, Gustavus Vassa, the African, Written by Himself* (1789), and Jacobs' *Incidents in the Life of a Slave Girl* (1861).

1935 Washington, Mary Helen. "Meditations on history: the slave woman's voice." In WASA: 3–15.

1936 Yellin, Jean Fagan. "Text and contexts of Harriet Jacobs' *Incidents in the Life of a Slave Girl: Written by Herself.*" In DAVC: 262–282.

1937 Yellin, Jean Fagan. "Written by herself: Harriet Jacobs' narrative." *Amer. Lit.* 25 1981: 479–486.

Annetta Jefferson

Poetry
1938 "The pumpkin time." *Black Scholar.* 12.5 Sept.–Oct. 1981: 33.

Eva Jessye

Poetry
1939 "A bag of peanuts." *Little Balkans Rev.* 1.4 Sum. 1981: 17–18.

1940 "To Grandmother Penny Jessye." *Little Balkans Rev.* 1.1 Aut. 1980: 22.

Terri L. Jewell (1954–)

Essay
1941 "Crawling around inside one Black writer." *Off Our Backs.* 13.6 June 1983: 18.

Poetry
1942 "Armed recruit." *Sinister Wisdom.* 28 1985: 45.

1943 "A brother returned." *Wind.* 14.52 1984: 28.

1944 "Confiding in open waters." *Wooster Rev.* 1.2 Nov. 1984: 56.

1945 "Covenant." *Black Amer. Lit. Forum.* 20.3 Fall 1986: 259–260.

1946 "Felled shadows." *Calyx.* 9.2–3 Wint. 1986: 90.

1947 "Gasoline on the roof." *Black Amer. Lit. Forum.* 20.3 Fall 1986: 257–259.

1948 "Ha'nt." *Wooster Rev.* 1.2 Nov. 1984: 57.

1949 "No news among us." *Black Amer. Lit. Forum.* 19.3 Fall 1985: 110.

1950 "Returning anymore." *Wind.* 14.52 1984: 28.
1951 "Salvaging blood, January 1983." *Black Amer. Lit. Forum.* 18.1 Spr. 1984: 35.
1952 "Sistah Flo." *Calyx.* 9.2-3 Wint. 1986: 91.
1953 "Teda." *Woman of Power.* 2 Sum. 1985: 48.
1954 "Theurgy." *Black Amer. Lit. Forum.* 18.1 Spr. 1984: 35.

Joanne Jimason

Poetry
1955 *Blowing the Blues Away.* Washington, DC: Common Ground, 1981.
1956 "It has been a long time." *Essence.* 12.6 Oct. 1981: 18.
1957 *Naked Against the Belly of the Earth.* Washington, DC: Common Ground, 1977.

Eloise McKinney Johnson

Essays
1958 "Egypt's Isis: the original Black madonna." Published in *Black Women in Antiquity.* Ivan Van Sertima, Ed. New Brunswick, NJ: Transaction Books: Journal of African Civilizations Ltd., 1984.
1959 "Langston Hughes and Mary McLeod Bethune." *Langston Hughes Rev.* 2.1 Spr. 1983: 1-12.
1960 "Tutankhamon and racism." *Black Art.* 2.2 Wint. 1978: 32-36.

Poetry
1961 "Aunt Mollie's quilts." *Black Dispatch* (Bay Area Association of Black Social Workers). 7.6 May-June 1981: 6.
1962 "Families at reunion time." *Black Dispatch* (Bay Area Association of Black Social Workers). 7.2 Sept.-Oct. 1980: 5.
1963 "Spelman College: one hundred years." *Spelman Messenger* (Spelman College). 97.3 Fall 1981: 38. Celebration Issue: 1881-1981.

Georgia Douglas Johnson (1886-1966)

Drama
1964 "Plumes." In FRAN: 74-78. One-act play, originally published in 1927.

Poetry
1965 "Conquest." *Essence.* 9.11 Mar. 1979: 17.
1966 "The heart of a woman." In STET: 58.
1967 "I want to die while you love me." *Ebony.* 36.10 Aug. 1981: 56.
1968 "I want to die while you love me." In STET: 58.

1969 "My little dreams." In STET: 59.
1970 "The poet speaks." *Essence.* 9.11 Mar. 1979: 17.
1971 "Smothered fires." In STET: 59.

Summary of Play
1972 Southgate, Robert L. In SOUT: 159-161. Summary of *A Sunday Morning in the South* (written in 1925).

Textual Criticism
1973 Berry, Linda S. "Georgia Douglas Camp Johnson." In MAIN: 407-409. Biography and bibliography.
1974 Fletcher, Winona. "Georgia Douglas Johnson." In DL51: 153-164. Includes biography and additional bibliography.
1975 Perry, Margaret. In PERM: 154-155. On various works.
1976 Stetson, Erlene. "Rediscovering the Harlem Renaissance: Georgia Douglas Johnson, 'The Negro poet'." *Obsidian.* 5 Spr. 1979: 26-34.

Helene Johnson (1907-)

Poetry
1977 "Bottled." In STET: 78-79.
1978 "Magalu." In STET: 79-80.
1979 "The road." In STET: 80.
1980 "Summer matures." In STET: 81-82.
1981 "Trees at night." In STET: 81.

Textual Criticism
1982 Patterson, Raymond R. "Helene Johnson." In DL51: 164-167. Biography and bibliography included.
1983 Perry, Margaret. In PERM: 160-162. On various works.
1984 Redmond, Eugene B. In REDM: 207-209, 331-332, 363. On various works.

Rosalie Jonas

Poetry
1985 "Ballade des belles milatraisses [the Octoroon Ball, New Orleans, 1840-1850]." In STET: 55-56.
1986 "Brother Baptis' on woman suffrage." In STET: 56.

Cheryl Jones

Poetry
1987 "I'm not that lonely." *Conditions 5.* 2.2 Aut. 1979: 71.

Gayl Jones (1949–)

Bibliography
1988 Mainiero, Lina. "Gayl Jones." In MAIN: 421–422. Some biography.
1989 Weixlmann, Joe. "A Gayl Jones bibliography." *Callaloo.* 7.1 Wint. 1984: 119–131.

Drama
1990 "The ancestors: a street play." *Yardbird Reader.* 5 1976: 246–252.

Essays
1991 "About my work." In EVAN: 233–235.

Novel
1992 *Eva's Man.* NY: Random, 1976.

Poetry
1993 "Alternative." *Callaloo.* 5.2 1979: 111.
1994 "Chance." *Callaloo.* 5.2 1979: 112.
1995 "Composition with guitar and apples." *Callaloo.* 5.3 1982: 85–88.
1996 "The day of the God." *Callaloo.* 5.3 1982: 54–58.
1997 "Deep song." In HARP: 376.
1998 "Foxes." *Callaloo.* 7.1 1984: 39–42.
1999 "Fur station." *First World.* 2.4 1980: 23.
2000 "The gathering." *Panache.* 16–17 1976: 54.
2001 *The Hermit-Woman.* Detroit: Lotus, 1983.
2002 "Love, another story." In ROCK: 7.
2003 "Many die here." In STET: 210–211.
2004 "March 31, 1970, part IV of *Journal.*" In STET: 205–209.
2005 "Mr. River's love story." *Callaloo.* 7.1 1984: 43–45.
2006 "Party." *Panache.* 16–17 1976: 55.
2007 "Satori." In STET: 210.
2008 *Song for Anninho.* Detroit: Lotus, 1981.
2009 "Tripart." In STET: 209.
2010 "Waiting for the miracle." *Callaloo.* 5.3 1982: 66–72.
2011 "Xarque." *First World.* 2.3 1979: 13.
2012 *Xarque and Other Poems.* Detroit: Lotus, 1985.

Short Fiction
2013 "Almeyda." In HARP: 349–351.
2014 "Almeyda." *Massachusetts Rev.* 18.4 Wint. 1977: 689–691.
2015 "Asylum." In WASH: 128–131.
2016 "Ensinança." In BARA: 174–176.
2017 "Goosens." *Callaloo.* 5.3 1982: 54–58.

2018 "Jevata." In WASH: 132–149.

2019 "Prophet powers." *Callaloo.* 5.3 1982: 80–84.

2020 "The roundhouse." In FISH: 230–236.

2021 "The siege." *Callaloo.* 5.3 1982: 89–94.

2022 "The shoemaker and the sadism of the Senhora." *Ploughshares.* 8.4 1982: 42–52.

2023 "Sticks and witches brooms." *Michigan Q. Rev.* 17.2 Spr. 1978: 205–208.

2024 "Those rock people." *Callaloo.* 5.3 1982: 59–65.

2025 *The White Rat: Stories.* NY: Random: 1977.

Summary of Novel

2026 Southgate, Robert L. In SOUT: 61–62. Summary of *Corregidora* (1974).

Textual Criticism and Interviews

2027 Beckles, Frances N. "Gayl Jones." In BECK: 36–41. Includes biography and bibliography.

2028 Bell, Roseann P. "Gayl Jones: a voice in the whirlwind." *Studia Africana.* 1.1 1977: 99–107.

2029 Bell, Roseann P. "Gayl Jones takes a look at *Corregidora* — an interview." In BELL: 282–287.

2030 Brown, Beth. *CLA J.* 28.1 Sept. 1984: 102–109. Rev. of *The Hermit-Woman.* Appears with other reviews.

2031 Byerman, Keith E. "Beyond realism: the fictions of Gayl Jones and Toni Morrison." In BYER: 171–216.

2032 Byerman, Keith E. "Black vortex: the gothic structure of *Eva's Man.*" *Melus.* 7.4 Wint. 1980: 93–101.

2033 Byerman, Keith E. "Gayl Jones." In DAVI: 128–135. On several works.

2034 Byerman, Keith E. "Intense behaviors: the use of the grotesque in *Eva's Man* and *The Bluest Eye.*" *CLA J.* 25.4 June 1982: 447–457.

2035 Cooke, Michael G. "Recent novels: women bearing violence." *Yale Rev.* 66.1 Aut. 1976: 146–155. Rev. of *Eva's Man.*

2036 Dixon, Melvin. *Obsidian.* 3.1 Spr. 1977: 72–74. Rev. of *Corregidora.*

2037 Dixon, Melvin. "Singing a deep song: language as evidence in the novels of Gayl Jones." In EVAN: 236–248.

2038 *Encore Amer. and Worldwide News.* June 7, 1976: 44. Rev. of *Eva's Man.*

2039 Gayle, Addison. "Black men and Black women: the literature of catharsis." *Black Books Bull.* 4.4 Wint. 1976: 48–52. Rev. of *Eva's Man.*

2040 Golden, Bernette. *Black World.* 25.4 Feb. 1976: 82. Rev. of *Corregidora.*

2041 Hairston, Loyle. *Freedomways.* 16.2 1976: 133–135. Rev. of *Eva's Man.*

2042 Harper, Michael S. "Gayl Jones: an interview." In HARP: 352–375.

2043 Harper, Michael S. "Gayl Jones: an interview." *Massachusetts Rev.* 18.4 Wint. 1977: 692–715.

2044 Harris, Janice. *Frontiers.* 5.3 Fall 1980: 1–5. Rev. of *Corregidora.*

2045 Harris, Jessica. *Essence.* 8.6 Oct. 1977: 54. Rev. of *The White Rat.*

2046 Harris, Trudier. "A spiritual journey: Gayl Jones's *Song for Anninho.*" *Callaloo.* 5.3 Oct. 1982: 105–111.

2047 Jordan, June. *N. Y. Times Book Rev.* May 16, 1976: 36–37. Rev. of *Eva's Man.*

2048 Lee, Valerie Gray. "The use of folktalk in novels by Black women writers." *CLA J.* 23.3 Mar. 1980: 266–272.

2049 Mano, D.K. "How to write two first novels with your knuckles." *Esquire.* 86.6 Dec. 1976: 62, 66. On *Corregidora* and *Eva's Man.*

2050 Rowell, Charles, Ed. "Gayl Jones, poet and fictionist." *Callaloo.* 5.3 Oct. 1982: 31–111. Special section of the periodical, including five short stories, two poems, and critical articles by Charles Rowell ("An interview. . ."), Jerry W. Ward, Jr. ("Escape from Trublem. . ."), and Trudier Harris ("A spiritual journey. . . *[Song for Anninho]*").

2051 Shattuck, Sandra D. *Conditions.* 13 1986: 192–198. Rev. of *Xarque, The Hermit Woman,* and *Song for Anninho.*

2052 Tate, Claudia C. "*Corregidora:* Ursa's blues medley." *Black Amer. Lit. Forum.* 13.4 Wint. 1979: 139–141.

2053 Tate, Claudia C. "Gayl Jones." In TATE: 89–99. On several works.

2054 Tate, Claudia C. "An interview with Gayl Jones." *Black Amer. Lit. Forum.* 13.4 Wint. 1979: 142–148.

2055 Updike, John. "Eva and Eleanor and Everywoman." *New Yorker.* Aug. 9, 1976: 74–77. On *Eva's Man.*

2056 Ward, Jerry W., Jr. "Escape from Trublem: the fiction of Gayl Jones." *Callaloo.* 5.3 Oct. 1982: 95–104.

2057 Ward, Jerry W., Jr. "Escape from Trublem: the fiction of Gayl Jones." In EVAN: 249–257.

Lucille Jones (1924–)

Interview

2058 Jones, Gayl. "Interview with Lucille Jones [her mother]." *Obsidian.* 3.3 Wint. 1977: 26–35.

Short Fiction

2059 "The boyish bob." *Obsidian.* 6.3 Wint. 1980: 95–97.

2060 "A dinner for Luther and Louis." *Obsidian.* 5.3 Wint. 1979: 67–69.

2061 "Everybody got into the act." *Obsidian.* 5.3 Wint. 1979: 64–66.

2062 "John and Nancy." *Obsidian.* 5.3 Wint. 1979: 72–74.

2063 "Luther." *Obsidian.* 3.3 Wint. 1977: 50–53.

2064 "The salesman." *Obsidian.* 5.3 Wint. 1979: 70–71.

2065 "Twenty-one B Street." *Obsidian.* 6.3 Wint. 1980: 82–94.

2066 "Vestina [Selections]." *Obsidian.* 3.3 Wint. 1977: 43–49.

Muriel Jones

Short Fiction
2067 "Misfits." *Conditions 5.* 2.2 Aut. 1979: 69.

Patricia Jones (1951–)

Poetry
2068 "Anoche." In MILE: 103.

2069 "Anoche." *Nimrod.* 21–22.2–1 1977: 127.

2070 "Bête noir." *Telephone.* 19 1983: 28–29.

2071 "Carrying on the blood." *Chrysalis.* 10 1980: 76–77.

2072 "Dedicated to Lori Sharpe." *Obsidian.* 5.1–2 Spr.–Sum. 1979: 115.

2073 "Eagle Rock." *Obsidian.* 5.1–2 Spr.–Sum. 1979: 113–114.

2074 "Feeling evil." *Essence.* 11.5 Sept. 1980: 14.

2075 "Fourteenth Street / New York [Excerpts]." *Conditions 2.* 1.2 Oct. 1977: 12.

2076 "Fourteenth Street / New York [Excerpts]." In MILE: 96–97.

2077 "I done got so thirsty that my mouth waters at the thought of rain." *Chrysalis.* 2 1977: 112–113.

2078 "I done got so thirsty that my mouth waters at the thought of rain." In MILE: 101–103.

2079 "I done got so thirsty that my mouth waters at the thought of rain." In STET: 249–251.

2080 "I've been thinking of Diana Sands." *Conditions 5.* 2.2 Aut. 1979: 26–28.

2081 "I've been thinking of Diana Sands." In SMIT: 106–109.

2082 "In like paradise / out like the blues." *Black Scholar.* 12.3 May–June 1981: 48–49.

2083 "It must be her heartbreak talking." *Obsidian.* 5.1–2 Spr.–Sum. 1979: 116.

2084 "LP." *Obsidian.* 5.1–2 Spr.–Sum. 1979: 115.

2085 "Mammies." *Heresies.* 5.2 1985: 39.

2086 "Mi Chinita." *Conditions 2.* 1.2 Oct. 1977: 9–11.

2087 "Mi Chinita." In MILE: 99–100.

2088 *Mythologizing Always: Seven Sonnets.* Guilford, CT: Telephone Books, 1981.

2089 "A no blues love poem." In MILE: 95.

2090 "Poem for David Murray." In MILE: 98.

2091 "Poem written on Rosh Hashanah / for Ted Greenwald." *Obsidian.* 5.1–2 Spr.–Sum. 1979: 118–119.

2092 "Sonnet / for Pedro Pietri." In MILE: 103.

2093 "Sonnet / for Pedro Pietri." *Nimrod.* 21–22.2–1 1977: 127.

2094 "Why I like movies [for Charlotte]." In STET: 251–252.

2095 "The woman who loved musicians." *Obsidian.* 5.1–2 Spr.–Sum. 1979: 117.

Jones, Sylvia *see* Baraka, Amina

Anasa Jordan

Poetry
2096 "Sweet Otis suite." In BARA: 177–179.

June Jordan (1936–)

Children's Stories
2097 *Kimako's Story*. Boston: Houghton Mifflin, 1981.

Essays
2098 *Civil Wars*. Boston: Beacon, 1981.

2099 Davis, Angela and Jordan, June. "Strong beyond all definitions. . ." *Women's Rev. of Books*. 4.10–11 July–Aug. 1987: 1, 19–21. Addresses given at a conference "Poetry and Politics: Afro-American Poetry Today" at Harvard University, March 1987.

2100 "'Don't you talk about my mama!'" *Essence*. 18.8 Dec. 1987: 53, 125–126, 128. On Black mothers and the Black family.

2101 "For the sake of a people's poetry: Walt Whitman and the rest of us." In JONE: 188–199.

2102 "In our hands." *Essence*. 16.1 May 1985: 50, 52. The work of women.

2103 "June Jordan." *Wilson Library Bull*. 53.2 Oct. 1978: 161–165. On her work.

2104 *On Call: Political Essays*. Boston: South End, 1985.

2105 "Second thoughts of a Black feminist." *Ms*. 5.8 Feb. 1977: 113–115.

2106 "Thinking about my poetry." *Chrysalis*. 4 1977: 105–109.

2107 "Where is the love?" *Essence*. 9.5 Sept. 1978: 62, 65–66.

2108 "Where is the love?" In BOWL: 29–31.

Poetry
2109 "Addenda to the Papal Bull (for Nicanor Parra)." *Thirteenth Moon*. 5.1–2 1980: 18.

2110 "Ah, momma." *Redbook*. 150 Dec. 1977: 74.

2111 "The Beirut jokebook." *Freedomways*. 22.4 1982: 223.

2112 "Blue ribbons for the baby girl." In BARA: 181.

2113 "Bullets or no bullets! The food is cooked an gettin cold." *Nimrod*. 21–22.2–1 1977: 129.

2114 "The difficult miracle of Black poetry in America or something like a sonnet for Phillis Wheatley." *Massachusetts Rev*. 27.2 Sum. 1986: 252–262. Essay on Phillis Wheatley, in poetic prose.

2115 "Feminism is not a narrow preoccupation." *Sojourner*. 10.8 June 1985: 16–17.

2116 "Free flight." *Essence*. 10.6 Oct. 1979: 16.

2117 "From sea to shining sea." *Feminist Studies.* 8.3 Fall 1982: 535–541.

2118 "From sea to shining sea." In SMIT: 223–229.

2119 "From 'The talking back of Miss Valentine Jones: poem number one'." *Ms.* 6.10 Apr. 1978: 58.

2120 "I must become a menace to my enemies." *Chrysalis.* 3 1977: 62–63.

2121 "If you saw a Negro lady." In FISH: 262–263.

2122 "If you saw a Negro lady." In KONE: 122–123.

2123 "In memoriam: Rev. Martin Luther King, Jr. (Part one)." In FISH: 263–264.

2124 "A last dialog on the left." In BARA: 182.

2125 *Living Room: New Poems.* NY: Thunder's Mouth, 1985.

2126 "Memoranda towards the Spring of seventy-nine." *Callaloo.* 5.2 1979: 76.

2127 "Meta-rhetoric." *Chrysalis.* 3 1977: 63.

2128 "The name of the poem is." *Transatlantic Rev.* 58–59 Feb. 1977: 98.

2129 *Niagara Falls.* Huntington, NY: A Poem a Month Club, 1977. A broadside.

2130 "Nineteen seventy-eight." *Black Scholar.* 10.3–4 Nov.–Dec. 1978: 22.

2131 "Nineteen seventy-seven: poem for Mrs. Fannie Lou Hamer." *Nimrod.* 21–22.2-1 1977: 128.

2132 "No more the chicken and the egg come." *Amer. Poetry Rev.* 6.1 Jan.–Feb. 1977: 25.

2133 "On the real world: Meditation 1." In BARA: 180–181.

2134 *Passion: New Poems, 1977–1980.* Boston: Beacon, 1980.

2135 "Poem about a night out: Michael: good-bye for a while." In DALE: 84–85.

2136 "Poem about my rights." *Essence.* 9.7 Nov. 1978: 22.

2137 "Poem for inaugural Rose." In DALE: 85.

2138 "Poem for Nana." In STET: 148–151.

2139 "Poem for Nana." *Nimrod.* 21–22.2-1 1977: 130.

2140 "Poem from the Empire State." In LONG: 735–736.

2141 "Poem in honor of South African women." *Ms.* 9.5 Nov. 1980: 47.

2142 "Poem in memory of Kimako Baraka." *Essence.* 15.3 July 1984: 130.

2143 "Poem number 2 for inaugural Rose." In DALE: 85–86.

2144 "Poem towards a final solution." In BARA: 183–184.

2145 "Poem towards the bottom line." *Little Magazine.* 11.3 Aut. 1977: 105.

2146 "Problems of translation: problems of language." In COOP: 194–197.

2147 "Problems of translation: problems of language." *Iowa Rev.* 12.2–3 Spr.–Sum. 1981: 194–197.

2148 "Relativity." *Essence.* 17.1 May 1986: 169.

2149 "A right to lifer in Grand Forks, North Dakota (poem for Sandy Donaldson)." *Shout in the Street.* 3.1 1982: 52.

2150 "Second poem from Nicarague libre: war zone." *Little Magazine.* 14.1–2 1983: 83.

2151 "Taking care." *Little Magazine.* 13.1–2 Spr.–Sum. 1979: 30–33.

2152 *Things That I Do in the Dark: Selected Poetry.* NY: Random, 1977.

2153 "This is a poem about Vieques, Puerto Rico." In DALE: 83–84.

2154 "To sing a song of Palestine (for Shulamith Koenig, an Israeli peace activist, 1982)." *Poetry East.* 9–10 Wint. 1982–Spr. 1983: 122–123.

2155 "Unemployment / monologue." *Little Magazine.* 13.1–2 1981: 30–32.

2156 "What happens." In LONG: 735.

2157 "Who would be free, themselves must strike the blow." *Northwest Rev.* 22.1–2 1984: 38.

Summary of Children's Story

2158 Southgate, Robert L. In SOUT: 83–84. Summary of *His Own Where* (1971).

Textual Criticism and Interviews

2159 Abbott, Dorothy. "Living standing up." *Women's Rev. of Books.* 3.9 June 1986: 6. Revs. of *Living Room* and *On Call.*

2160 Bambara, Toni Cade. *Ms.* 9.10 Apr. 1981: 40–42. Rev. of *Civil Wars.*

2161 Bowen, Angela. *Conditions.* 13 1986: 147–153. Rev. of *On Call.*

2162 Boyd, Melba Joyce. *Black Scholar.* 16.3 May–June 1985: 48–49. Rev. of *Living Room.*

2163 Boyd, Melba Joyce. "The Whitman awakening in June Jordan's poetry." *Obsidian.* 7.2–3 Sum.–Wint. 1981: 226–228. Rev. of *Passion: New Poems, 1977–1980.*

2164 Carruth, Hayden. *N.Y. Times Book Rev.* Oct. 9, 1977: 15. Rev. of *Things That I Do in the Dark.*

2165 Daniels, Gabrielle. *Off Our Backs.* 11.2 Feb. 1981: 19. Rev. of *Passion: New Poems, 1977–1980.*

2166 Davis, Enid. "Easy readers: *New Life: New Room.*" In DAVE: 97. On a children's book written in 1975.

2167 DeMontreville, Doris and Elizabeth D. Crawford. In DEMO: 204–205. Biography and bibliography.

2168 DeVeaux, Alexis. "Creating soul food: June Jordan." *Essence.* 11.12 Apr. 1981: 82–83, 138, 140, 143, 145, 147–148, 150.

2169 Diaz-Diocaretz, Myriam. *Thirteenth Moon.* 5.1–2 1980: 147–155. Rev. of *Passion: New Poems, 1977–1980.*

2170 Dong, S. "PW interviews June Jordan." *Publishers Weekly.* May 1, 1981: 12–13.

2171 Erickson, Peter. "June Jordan." In DL38: 146–162. Includes biography and additional bibliography.

2172 Erickson, Peter. "The Love Poetry of June Jordan." *Callaloo.* 26 Wint. 1986: 221–234.

2173 Hacker, Marilyn. *Chrysalis.* 10 1980: 114–121. General criticism, including comments on *Things That I Do in the Dark,* pp. 119–121.

2174 Hammond, Karla. "Interview with June Jordan." In DALE: 90–94.

2175 Kaye, Marilyn. *School Library J.* 28.1 Sept. 1981: 110. Rev. of *Kimako's Story.*

2176 Kazi-Ferrouillet, Kuumba. *Black Collegian.* 16.2 Nov.–Dec. 1985: 46. Rev. of *Living Room.*

2177 Larkin, Joan. *Ms.* 9.9 Mar. 1981: 78. Rev. of *Passion: New Poems, 1977-1980.*

2178 Martin, Ruby. *Reading Teacher.* 30.7 Apr. 1977: 824-825. Rev. of *New Life: New Room.*

2179 Mberi, Antar Sudan Katara. *Freedomways.* 17.3 1977: 180-181. Rev. of *Things That I Do in the Dark.*

2180 McHenry, S. *Nation.* Apr. 11, 1981: 437-438. Rev. of *Civil Wars.*

2181 Miles, Sara. "This wheel's on fire: the poetry of June Jordan." In DALE: 87-89.

2182 Pinckney, Darryl. *N.Y. Times Book Rev.* Aug. 9, 1981: 8. Revs. of *Civil Wars* and *Passion: New Poems, 1977-1980.*

2183 Roebuck, Marcia V. *Encore Amer. and Worldwide News.* 9.9 Dec. 1981: 38. Rev. of *Kimako's Story.*

2184 Thompson, Mildred. *Black Scholar.* 12.1 Jan.-Feb. 1981: 96. Rev. of *Passion: New Poems, 1977-1980.*

2185 Turner, Jenny. *New Statesman.* June 5, 1987: 38. Rev. of *On Call.*

2186 Wilkinson, Brenda. *N.Y. Times Book Rev.* Apr. 18, 1982: 38. Rev. of *Kimako's Story.*

2187 Wilson, Judith. *Essence.* 12.5 Sept. 1981: 17. Rev. of *Civil Wars.*

Rose Jourdain (1932-)

Novel
2188 *Those the Sun Has Loved.* NY: Doubleday, 1978.

Textual Criticism
2189 Giovanni, Nikki. *Encore Amer. and Worldwide News.* 9.1 Jan. 1980: 45. Rev. of *Those the Sun Has Loved.*

Sybil Kein

Poetry
2190 "Bessie Smith." *Essence.* 17.3 July 1986: 121.

2191 "Billie." *Essence.* 16.3 July 1985: 107.

2192 "Chestnut lilies." *Beloit Poetry J.* 29.2 Wint. 1978-1979: 26.

2193 *Delta Dancer: New and Selected Poems.* Detroit: Lotus, 1984.

2194 "Flowers." *Essence.* 18.5 Sept. 1987: 157.

2195 *Gombo People: New Orleans Creole Poetry.* New Orleans: Leo J. Hall, 1981.

2196 "Mo Oulé mourri dan lac lá." *Beloit Poetry J.* 29.2 Wint. 1978-1979: 25.

2197 "Now." *Obsidian.* 7.2-3 Sum.-Wint. 1981: 144. Translated by author from Louisiana Creole.

2198 "The river." *Obsidian.* 7.2-3 Sum.-Wint. 1981: 143. Translated by author from Louisiana Creole.

2199 "Shame." *Obsidian.* 7.2-3 Sum.-Wint. 1981: 145. Translated by author from Louisiana Creole.

2200 "To the widow Paris." *Obsidian.* 7.2-3 Sum.-Wint. 1981: 142. Translated by author from Louisiana Creole.
2201 *Visions from the Rainbow.* Flint, MI: N.D. Hosking, 1979.

Dolores Kendrick

Poetry
2202 "Catching water." *Open Places.* 34 Aut.-Wint. 1982: 12-13.
2203 "Dead asters (for Cabot Lyford)." *Open Places.* 34 Aut.-Wint. 1982: 14.
2204 "Frustrated genius." *Beloit Poetry J.* 29.2 Wint. 1978-1979: 47.
2205 "Jesus, looking for an aspirin." *Open Places.* 34 Aut.-Wint. 1982: 15-16.
2206 "Josephine in the Jeu de Paume." *Beloit Poetry J.* 29.2 Wint. 1978-1979: 46.
2207 *Now Is the Thing to Praise: Poems.* Detroit: Lotus, 1984.
2208 "The snow bird." *Open Places.* 34 Aut.-Wint. 1982: 10-11.

Textual Criticism
2209 Brown, Beth. *CLA J.* 29.2 Dec. 1985: 252-254. Rev. of *Now Is the Thing to Praise.*

Adrienne Kennedy (1931-)

Autobiography
2210 *People Who Led to My Plays.* NY: Knopf, 1987.

Drama
2211 "A movie star has to star in black and white." In WORD: 51-68.

Summary of Play
2212 Southgate, Robert L. In SOUT: 128-129. Summary of *The Owl Answers* (1963).

Textual Criticism and Interviews
2213 Benston, Kimberly W. "*Cities in Bezique:* Adrienne Kennedy's expressionistic vision." *CLA J.* 20.2 Dec. 1976: 235-244. *Cities in Bezique* (1969) is comprised of two plays, *The Owl Answers* and *A Beast Story.*
2214 Cohn, Ruby. "Black on Black: Baraka, Bullins, Kennedy." In COHN: 95, 108-115.
2215 Curb, Rosemary K. "Fragmented selves in Adrienne Kennedy's *Funnyhouse of a Negro* and *The Owl Answers.*" *Theatre J.* 32 May 1980: 180-195.
2216 Curb, Rosemary K. "'Lesson I bleed'." In CHIN: 50-56.
2217 Fabre, Geneviève. "The new Black theatre: achievements and problems." *Caliban.* 15 1978: 121-129.
2218 Kennedy, Adrienne and Margaret B. Wilkerson. "Adrienne Kennedy: reflections." *City Arts Monthly.* Feb. 1982: 39.

2219 Koenig, Rachel. "Revolutions on stage." *Women's Rev. of Books.* 5.1 Oct. 1987: 14–15. Rev. of *People Who Led to My Plays.*

2220 Lehman, Lisa, Ed. "A growth of images." *Drama Rev.* 21.4 Dec. 1977: 41–48. Transcript of a recorded interview.

2221 Olauson, Judith. In OLAU: 109–114. On several works.

2222 Wilkerson, Margaret B. In DL38: 162–169. Biography and bibliography included.

Aneb Kgositsile (Gloria Larry House)

Poetry
2223 *Blood River.* Detroit: Broadside, 1983.

Jamaica Kincaid (1949–)

Novels
2224 *Annie John.* NY: Farrar, 1985.

Short Fiction
2225 *At the Bottom of the River.* NY: Farrar, 1984.
2226 "The circling hand." *New Yorker.* Nov. 21, 1983: 50–57.
2227 "Columbus in chains." *New Yorker.* Oct. 10, 1983: 48–52.
2228 "Figures in the distance." *New Yorker.* May 9, 1983: 40–42.
2229 "Gwen." *New Yorker.* Apr. 16, 1984: 45–51.
2230 "The long rain." *New Yorker.* July 30, 1984: 28–36.
2231 "The red girl." *New Yorker.* Aug. 8, 1983: 32–38.
2232 "Somewhere, Belgium." *New Yorker.* May 14, 1984: 44–51.
2233 "A walk to the jetty." *New Yorker.* Nov. 5, 1984: 45–51.

Textual Criticism
2234 Allen, Zita. *Freedomways.* 25.2 1985: 116–119. Rev. of *Annie John.*
2235 Cole, Diane. *Ms.* 13.10 Apr. 1985: 14. Rev. of *Annie John.*
2236 Freeman, S. *Ms.* 12.7 Jan. 1984: 15–16. Rev. of *At the Bottom of the River.*
2237 Milton, E. *N. Y. Times Book Rev.* Jan. 15, 1984: 22. Rev. of *At the Bottom of the River.*
2238 Tyler, Anne. "Mothers and mysteries." *New Republic.* Dec. 31, 1983: 32–33. Rev. of *At the Bottom of the River.*
2239 VanWyngarden, Bruce. *Saturday Rev.* 11.3 May–June 1985: 68. Rev. of *Annie John.*
2240 White, Evelyn C. *Women's Rev. of Books.* 3.2 Nov. 1985: 11. Rev. of *Annie John.*

Kunjufu, Johari M. *see* Amini, Johari

Pinkie Gordon Lane (1923-)

Bibliography
2241 *A Literary Profile to 1977.* Baton Rouge, LA: P.G. Lane, 1977.

Poetry
2242 "Baton Rouge No. 2." *Southern Rev.* 13.2 Apr. 1977: 352.

2243 "Betrayal: on the loss of a friend." *Callaloo.* 5.2 Feb. 1979: 96.

2244 "Children." *Black Amer. Lit. Forum.* 20.3 Fall 1986: 293.

2245 "Four love poems: I. Love poem, II. Leaving, III. Shadows, IV. What matters after all." *Black Scholar.* 15.6 Nov.-Dec. 1984: 60.

2246 "Girl at the window." *Black Scholar.* 10.3-4 Nov.-Dec. 1978: 17.

2247 *I Never Scream: New and Selected Poems.* Detroit: Lotus, 1985.

2248 "Kaleidoscope: leaving Baton Rouge." *Nimrod.* 21-22.2-1 1977: 140.

2249 "Lake Murry." *Southern Rev.* 13.2 Apr. 1977: 351-352.

2250 "Leaves." *Obsidian.* 3.3 Wint. 1977: 54.

2251 "Listenings." *Obsidian.* 3.3 Wint. 1977: 56.

2252 "Listenings." *South and West.* 14 Fall 1977: 18-21.

2253 "Love poem." *Black Scholar.* 9.3 Nov. 1977: 29.

2254 "Midnight song." *Black Scholar.* 9.3 Nov. 1977: 28.

2255 "Migration." *Callaloo.* Feb. 1978: 6.

2256 "Migration." In STET: 231-232.

2257 *The Mystic Female.* Fort Smith, Arkansas: South and West, 1978.

2258 "The mystic female." *Callaloo.* Feb. 1978: 90.

2259 "Nocturne." In STET: 233.

2260 "Old photo from a family album: 1915." *Southern Rev.* 21.3 July 1985: 862-863.

2261 "On being head of the English Department." In STET: 228-229.

2262 "Opossum." *Obsidian.* 3.3 Wint. 1977: 55.

2263 "Poem for Lois: an elegy." *Callaloo.* 1 Dec. 1976: 18.

2264 "Poems to my father." *Black Amer. Lit. Forum.* 20.3 Fall 1986: 289-293.

2265 "The privacy report." *Ms.* 8.7 Jan. 1980: 29.

2266 "Renewal." *Callaloo.* 5.2 Feb. 1979: 88.

2267 "Sexual privacy of women on welfare." In STET: 230-231.

2268 "Sexual privacy of women on welfare." *Nimrod.* 21-22.2-1 1977: 141.

2269 "Silence." *Black Scholar.* 10.3-4 Nov.-Dec. 1978: 17.

2270 "Southern University." *Southern Rev.* 13.2 Apr. 1977: 353-354.

2271 "Two poems for Gordon." *Southern Rev.* 21.3 July 1985: 860-861.

2272 "When you read this poem." *Black Scholar.* 9.3 Nov. 1977: 29.

2273 "When you read this poem." In STET: 229-230.

2274 "While sitting in the airport waiting room." *Callaloo.* 1 Dec. 1976: 15.

2275 "Who is my brother?" In STET: 232.

Textual Criticism
2276 Bogus, S. Diane. *Black Scholar.* 11.5 May-June 1980: 82-83. Rev. of *The Mystic Female.*

2277 Craig, Marilyn B. "Pinkie Gordon Lane." In DL41: 212–216. Biography and bibliography included.

2278 Forbes, Calvin. "Quiet poems to shut out the noise." *Obsidian.* 5.3 Wint. 1979: 117. Rev. of *The Mystic Female.*

2279 Kilgore, James C. *CLA J.* 23.3 Mar. 1980: 372–374. Rev. of *The Mystic Female.*

2280 Newman, Dorothy W. "Lane's *Mystic Female.*" *Callaloo.* 5.2 Feb. 1979: 153–155.

2281 Roland, Lillian D. *Black Amer. Lit. Forum.* 20.3 Fall 1986: 294–298. Rev. of *I Never Scream.*

Nella Larsen (1893–1963)

Bibliography

2282 Perry, Margaret. "Nella Larsen." In PERH: 116–118. Includes commentary.

2283 Wall, Cheryl A. "Nella Larsen." In MAIN: 507–509. Includes biography.

Miscellaneous

2284 Clark, William Bedford. "The letters of Nella Larsen to Carl Van Vechten: a survey." *Resources for Amer. Literary Study.* 8 Fall 1978: 193–199.

Novel

2285 "Helga Crane." In WASA: 174–233. Excerpt from *Quicksand* (1928).

Summary of Novel

2286 Southgate, Robert L. In SOUT: 132–134. Summary of *Quicksand.*

Textual Criticism

2287 Bell, Bernard W. "Nella Larsen." In BELA: 109–112. On several works.

2288 Cary, Meredith. In CARY: 113–120. On *Quicksand.*

2289 Cooke, Michael G. "Self-veiling: James Welden Johnson, Charles Chesnutt, and Nella Larsen." In COOK: 43–70.

2290 Davis, Thadious M. "Nella Larsen." In DL51: 182–192. Includes biography and additional bibliography.

2291 Joyce, Joyce Ann. "Nella Larsen's *Passing:* a reflection of the American dream." *Western J. of Black Studies.* 7.2 Sum. 1983: 68–73.

2292 Lewis, Vashti Crutcher. "Nella Larsen's use of the near-white female in *Quicksand* and *Passing.*" *Western J. of Black Studies.* 10.3 Fall 1986: 137–142. *Passing* was published in 1929, a year after *Quicksand.*

2293 Noble, Jeanne. In NOBL: 162–164. On several works.

2294 Perry, Margaret. In PERM: 73–79. On several works.

2295 Ramsey, Priscilla. "Freeze the day: a feminist reading of Nella Larsen's *Quicksand* and *Passing.*" *Afro-Americans in New York Life and History.* 9.1 1985: 27–41.

2296 Ramsey, Priscilla. "A study of Black identity in 'passing' novels of the nineteenth and early twentieth centuries." *Studies in Black Lit.* 7 Wint. 1976: 1–7.

2297 Singh, Amritjit. In SING: 92–93, 98–100, 100–104. On a number of works.

2298 Tate, Claudia. "Nella Larsen's *Passing:* a problem of interpretation." *Black Amer. Lit. Forum.* 14.4 Wint. 1980: 142–146.

2299 Wall, Cheryl A. "Passing for what? Aspects of identity in Nella Larsen's novels." *Black Amer. Lit. Forum.* 20.1–2 Spr.–Sum. 1986: 97–111.

2300 Washington, Mary Helen. "Lost women: Nella Larsen — mystery woman of the Harlem Renaissance." *Ms.* 9.6 Dec. 1980: 44, 47–48, 50.

2301 Washington, Mary Helen. "The Mulatta trap: Nella Larsen's women of the 1920's." In WASA: 159–167.

Latimore, Jewel Christine McLawler *see* Amini, Johari

Jennifer Blackman Lawson

Editing
2302 Lawson, Jennifer Blackman and Dorothy Randall-Tsuruta, Eds. *High Expectations: Poems for Black Women.* Pittsburgh, CA: Los Medans, 1977.

Poetry
2303 *Blackbird in My Tree: A Collection of Poems.* Palo Alto, CA: Zikawuna, 1979.

2304 "Ella Mae." *Essence.* 11.1 May 1980: 102.

Short Fiction
2305 "Early morning calls." *Essence.* 7.4 Aug. 1976: 54–55, 90.

Andrea Lee (1953–)

Non-Fiction
2306 "Russia observed — the real life." *Vogue.* 171 Aug. 1981: 288–289. Excerpt from *The Russian Journal.*

2307 *The Russian Journal.* NY: Random, 1981. About social life and customs in the Soviet Union.

Novel
2308 *Sarah Phillips.* NY: Random, 1984.

Short Fiction
2309 "The days of the Thunderbirds." *New Yorker.* July 9, 1984: 34–42.

2310 "Fine points." *New Yorker.* May 21, 1984: 38–41.

2311 "Gypsies." *New Yorker.* June 18, 1984: 37–39.

2312 "Negatives." *New Yorker.* Oct. 1, 1984: 34–38.

Textual Criticism and Interviews

2313 Booker, Christopher. *New Republic.* Feb. 24, 1982: 36. Rev. of *The Russian Journal.*

2314 Brown, Archie. *Times (London) Literary Suppl.* Aug. 13, 1982: 891. Rev. of *The Russian Journal.*

2315 Clemons, W. *Newsweek.* Oct. 19, 1981: 101–102. Rev. of *The Russian Journal.*

2316 Hazelton, Nika. *National Rev.* Sept. 3, 1982: 1095. Rev. of *The Russian Journal.*

2317 Jacoby, Susan. *N.Y. Times Book Rev.* Oct. 25, 1981: 11. Rev. of *The Russian Journal.*

2318 Leonard, John. *N.Y. Times Book Rev.* Oct. 25, 1981: 11. Rev. of *The Russian Journal.*

2319 Murrell, Elizabeth V. *Freedomways.* 25.2 1985: 119–120. Rev. of *Sarah Phillips.*

2320 Obolensky, Laura. *New Republic.* Nov. 19, 1984: 41–42. Rev. of *Sarah Phillips.*

2321 Patterson, M.L. *Freedomways.* 22.2 1982: 116. Rev. of *The Russian Journal.*

2322 Rasmussen, Carol. *Library J.* Oct. 1, 1981: 1920. Rev. of *The Russian Journal.*

2323 Rein, R.K. "American student comes home from Russia with love, and a bittersweet memoir." *People Weekly.* Nov. 23, 1981: 101–102. Interview.

2324 Shreve, Susan R. *N.Y. Times Book Rev.* Nov. 18, 1984: 13. Rev. of *Sarah Phillips.*

2325 Sisco, Ellen. *School Library J.* 28.6 Feb. 1982: 95–96. Rev. of *The Russian Journal.*

2326 Taylor, Linda. *Times (London) Literary Suppl.* Apr. 5, 1985: 376. Rev. of *Sarah Phillips.*

2327 Washington, Mary Helen. *Women's Rev. of Books.* 2.6 Mar. 1985: 3–4. Rev. of *Sarah Phillips.*

2328 Williams, Sherley A. "Roots of privilege, new Black fiction." *Ms.* 13.12 June 1985: 69–72. Revs. of Gloria Naylor's *Linden Hills,* Lee's *Sarah Phillips,* and Ntozake Shange's *Betsey Brown.*

Audrey Lee

Short Fiction

2329 "Eulogy for a public servant." *Black World.* 25.3 Jan. 1976: 54–57.

Rikki Lights (1952–)

Poetry

2330 *Dog Moon.* NY: Sunbury, 1976.

2331 "Gut riddle." *Essence.* 8.8 Dec. 1977: 32.

2332 "Lyriclicks." *Essence.* 8.8 Dec. 1977: 32.

Short Fiction

2333 "Medicine man." In HOFF: 126–136.

Textual Criticism

2334 Bethel, Lorraine. *Conditions 3.* 1.3 Spr. 1978: 121–129. Rev. of *Dog Moon.*

2335 Hamilton, Stephanie. "The 100-watt Rikki Lights." *Encore Amer. and Worldwide News.* June 6, 1977: 46. Biography and criticism.

Abbey Lincoln (Aminata Moseka)

Poetry

2336 "I am the weaver." In BARA: 185–186.
2337 "In the middle." In BARA: 188.
2338 "A name change." In BARA: 189–190.
2339 "On being high." In BARA: 187–188.

Myrtle Smith Livingston

Summary of Play

2340 Southgate, Robert L. In SOUT: 72–73. Summary of *For Unborn Children* (1926).

Elouise Loftin (1950–)

Poetry

2341 "Deeper." *Essence.* 8.7 Nov. 1977: 34. Written under the name "Hanna."
2342 "Jumbish-one." *Essence.* 8.7 Nov. 1977: 34. Written under the name "Hanna."
2343 "Pigeon." In ADOF: 69–70.
2344 "Who are the happy." *Essence.* 8.7 Nov. 1977: 112. Written under the name "Hanna."

Textual Criticism

2345 *Encore Amer. and Worldwide News.* April 5, 1976: 44. Rev. of *Barefoot Necklace* (poetry, 1975).

Pearl Cleage Lomax (1948–)

Poetry

2346 "Jesus drum." In ADOF: 28–29.
2347 "Mississippi born." In ADOF: 47–48.
2348 "Poem." In ADOF: 118–119.

Long, Naomi Cornelia *see* **Madgett, Naomi Long**

Audre Lorde (1934–)

Autobiography

2349 *The Cancer Journals.* Argyle, NY: Spinsters, Ink, 1980.

2350 *Zami: A New Spelling of My Name.* Watertown, MA: Persephone, 1982.

Editing

2351 Clifton, Lucille; Anna Khalil; Audre Lorde, Eds. *Hoo-Doo 5.* DeRidder, LA: Energy Black South, 1976. Special women's issue.

Essays

2352 "Abortion." In COOP: 223–231.

2353 "Abortion." *Iowa Rev.* 12.2–3 1981: 223–231.

2354 "Audre Lorde: a new spelling of our name." *Sojourner.* 10.5 Mar. 1985: 16–17.

2355 "Black women's anger." *Essence.* 14.6 Oct. 1983: 90–92, 155–156, 158. From *Sister Outsider.*

2356 "Breast cancer: a Black lesbian feminist experience." *Sinister Wisdom.* 10 Sum. 1979: 44–61.

2357 "Breast cancer: power vs. prosthesis." In DELA: 49–50.

2358 "The erotic as power." *Chrysalis.* 9 Fall 1979: 29–31.

2359 "The erotic as power." *Ms.* 11.6 Dec. 1982: 78.

2360 "I've been standing on this street corner a hell of a long time!" In VIDA: 222–225. On being Black and lesbian in the 1950's.

2361 "Keynote address: the uses of anger." *Women's Studies Q.* 9.3 Fall 1981: 7–10. National Women's Studies Association Convention, 1981.

2362 "Man child: a Black lesbian feminist's response." *Conditions 4.* 2.1 Wint. 1979: 30–36. On Lorde's relationship with her son.

2363 "The master's tools will never dismantle the master's house." In MORA: 98–101. On racism and homophobia.

2364 "My mother's mortar." *Sinister Wisdom.* 8 Wint. 1979: 54–61.

2365 "My words will be there." In EVAN: 261–268. On her writing.

2366 "Of sisters and secrets." In CRUA: 186–195.

2367 "An open letter to Mary Daly." In MORA: 94–97. On racism and feminism.

2368 "Poetry is not a luxury." In EISE: 125–127.

2369 "Scratching the surface: some notes on barriers to women and loving." *Black Scholar.* 9.7 Apr. 1978: 31–35.

2370 *Sister Outsider: Essays and Speeches.* Trumansburg, NY: The Crossing, 1984.

2371 "Sister outsiders." *Heresies.* 4.3 1982: 15–16. From ZAMI.

2372 "Sisterhood and survival." *Black Scholar.* 17.2 Mar.–Apr. 1986: 5–7. Keynote address, Black Women Writers and the Diaspora Conference, E. Lansing, MI, Oct. 1985.

2373 "There is no hierarchy of oppressions." *Interracial Books for Children Bull.* 14.3–4 1983: 9. On homophobia.

2374 "The transformation of silence into language and action." *Sinister Wisdom.* 6 Sum. 1978: 11–15. Remarks given at the Lesbians and Literature Panel, 1977 Modern Language Association Convention, Chicago.

2375 *The Uses of the Erotic: The Erotic as Power.* Brooklyn: Out and Out, 1978. Pamphlet No. 3.

2376 "Uses of the erotic: the erotic as power." In LEDE: 295–301. Paper given at the Fourth Berkshire Conference on the History of Women, Mt. Holyoke College, Aug. 25, 1978.

Non-Fiction

2377 *Apartheid U.S.A.* NY: Kitchen Table: Women of Color, 1986.

2378 *I Am Your Sister: Black Women Organizing Across Sexualities.* NY: Kitchen Table: Women of Color, 1980. Freedom Organizing Series, No. 3.

2379 Lorde, Audre and Merle Woo. *Apartheid U.S.A.* and *Our Common Enemy, Our Common Cause: Freedom Organizing in the Eighties.* NY: Kitchen Table: Women of Color, 1986. Freedom Organizing Series, No. 2.

Poetry

2380 "Bazaar." *Denver Q.* 16.1 Spr. 1981: 35.

2381 *Between Our Selves.* Point Reyes, CA: Eidolon, 1976.

2382 "Between ourselves." *Denver Q.* 16.1 Spr. 1981: 29–31.

2383 "A birthday memorial to seventh street." In ADOF: 72–75.

2384 *The Black Unicorn.* NY: Norton, 1978.

2385 "The Black unicorn." *Amer. Poetry Rev.* 6.6 Nov.–Dec. 1977: 35.

2386 "Chain." *Chrysalis.* 1 1977: 46–47.

2387 "Chain." In STET: 199–201.

2388 *Chosen Poems — Old and New.* NY: Norton, 1982.

2389 "Chorus." *Denver Q.* 16.1 Spr. 1981: 28.

2390 *Coal.* NY: Norton, 1976.

2391 "Coal." In ADOF: 217–218.

2392 "Coal." In GILN: 2250.

2393 "Coal." In STET: 198.

2394 "Coniagui women." In GILN: 2253–2254.

2395 "Coniagui women." *New Yorker.* Nov. 28, 1977: 84.

2396 "Contact lenses." *Denver Q.* 16.1 Spr. 1981: 32.

2397 "Conversation in crisis." In FISH: 278.

2398 "Dahomey." In LONG: 728.

2399 "Dahomey." *Sinister Wisdom.* 4 Fall 1977: 14.

2400 "Eulogy for Alvin Frost." In ADOF: 211–214.

2401 "The evening news." *Denver Q.* 16.1 Spr. 1981: 34.

2402 "The evening news." In DALE: 13–14.

2403 "Fog report." *Women / Poems.* 4 1976: [no page listed].

2404 "For Assata." *Thirteenth Moon.* 4.1 1978: 25.

2405 "For each of you." In ADOF: 238–239.

2406 "From the House of Yamanja." *Amer. Poetry Rev.* 6.6 Nov.–Dec. 1977: 35.

2407 "From the House of Yamanja." In GILN: 2252-2253.

2408 "Harriet." In STET: 202-203.

2409 "Harriet: for my sisters." *Essence*. 8.2 June 1977: 48.

2410 "Letter for Jan." *Thirteenth Moon*. 4.1 1978: 23-24.

2411 *Litany for Survival*. Watsonville, CA: Blackwells, 1981. Broadside.

2412 "Meet." *Sinister Wisdom*. 3 Spr. 1977: 4.

2413 "Morning is a time for miracles." In DALE: 14.

2414 "Movement song." In ADOF: 155-156.

2415 "Naturally." In ADOF: 218-219.

2416 "Naturally." In SIMC: 63.

2417 "Naturally." In STET: 203-204.

2418 "Need." *Black Scholar*. 12.3 May-June 1981: 37-40. Rpt. in 12.6 (Nov.-Dec. 1981): 35-38.

2419 "Need." *Black Collegian*. 10.5 Apr.-May 1980: 117-119.

2420 "Need." *Heresies*. 2.4 [Sum.] 1979: 112-113.

2421 "Need: a chorale of Black women's voices." In BARA: 191-197.

2422 "Need: a chorale of Black women's voices." In DELA: 63-67.

2423 "Now that I am forever with child." In GILN: 2251-2252.

2424 "October." In DALE: 13.

2425 "The old days." *Sinister Wisdom*. 1.2 Fall 1976: 4.

2426 "On a night of the full moon." In GILN: 2250-2251.

2427 "One year to life on the Grand Central shuttle." In ADOF: 71-72.

2428 *Our Dead Behind Us: Poems*. NY: Norton, 1986.

2429 "Outside." *Amer. Poetry Rev*. 6.1 Jan.-Feb. 1977: 26.

2430 "Outside." *Essence*. 11.1 May 1980: 103.

2431 "Oya." In ADOF: 29-30.

2432 "Paperweight." In FISH: 279.

2433 "A poem for women in rage." In COOP: 220-222.

2434 "A poem for women in rage." *Iowa Rev*. 12.2-3 Spr.-Sum. 1981: 220-222.

2435 "Poems are not luxuries." *Chrysalis*. 3 1977: 7-9.

2436 "Portrait." *Poetry Now*. 19 1978: 17.

2437 "Rites of passage." In ADOF: 197.

2438 "Rooming houses are old women." In FISH: 280.

2439 "Rooming houses are old women." In LONG: 730.

2440 "Scar." *Epoch*. 26.3 Spr. 1977: 256-258.

2441 "School note." *Poetry Now*. 19 1978: 17.

2442 "The seventh sense." *Essence*. 14.8 Dec. 1983: 17.

2443 "Sisters in arms." *Parnassus*. 12-13.2-1 Spr.-Sum.-Fall-Wint. 1985: 223-224.

2444 "Sisters in arms." *Sojourner*. 10.5 Mar. 1985: 17.

2445 "Soho Cinema." *Parnassus*. 12-13.2-1 Spr.-Sum.-Fall-Wint. 1985: 225-226.

2446 "Solstice." In BELL: 375-376.

2447 "Summer oracle." In STET: 201-202.

2448 "Timepiece." *Denver Q*. 16.1 Spr. 1981: 33.

2449 "To Desi as Joe as Smoky the lover of 115th Street." In ADOF: 100-101.

2450 "To my daughter the junkie on a train." In ADOF: 99-100.

2451 "To the poet that happens to be Black and the Black poet who happens to be a woman." *Sojourner.* 10.5 Mar. 1985: 16.

2452 "Touring." *Some.* 9 1978: 71.

2453 "A trip on the Staten Island ferry." In ADOF: 70-71.

2454 "The trollop maiden." *Sinister Wisdom.* 3 Spr. 1977: 27.

2455 "Woman." *Sinister Wisdom.* 4 Spr. 1977: back page.

2456 "A woman speaks." In LONG: 729.

2457 "The woman thing." In STET: 204-205.

2458 "The women of Dan dance with swords in their hands to mark the time when they were warriors." In GILN: 2254-2255.

Short Fiction

2459 "The beginning." In BULK: 255-272.

2460 "Of sisters and secrets." *Callaloo.* 2.3 1979: 67-73.

2461 "Tar beach." *Conditions 5.* 2.2 Aut. 1979: 34-47.

2462 "Tar beach." In SMIT: 145-158.

Textual Criticism and Interviews

2463 Baldwin, James and Audre Lorde. "Revolutionary hope: a conversation between James Baldwin and Audrey Lorde." *Essence.* 15.8 Dec. 1984: 72-74, 129, 133.

2464 Barale, Michele Aina. *Frontiers.* 8.1 1984: 71-73. Rev. of *Zami* and *Sister Outsider.*

2465 Bethel, Lorraine. *Gay Community News.* Feb. 10, 1979: Book Supplement 1, 5, 6. Rev. of *The Black Unicorn.*

2466 Bovoso, Carole. *Essence.* 13.11 Mar. 1983: 20. Rev. of *Zami.*

2467 Bowen, Angela. *Sojourner.* 10.5 Mar. 1985: 33-34. Rev. of *Sister Outsider.*

2468 Bowen, Angela. *Woman of Power.* 2 Sum. 1985: 84. Rev. of *Sister Outsider.*

2469 Brooks, Jerome. "In the name of the father: the poetry of Audre Lorde." In EVAN: 269-276.

2470 Bulkin, Elly. "'Kissing againt the light': a look at lesbian poetry." *Radical Teacher.* 10 Dec. 1978: 7-17.

2471 Carruthers, Mary J. "The re-vision of the muse: Adrienne Rich, Audre Lorde, Judy Grahn, and Olga Broumas." *Hudson Rev.* 36 Sum. 1983: 293-322.

2472 Christian, Barbara. "The dynamics of difference: book review of Audre Lorde's *Sister Outsider.*" In CHRF: 205-210.

2473 Christian, Barbara. "No more buried lives: the theme of lesbianism in Audre Lorde's *Zami,* Gloria Naylor's *The Women of Brewster Place,* Ntozake Shange's *Sassafras, Cypress and Indigo,* and Alice Walker's *The Color Purple.*" In CHRF: 187-204.

2474 Christian, Barbara. "No more buried lives: the theme of lesbianism in Lorde, Naylor, Shange, Walker." *Feminist Issues.* 5 Spr. 1985: 3-20.

2475 Christian, Barbara. *Women's Rev. of Books.* 1.11 Aug. 1984: 6-7. Rev. of *Sister Outsider.*

2476 Clarke, Cheryl. *Conditions 8.* 3.2 Spr. 1982: 148–154. Rev. of *The Cancer Journals.*

2477 Cornwell, Anita. "'So who's giving guarantees?' An interview with Audre Lorde." *Sinister Wisdom.* 4 Fall 1977: 15–21.

2478 Daniell, Rosemary. *N.Y. Times Book Rev.* Dec. 19, 1982: 12. Revs. of *Chosen Poems — Old and New* and *Zami.*

2479 DeShazer, Mary K. "'Sisters in pain': the warrior muse of Audre Lorde." In DESH: 170–195.

2480 Gilbert, Sandra M. "On the edge of the estate." *Poetry.* 129 Feb. 1977: 296–301.

2481 Gould, Jean. "Audre Lorde." In GOUL: 288–296. On several works.

2482 Gullickson, Gay L. *Off Our Backs.* 11.7 July 1981: 22. Rev. of *The Cancer Journals.*

2483 Hammond, Karla. "Audre Lorde: interview." *Denver Q.* 16.1 Spr. 1981: 10–27.

2484 Hammond, Karla. "An interview with Audre Lorde." *Amer. Poetry Rev.* 9.2 1980: 18–21.

2485 Hull, Gloria T. *Conditions 1.* 1.1 Apr. 1977: 97–100. Rev. of *Between Ourselves.*

2486 Hull, Gloria T. and Geraldine M. McIntosh. "The brightest day . . . The loudest thunder." *Sinister Wisdom.* 18 1981: 92–96. Rev. of *The Cancer Journals.*

2487 Johnson, Joe. *Crisis.* 92.9 Nov. 1985: 10, 12, 47, 48. Rev. of *Zami.*

2488 Joseph, Gloria I. *Black Scholar.* 14.4–5 Sept.–Oct. 1983: 48–49. Rev. of *Zami.*

2489 Kunjufu, Johari M. *Black Books Bull.* 5.1 Spr. 1977: 49. Rev. of *Between Our Selves.*

2490 Larkin, Joan. "Full stature: Audre Lorde." In DALE: 15–17. On several works.

2491 Lorde, Audre and Adrienne Rich. "An interview with Audre Lorde." *Signs.* 6.4 Sum. 1981: 713–736.

2492 Martin, Joan. "The unicorn is Black: Audre Lorde in retrospect." In EVAN: 277–291.

2493 Mberi, Antar S.K. *Freedomways.* 16.3 1976: 194–196. Rev. of *Coal.*

2494 McAnnally-Knight, Mary. *Obsidian.* 4.2 Sum. 1978: 98–100. Rev. of *Between Our Selves.*

2495 McClaurin, Irma. *Obsidian.* 3.1 Spr. 1977: 69–71. Rev. of *The New York Head Shop and Museum* (1974).

2496 McClaurin-Allen, Irma. "Audre Lorde." In DL41: 217–222. Includes biography and additional bibliography.

2497 McHenry, Susan. *Ms.* 11.8 Feb. 1983: 26. Rev. of *Zami.*

2498 McHenry, Susan. *Ms.* 9.10 Apr. 1981: 42. Rev. of *The Cancer Journals.*

2499 Moira, Fran and Lorraine Sorrel. "Audre Lorde: lit from within." *Off Our Backs.* 12.4 Apr. 1982: 2–3, 11. An interview.

2500 Parkerson, Michelle. *Off Our Backs.* 13.5 May 1983: 25. Rev. of *Zami.*

2501 Rich, Adrienne. "Interview with Audre Lorde." In DALE: 18–21.

2502 Rushing, Andrea Benton. "A creative use of African sources." *Obsidian.* 5.3 Wint. 1979: 114–116. Rev. of *The Black Unicorn.*

2503 Rushing, Andrea Benton. *Ms.* 7.7 Jan. 1979: 43. Rev. of *The Black Unicorn.*

2504 Shariat, Fahamisha. *Conditions 5.* 2.2 Aut. 1979: 173–176. Rev. of *The Black Unicorn.*

2505 Stepto, Robert B. "Audre Lorde: the severed daughter." In BLOO: 289–294. On *The Black Unicorn.*

2506 Stepto, Robert B. "The phenomenal woman and the severed daughter." *Parnassus.* 8.1 Fall–Wint. 1979: 315–320. Revs. of Maya Angelou's *And Still I Rise* and Lorde's *The Black Unicorn.*

2507 Tate, Claudia, Ed. In TATE: 100–116. On a number of works.

2508 Winter, Nina. In WINT: 71–81. Influences on Lorde's creativity.

Esther Louise

Poetry

2509 "Enough." In BARA: 198.

2510 "Equity." *Essence.* 16.6 Oct. 1985: 124.

2511 "For us." In BARA: 201.

2512 "It's all in the name." In BARA: 199.

2513 "Jesus' song." *Essence.* 9.12 Apr. 1979: 17.

2514 "Jesus' song." *Obsidian.* 6.1–2 Spr.–Sum. 1980: 169.

2515 "On predestination." *Essence.* 9.12 Apr. 1979: 18.

2516 "On predestination." *Obsidian.* 6.1–2 Spr.–Sum. 1980: 169.

2517 "Running to gone." In BARA: 200.

2518 "Swinging doors of knocking-wood cowards." *Essence.* 11.8 Dec. 1980: 20.

2519 "Swinging doors of knocking-wood cowards." *Obsidian.* 6.1–2 Spr.–Sum. 1980: 170–173.

2520 "Tokens for 't'." In BARA: 201–202.

Oyoko Loving

Poetry

2521 "Ritual." In BELL: 355.

Naomi Long Madgett (1923–)

Miscellaneous

2522 *Deep Rivers, a Portfolio: Twenty Contemporary Black American Poets.* Detroit: Lotus, 1978. Poems on posters, for use in the classroom. Teachers' guide by Madgett.

Non-Fiction

2523 *A Student's Guide to Creative Writing.* Detroit: Penway, 1980. Writing short fiction and poetry, for college and advanced high school.

Poetry

2524 "Black poet." *Obsidian.* 7.1 Spr. 1981: 36.

2525 "Black woman." In FISH: 256.

2526 "Black woman." In STET: 130–131.

2527 *Blacksongs, Series I: Four Poetry Broadsides by Black Women.* Detroit: Lotus, 1977. Includes Madgett's "Woman with flower," Jill W. Boyer's "Sun song," Louise Robinson's "Woman-song," and Paulette C. White's "Lost your momma."

2528 "Deacon Morgan." In STET: 127.

2529 *Exits and Entrances.* Detroit: Lotus, 1978.

2530 "Exits and entrances." In STET: 128.

2531 "Fifth Street Exit, Richmond." *Callaloo.* 5.2 1979: 81–83.

2532 "Her story." In KONE: 148–149.

2533 "Memorial." *Great Lakes Rev.* 6.1 Sum. 1979: 73.

2534 "Midway." In STET: 128–129.

2535 "New day." In STET: 130.

2536 "Nocturne." In SIMC: 67.

2537 "Offspring." *Essence.* 15.5 Sept. 1984: 176.

2538 "Offspring." In FISH: 255.

2539 "Packrat." *Callaloo.* 5.2 1979: 52.

2540 *Phantom Nightingale: Juvenilia: Poems 1934–1943.* Detroit: Lotus, 1981.

2541 "Soon I will be done." *Callaloo.* 5.2 1979: 27.

2542 "Soon I will be done." *Great Lakes Rev.* 6.1 Sum. 1979: 72.

2543 "The sun do move." *Obsidian.* 7.1 Spr. 1981: 37.

2544 "The survivors." *Callaloo.* 5.2 1979: 78.

2545 "Ten." *Obsidian.* 7.1 Spr. 1981: 36.

2546 "Tree of heaven (Ailanthus Altissima)." In SIMC: 85.

2547 "Twice a child (for my mother at ninety)." *Great Lakes Rev.* 6.1 Sum. 1979: 74.

2548 "Twice a child (for my mother at ninety)." In DALL: 90.

2549 "Women (To Femi Sodipo and my African-American ancestors)." In STET: 129.

2550 "Writing a poem." In FISH: 256.

Textual Criticism

2551 Boyd, Melba. *Black Scholar.* 11.4 Mar.–Apr. 1980: 84–85. Rev. of *Exits and Entrances.*

2552 Ward, Jerry W. *New Orleans Rev.* 5.1 1976: 93–94. Rev. of *Pink Ladies in the Afternoon* (1972).

Jabari Mahiri

Children's Stories

2553 *The Day They Stole the Letter J.* Chicago: Third World, 1981.

Textual Criticism
2554 Shauri, Dhamana. *Black Books Bull.* 7.2 1981: 55–56. Rev. of *The Day They Stole the Letter J.*

Barbara J. Mahone (1944–)

Biography
2555 Eanes, Marcie. "Essence women: Barbara J. Mahone." *Essence.* 14.8 Dec. 1983: 56.

Poetry
2556 "Colors for mama." In ADOF: 36.
2557 "Sugarfields." In ADOF: 37.

Deborah Major

Editing
2558 *Ascension II.* San Francisco: San Francisco African American Historical and Cultural Society, 1983. Twentieth-century poetry by Afro-Americans.

Poetry
2559 "Progress report." *Black Scholar.* 12.5 Sept.–Oct. 1981: 17.
2560 "Two young men meet oppression one last time." *Black Scholar.* 11.5 May–June 1980: 71.

Julianne Malveaux (1953–)

Essays
2561 "Black women on white campuses." *Essence.* 10.4 Aug. 1979: 78.
2562 "Three views of Black women—the myths, the statistics, and a personal statement." *Heresies.* 2.4 [Sum.] 1979: 50–55.

Non-Fiction
2563 Simms, Margaret C. and Julianne M. Malveaux, Eds. *Slipping Through the Cracks: The Status of Black Women.* New Brunswick, NJ: Transaction, 1986. Politics and economy.

Poetry
2564 "Don't take up with nobody you meet on a train." *Essence.* 11.10 Feb. 1981: 19.

Paule Marshall (1929–)

Essays

2565 "Characterizations of Black women in the American novel." In BOWL: 76–79.

2566 "Shaping the world of my art." *Women's Studies Q.* 9.4 Wint. 1981: 23–24.

2567 "Ties that bind." *Essence.* 16.1 May 1985: 64, 66. On marriage and maintaining the family.

Novels

2568 *Praisesong for the Widow* [Excerpt]. *Ms.* 11.8 (Feb. 1983): 49, 52, 79–80.

2569 *Praisesong for the Widow.* NY: Putnam, 1983.

Short Fiction

2570 "Barbados." In BARA: 203–217.

2571 "Brooklyn." In FISH: 214–229.

2572 *Merle: A Novella and Other Stories.* NY: Feminist, 1983.

2573 "Reena." In HAMA: 264–283.

2574 *Reena and Other Stories.* Old Westbury, NY: Feminist, 1983.

2575 "Return of the native." In BELL: 314–321.

2576 "To Da-duh, in memoriam." In LONG: 604–613.

Summary of Novel

2577 Southgate, Robert L. In SOUT: 49–50. Summary of Marshall's *Brown Girl, Brownstones* (1959).

Textual Criticism and Interviews

2578 Bond, Jean Carey. *Freedomways.* 22.2 1982: 110–112. Rev. of *Brown Girl, Brownstones.*

2579 Bovoso, Carole. *Essence.* 13.12 Apr. 1983: 19. Rev. of *Praisesong for the Widow.*

2580 Brown, Lloyd W. "Mannequins and mermaids—the contemporary writer and sexual images in the consumer culture." *Women's Studies.* 5.1 1977: 1–12.

2581 Christian, Barbara. "Pass it on." In CHRW: 239–252. Comparative study of Marshall, Toni Morrison, and Alice Walker.

2582 Christian, Barbara. "Paule Marshall." In DL33: 161–170. Includes biography and additional bibliography.

2583 Christian, Barbara. "Paule Marshall: a literary biography." In CHRF: 103–117.

2584 Christian, Barbara. "Ritualistic process and the structure of Paule Marshall's *Praisesong for the Widow.*" *Callaloo.* 6.2 Spr.–Sum. 1983: 74–84. Treatment of West Indians.

2585 Christian, Barbara. "Ritualistic process and the structure of Paule Marshall's *Praisesong for the Widow.*" In CHRF: 149–158.

2586 Christian, Barbara. "Sculpture and space: the interdependency of character and culture in the novels of Paule Marshall." In CHRW: 80–136.

2587 Collier, Eugenia. "The closing of the circle: movement from division to wholeness in Paule Marshall's fiction." In EVAN: 295-315.

2588 Collins, Martha. *Sojourner.* 10.6 Apr. 1985: 34. Rev. of *The Chosen Place, The Timeless People.*

2589 Cook, John. "Whose child? the fiction of Paule Marshall." *CLA J.* 24.1 Sept. 1980: 1-15.

2590 Denniston, Dorothy L. "Early short fiction by Paule Marshall." *Callaloo.* 6.2 Spr.-Sum. 1983: 31-45. On the short story "The valley between."

2591 DeVeaux, Alexis. "Paule Marshall, in celebration of our triumph." *Essence.* 10.1 May 1979: 70-71, 96, 98, 123-124, 126, 128, 131, 133, 135, 137. On several works.

2592 Eko, Ebele O. "Oral tradition: the bridge to Africa in Paule Marshall's *Praisesong for the Widow.*" *Western J. of Black Studies.* 10.3. Fall 1986: 143-147.

2593 "Great books we never finished reading." *N.Y. Times Book Rev.* June 3, 1984: 47. Interview.

2594 Harris, Trudier. "No outlet for the blues: Silla Boyce's plight in *Brown Girl, Brownstones.*" *Callaloo.* 6.2 Spr.-Sum. 1983: 57-67. Treatment of West Indians as immigrants.

2595 Holloway, Clayton G. *CLA J.* 27.4 June 1984: 460-461. Rev. of *Praisesong for the Widow.*

2596 Hull, Gloria T. "To be a Black woman in America: a reading of Paule Marshall's *Reena.*" *Obsidian.* 4.3 Wint. 1978: 5-15.

2597 Jefferson, Margo. "A Black woman's odyssey." *Nation.* Apr. 2, 1983: 403-404. Rev. of *Praisesong for the Widow.*

2598 Kazi-Ferrouillet, Kuumba and Karima A. Belle. *Black Collegian.* 15.1 Sept.-Oct. 1984: 64. Rev. of *Praisesong for the Widow.*

2599 Killens, John Oliver. *Crisis.* 90.7 Aug.-Sept. 1983: 49-50. Rev. of *Praisesong for the Widow.*

2600 Kubitschek, Missy Dehn. "Paule Marshall's women on quest." *Black Amer. Lit. Forum.* 21.1-2 Spr.-Sum. 1987: 43-60.

2601 Lacovia, R.M. "Migration and transmutation in the novels of McKay, Marshall, and Clarke." *J. of Black Studies.* 7.4 June 1977: 437-454.

2602 Lodge, S.A. "*Publishers Weekly* interviews Paule Marshall." *Publishers Weekly.* Jan. 20, 1984: 90-91.

2603 Marshall, Paule and Maryse Condé. "Return of a native daughter: an interview with Paule Marshall and Maryse Condé." *Sage.* 3 Fall 1986: 52-53. Translation, by John Williams, of an interview in *Politique Africaine,* Sept. 1984.

2604 McCluskey, John, Jr. "And called every generation blessed: theme, setting, and ritual in the works of Paule Marshall." In EVAN: 316-334.

2605 McHenry, Susan. *Ms.* 10.5 Nov. 1981: 47. Rev. of *Brown Girl, Brownstones.*

2606 Ogunyemi, Chikwenye Okonjo. "The old order shall pass: the examples of 'Flying home' and 'Barbados'." *CLA J.* 25.3 Mar. 1982: 303-314.

2607 Pannill, Linda. "From the 'Wordshop': the fiction of Paule Marshall." *Melus.* 12.2 Sum. 1985: 63-73.

2608 Pinckney, D. *N.Y. Rev. of Books.* Apr. 28, 1983: 26-30. Revs. of *Brown Girl, Brownstones* and *Praisesong for the Widow.*

2609 Pollard, Velma. "Cultural connections in Paule Marshall's *Praisesong for the Widow.*" *World Lit. Written in English.* 25.2 Aut. 1985: 285–298.

2610 Ravell-Pinto, Thelma. *J. of Black Studies.* 17.4 June 1987: 509–511. Rev. of *Praisesong for the Widow.*

2611 Rushin, Kate. "Paule Marshall: stages in a writer's life." *Sojourner.* 10.6 Apr. 1985: 16–17.

2612 Sandiford, Keith A. "Paule Marshall's *Praisesong for the Widow:* The reluctant heiress, or Whose life is it anyway?" *Black Amer. Lit. Forum.* 20.4 Wint. 1986: 371–392.

2613 Schneider, Deborah. "A search for selfhood: Paule Marshall's *Brown Girl, Brownstones.*" In BRUC: 53–73.

2614 Sheffey, Ruthe T. *Langston Hughes Rev.* 4.1 1986: 55–57. Rev. of *Praisesong for the Widow.*

2615 Simmons, Sheila M. *Sojourner.* 9.8 Apr. 1984: 21. Rev. of *Reena and Other Stories.*

2616 Skerrett, Joseph T., Jr. "Paule Marshall and the crisis of middle years: *The Chosen Place, The Timeless People.*" *Callaloo.* 6.2 Spr.–Sum. 1983: 68–73.

2617 Spillers, Hortense J. "*Chosen Place, Timeless People:* some figurations on The New World." In PRYS: 151–175. On Marshall's 1969 novel.

2618 Talbert, E. Lee. "The poetics of prophecy in Paule Marshall's *Soul Clap Hands and Sing.*" *Melus.* 5.1 Spr. 1978: 49–56.

2619 Troester, Rosalie Riegle. "Turbulence and tenderness: mothers, daughters, and 'othermothers' in Paule Marshall's *Brown Girl, Brownstones.*" *Sage.* 1.2 Fall 1984: 13–16.

2620 Tyler, A. *N.Y. Times Book Rev.* Feb. 20, 1983: 7. Rev. of *Praisesong for the Widow.*

2621 Wade-Gayles, Gloria. "The truths of our mothers' lives: mother-daughter relationships in Black women's fiction." *Sage.* 1.2 Fall 1984: 8–12. *Brown Girl, Brownstones* compared to Dorothy West's *The Living Is Easy* and Toni Morrison's *The Bluest Eye.*

2622 Waniek, Marilyn Nelson. "Paltry things: immigrants and marginal men in Paule Marshall's short fiction." *Callaloo.* 6.2 Spr.–Sum. 1983: 46–56.

2623 Washington, Mary Helen. "I sign my mother's name: Alice Walker, Dorothy West, Paule Marshall." In PERR: 144–150.

2624 Waxman, Barbara F. "The widow's journey to self and roots: aging and society in Paule Marshall's *Praisesong for the Widow.*" *Frontiers.* 9.3 1987: 94–99.

2625 Willis, Susan. "Paule Marshall's relationship to Afro-American culture." In WILL: 53–82.

Sharon Stockard Martin

Drama
2626 "The moving violation." In OSTR: 123–153.

Judi Ann Mason (1955–)

Biography
2627 Stinson, Patricia. "*Essence* women." *Essence.* 8.7 Nov. 1977: 6. Short article on Mason as a playwright. Among the plays that Mason has written is *Livin Fat* (1974).

Short Fiction
2628 "Smells that go boom." *Essence.* 11.4 Aug. 1980: 86–87, 135, 138, 140, 142–144.

Sharon Bell Mathis (1937–)

Bibliography
2629 Roginski, Jim, Comp. "Sharon Bell Mathis." In ROGI: 182–183.

Children's Story
2630 *Cartwheels.* NY: Scholastic, 1977.

Essay
2631 "*The Slave Dancer* is an insult to Black children." In MACD: 146–148. On Paula Fox's 1973 children's book.

Summary of Children's Story
2632 Southgate, Robert L. In SOUT: 161–162. Summary of *Teacup Full of Roses* (1972).

Textual Criticism
2633 DeMontreville, Doris and Elizabeth D. Crawford, Eds. "Sharon Bell Mathis." In DEMO: 255–256. Biography with list of the author's works.
2634 Foster, Frances Smith. "Sharon Bell Mathis." In DL33: 170–173. Includes biography and additional bibliography.

Raymina Mays

Short Fiction
2635 "Lerna's mother, Verda Lee." *Essence.* 11.11 Mar. 1981: 76, 112.
2636 "LeRoy's birthday." In SMIT: 168–170.

Malkia M'Buzi

Poetry
2637 "Lament." In BARA: 218.
2638 "Tree women quest for sun..." In BARA: 219–220.

Irma McClaurin (1952–)

Poetry

2639 "Africa." *Nimrod.* 21–22.2–1 1977: 155.

2640 "Children's Cycle II." *Nimrod.* 21–22.2–1 1977: 154.

2641 "I, woman." *Obsidian.* 3.2 Sum. 1977: 55.

2642 "I, woman." In STET: 197.

2643 "The mask." In STET: 195–196.

2644 "Old age sequence (for Gwendolyn Brooks)." *Black Amer. Lit. Forum.* 21.3 Fall 1987: 252.

2645 "Poem for a strung-out friend." *Nimrod.* 21–22.2–1 1977: 153.

2646 "Return." *Nimrod.* 21–22.2–1 1977: 155.

2647 "To a gone era (my college days—class of '73)." In STET: 196–197.

2648 "Zenzile (self-made woman)." *Greenfield Rev.* 5.3–4 Wint. 1976–1977: 71.

Chirlane McCray

Essay

2649 "I am a lesbian." *Essence.* 10.5 Sept. 1979: 90–91, 157, 161, 164, 166.

Poetry

2650 "I used to think." *Conditions 5.* 2.2 Aut. 1979: 29–30.

2651 "I used to think." In SMIT: 57–59.

2652 "Two love poems for Sekou: 2." *Essence.* 10.10 Feb. 1980: 59.

Colleen J. McElroy (1935–)

Poetry

2653 *Bone Flames: Poems.* NY: Harper, 1987.

2654 "Breaking the Kula Ring." *Chowder Rev.* 9 Fall–Wint. 1977: 34–35.

2655 "Caledonia." In STET: 288–289.

2656 "Catacombs: dream poem number one." In DALW: 70.

2657 "The circus of the city." *Southern Poetry Rev.* 24.2 Aut. 1984: 61–62.

2658 "Confessions of a woman who sucks baby toes." *Nimrod.* 30.2 Spr.-Sum. 1987: 119–120.

2659 "Dancing with the fifth horseman." In FISH: 268–270.

2660 "Defining it for Vanessa." In FISH: 267–268.

2661 "Dreams of Johnson Grass." *Southern Poetry Rev.* 20.1 Spr. 1980: 11.

2662 "Etymologies." *Portland Rev.* 27.2 1981: 25.

2663 "The female as taken from freshman essays." *Massachusetts Rev.* 24.2 Sum. 1983: 314–316.

2664 "Flight." In DALW: 69.

2665 "For want of a male the shoe was lost." *Nimrod.* 30.2 Spr.-Sum. 1987: 116.

2666 "From blue waters." *Southern Poetry Rev.* 20.1 Spr. 1980: 13.

2667 "How long does it take to get away from it all (for Kathy Newbreast)." *Thirteenth Moon.* 7.1-2 1983: 9-10.

2668 "How to become a mistress." *Aspen Anthology.* 1 Wint. 1976: 51.

2669 "It ain't the blues that blows an ill wind (Valaida Snow: circa 1930)." *Black Warrior Rev.* 11.1 Aut. 1984: 40-41.

2670 "Landscapes and still life." *Callaloo.* 1.4 1978: 77.

2671 *Lie and Say You Love Me.* Tacoma, WA: Circinatum, 1981.

2672 "Lie and say you love me." *Portland Rev.* 27.2 1981: 26.

2673 "Living here ain't easy." *Epoch.* 32.2 Wint.-Spr. 1983: 132-133.

2674 *Looking for a Country Under Its Original Name: Poems.* Yakima, WA: Blue Begonia, 1984.

2675 "Looking for a country under its original name." In STET: 290-291.

2676 "Looking into the eyes." *Portland Rev.* 27.2 1981: 27.

2677 "Lothar's wife." *Calyx.* 5.1 1980: 51.

2678 "Memoirs of American speech." In SKLA: 145-146. From her *Winters Without Snow.*

2679 "Monologue for Saint Louis." *Calyx.* 5.1 1980: 50.

2680 "Moon, razor, eye." *Georgia Rev.* 39.3 Fall 1985: 523.

2681 "Morning in Argentina (for Helen)." In DALW: 69-70.

2682 *Music from Home: Selected Poems.* Carbondale: S. Illinois Univ., 1976.

2683 "A poem for my old age." *Nimrod.* 21-22.2-1 1977: 156.

2684 "The privilege of choice." *Thirteenth Moon.* 7.1-2 1983: 7-8.

2685 "Pulsing." *South Dakota Rev.* 16.3 Aut. 1978: 7-8.

2686 *Queen of the Ebony Isles.* NY: Harper, 1984.

2687 "Runners." *Callaloo.* 1.4 1978: 1.

2688 "Ruth." In STET: 286-288.

2689 "Shelley at Sequim Inlet." *Manhattan Rev.* 3.2 Wint. 1984-1985: 72.

2690 "Six. Stimulus-Response." *Poetry Northwest.* 17.3 Aut. 1976: 23.

2691 "Speech: I." *Xanadu.* 4 1977: 18.

2692 "Sweet with wonder, my feet upon air." *Nimrod.* 30.2 Spr.-Sum. 1987: 117-118.

2693 "There are no absolutes." *Xanadu.* 4 1977: 16.

2694 "This is the poem I never meant to write." *Poetry Northwest.* 19.3 1978: 30-31.

2695 "To the lady holding the MGM torch." *Callaloo.* 1.4 1978: 82-83.

2696 "Try to understand papa." *Encore Amer. and Worldwide News.* Jan. 17, 1977: 47.

2697 "Velasquez' Juan de Pareja." *Missouri Rev.* 6.2 Wint. 1983: 16-17.

2698 "The ways of women." *Kansas Q.* 14.3 Sum. 1982: 45.

2699 "What I'd least like to remember." *Manhattan Rev.* 3.2 Wint. 1984-1985: 73.

2700 "When poets dream." In DALW: 70.

2701 "Where iguanas still live." In FISH: 271-272.

2702 "While poets are watching (for Quincy Troupe)." *Ploughshares.* 7.1 1981: 88-90.

2703 "Why Tu Fu does not speak of the Nubian." *Nimrod.* 21-22.2-1 1977: 159.

2704 *Winters Without Snow.* NY: Reed, 1979.
2705 "With Bill Pickett at the 101 Ranch." *Callaloo.* 9.1 Wint. 1986: 100.
2706 "A woman's song." In STET: 291-293.
2707 "A woman's song." *Obsidian.* 3.1 Spr. 1977: 57-58.
2708 "Zeta and Xerosis." *South Dakota Rev.* 16.3 Aut. 1978: 5-6.

Short Fiction
2709 *Jesus and Fat Tuesday, and Other Short Stories.* Berkeley, CA: Creative Arts, 1987.
2710 "Remember me to Harris." *Callaloo.* 2.3 1979: 9-21.
2711 "Sun, wind and water." *Callaloo.* 4.1-3 1981: 39-46.

Textual Criticism
2712 Ahrold, Kyle. *Encore Amer. and Worldwide News.* Jan. 17, 1977: 46-47. Rev. of *Music from Home.*
2713 Begnal, K. *Choice.* 25.4 Dec. 1987: 622. Rev. of *Jesus and Fat Tuesday.*
2714 Broussard, Mercedese. "Home again." *Callaloo.* 5.2 1979: 161-163. Rev. of *Music from Home.*
2715 Colman, Cathy A. *N.Y. Times Book Rev.* Sept. 6, 1987: 16. Rev. of *Jesus and Fat Tuesday.*
2716 Drew, Bet-tina. *Library J.* Nov. 15, 1987: 84. Rev. of *Bone Flames.*
2717 Hernton, Calvin. "The tradition." *Parnassus.* 12-13.2-1 Spr.-Sum.-Fall-Wint. 1985: 537-541. Rev. of *Queen of the Ebony Isles.*
2718 Jones, Robert B., Jr. *Chowder Rev.* 8 1977: 79-81. Rev. of *Music from Home.*
2719 Miller, R.B. *Choice.* 22.8 Apr. 1985: 1159. Rev. of *Queen of the Ebony Isles.*

McMichael, Michelle *see* Zimele-Keita, Nzadi

Terry McMillan

Novel
2720 *Mama.* Boston: Houghton, 1987.
2721 *Mama* [Excerpt]. *Essence.* 17.12 Apr. 1987: 72-74, 125, 131.

Textual Criticism
2722 Blythe, Will. *N.Y. Times Book Rev.* Feb. 22, 1987: 11. Rev. of *Mama.*
2723 Giddings, Paula. *Essence.* 17.11 Mar. 1987: 28. Rev. of *Mama.*
2724 Lockwood, Frank. "Terry McMillan at Radcliffe." *Second Century (Radcliffe News).* 8.2 Apr. 1987: 5.
2725 *New Yorker.* Mar. 16, 1987: 104. Rev. of *Mama.*

Rosemari Mealy

Poetry
2726 *Lift These Shadows from Our Eyes: Poems.* Cambridge, MA: West End, 1978.

2727 "A love poem to an African freedom fighter." In BARA: 221–222.
2728 "New chapters for our history." In BARA: 223–229.
2729 "Untitled [Spring comes slowly]." In BARA: 222.

Louise Meriwether (1923–)

Short Fiction
2730 "A happening in Barbados." In KOPO: 272–281. Written in 1968.
2731 "Lydia." *Freedomways.* 25.2 1985: 81–89.
2732 "A man called Jethro." In BARA: 230–242.
2733 "Robert and Hannah." *Essence.* 16.10 Feb. 1986: 70–72, 74, 128, 132.

Summary of Novel
2734 Southgate, Robert L. In SOUT: 65–66. Summary of *Daddy Was a Number Runner* (1970).

Textual Criticism
2735 Commire, Anne. "Louise Meriwether." In CO31: 143. Biography and some bibliography.
2736 Dandridge, Rita B. "Louise Meriwether." In DL33: 182–186. Includes biography and additional bibliography.

May Miller (1899–)

Children's Poetry
2737 *Halfway to the Sun.* Washington, D.C.: Washington Writers, 1981.

Poetry
2738 "Blazing accusation." *Beloit Poetry J.* 29.2 Wint. 1978–1979: 14.
2739 "Child in the night." In SIMC: 96.
2740 "Death is not master." In FISH: 257.
2741 "Gift from Kenya." In STET: 112.
2742 "Love on the Cape." *Beloit Poetry J.* 29.2 Wint. 1978–1979: 15.
2743 "Not that far." In STET: 113–117.
2744 "Nuptial calendar." *Beloit Poetry J.* 29.2 Wint. 1978–1979: 16.
2745 "Place in the morning." In FISH: 258.
2746 *The Ransomed Wait.* Detroit: Lotus, 1983.
2747 "The scream." In FISH: 258.
2748 "Three scenes for all men." In SIMC: 97.

Textual Criticism
2749 Brown, Beth. *CLA J.* 28.1 Sept. 1984: 102–109. Rev. of *The Ransomed Wait.*
2750 Stoelting, Winifred L. "May Miller." In DL41: 241–247. Biography and bibliography included.

2751 Zu-Bolton, Ahmos, II and Kirsten Mullen. "Review: *The Clearing and Beyond* (poetry, 1972). . ." *Obsidian.* 3.1 Spr. 1977: 75–78.

Arthenia J. Bates Millican (1920–)

Essays
2752 "Fire as the symbol of a leadening existence." In ODAN: 170–180. On James Baldwin.

Poetry
2753 *Such Things from the Valley.* Norfolk, VA: Millican, 1977.

Textual Criticism and Interviews
2754 Parker, Bettye J. "Reflections: Arthenia Bates Millican." In BELL: 201–208. Interview in which Dr. Millican comments on various topics.
2755 Smith, Virginia Whatley. "Arthenia J. Bates Millican." In DL38: 195–201. Biography and bibliography included.
2756 Ward, Jerry. "Legitimate resources of the soul: an interview with Arthenia Bates Millican." *Obsidian.* 3.1 Spr. 1977: 14–34.

Karen L. Mitchell

Poetry
2757 "About 1929." *Thirteenth Moon.* 7.1–2 1983: 122–123.
2758 "Belly edge." *Thirteenth Moon.* 6.1–2 1982: 42–43.
2759 "Birmingham, Alabama, 1963." *Open Places.* 27 Spr. 1979: 32–33.
2760 "Birmingham, Alabama, 1963." *Open Places.* 31–32 Aut. 1981: 136–137.
2761 *Blackberry Pickin'.* Columbia (?), MO: Mitchell, 1976.
2762 "The eating hill." *Thirteenth Moon.* 6.1–2 1982: 37–39.
2763 "For Michael." *Essence.* 11.3 July 1980: 15.
2764 "For Michael." *Open Places.* 27 Spr. 1979: 37.
2765 "My mother bakes cookies." *Obsidian.* 6.1–2 Spr.–Sum. 1980: 220.
2766 "The paper woman." *Thirteenth Moon.* 7.1–2 1983: 124–125.
2767 "Returning." *Open Places.* 27 Spr. 1979: 34–35.
2768 "Sometimes." *Thirteenth Moon.* 6.1–2 1982: 40–41.
2769 "Tree stillness." *Open Places.* 27 Spr. 1979: 36.
2770 "Visit." *Obsidian.* 6.1–2 Spr.–Sum. 1980: 218–219.
2771 "Where have all the Black sheep gone? They have gone grazing in the fields." *Obsidian.* 6.1–2 Spr.–Sum. 1980: 217–218.

Barbara J. Molette (1940–)

Drama
2772 Molette, Carlton and Barbara Molette. "Noah's ark." In OSTR: 177–196.

Essays

2773 "Black heroes and Afrocentric values in theatre." *J. of Black Studies.* 15.4 June 1985: 447–462. Includes criticism on Black women playwrights.

2774 "They speak. Who listens? Black women playwrights." *Black World.* 25.6 Apr. 1976: 28–34. Historical viewpoint.

Non-Fiction

2775 Molette, Carlton W. and Barbara J. Molette. *Black Theatre: Premise and Presentation.* Bristol, IN: Wyndham Hall, 1986.

Cynthia B. Moore

Poetry

2776 "A reflection." *Essence.* 17.10 Feb. 1987: 123.

Opal Moore

Essays

2777 "False flattery and thin history: a study of three novels for children." In MACC: 129–143. On the trilogy *Jump Ship to Freedom, War Comes to Willy Freeman,* and *Who Is Carrie?* by James Lincoln and Christopher Collier.

2778 "Picture books: the un-text." In MACC: 183–191. On images of Black people in *Ben's Trumpet* by Rachel Isadora and *Big Sixteen* by Mary Calhoun.

Poetry

2779 "Landscapes: shakin'." *Black Amer. Lit. Forum.* 19.3 Fall 1985: 113.

Short Fiction

2780 "A small insolence." *Callaloo.* 8.2 Spr.–Sum. 1985: 304–309.

Maria K. Mootry (1944–)

Editing

2781 Jones, Joyce; Mary McTaggart; Maria Mootry, Eds. *The Otherwise Room.* Carbondale, IL: Poetry Factory, 1981.

2782 Jones, Joyce; Mary McTaggart; Maria Mootry, Eds. *Sestina: Six Women Poets.* Carbondale, IL: Poetry Factory, 1983.

2783 Mootry, Maria and Gary Smith, Eds. *A Life Distilled: Gwendolyn Brooks, Her Poetry and Fiction.* Urbana: Univ. of Illinois, 1987.

Essays

2784 "Love and death in the Black pastoral." *Obsidian.* 3.2 Sum. 1977: 5–11.

Non-Fiction
2785 *The Crisis of Feminist Criticism: A Case Study of Lorraine Hansberry's Feminine Triads in "Raisin" and "Sign."* Urbana: Univ. of Illinois, 1982(?). Afro Scholar Working Papers, vol. 16.

Poetry
2786 "A palace of strangers: a female Chicago artist confronts Sally Mae Hunter, bag lady of the streets." *Open Places.* 37 Spr.–Sum. 1984: 24–27.

2787 "To Winnie on Ecumenical Day." *Open Places.* 41 Spr. 1986: 65–69.

Toni Morrison (1931–)

Bibliography
2788 Fikes, Robert, Jr. "Echoes from small town Ohio: a Toni Morrison bibliography." *Obsidian.* 5.1–2 Spr.–Sum. 1979: 142–148.

2789 Martin, Curtis. "A bibliography of writings by Toni Morrison." In RAIN: 205–207.

2790 Mekkawi, Mod. *Toni Morrison: A Bibliography.* Washington, D.C.: Founders Graduate Library (Howard Univ.), 1986.

Essays
2791 "City limits, village values: concepts of neighborhood in Black fiction." In JAYE: 35–44.

2792 "A knowing so deep." *Essence.* 16.1 May 1985: 230. An essay on women.

2793 "Memory, creation, and writing." *Thought.* 59.235 Dec. 1984: 385–390. On *Tar Baby.*

2794 "Rootedness: the ancestor as foundation." In EVAN: 339–345. On her writing.

2795 "Toni Morrison on Cinderella's stepsisters." *Ms.* 8.3 Sept. 1979: 41–42.

2796 "Writers together." *Nation.* Oct. 24, 1981: 396–397. A speech given on Oct. 9, 1981 at the American Writers Congress, New York.

Novels
2797 *Beloved.* NY: Knopf, 1987.

2798 *The Bluest Eye.* In GILN: 2068–2184. Originally published in 1970.

2799 *The Bluest Eye* [Excerpt]. In LONG: 672–686.

2800 "Nineteen hundred twenty-one." In FISH: 237–247. Excerpt from *Sula* (1973).

2801 *Song of Solomon.* NY: Knopf, 1977.

2802 *Song of Solomon* [Excerpt]. *Redbook.* 149 Sept. 1977: 237–260.

2803 *Sula* [Excerpt]. In HARP: 212.

2804 *Tar Baby.* NY: Knopf, 1981.

2805 *Tar Baby* [Excerpt]. *Essence.* 12.1 May 1981: 90–92, 152, 156, 158, 161, 164, 166.

Poetry
2806 "The big box." *Ms.* 8.8 Mar. 1980: 57–58. In the column "Stories for Free Children."

Short Fiction
2807 "Eva Peace." In WASH: 156–167.
2808 "Recitatif." In BARA: 243–261.

Summary of Novel
2809 Southgate, Robert L. In SOUT: 158–159. Summary of *Sula* (1973).

Textual Criticism and Interviews
2810 Abel, Elizabeth. "(E)merging identities: the dynamics of female friendship in contemporary fiction by women." *Signs.* 6.3 Spr. 1981: 413–435. Pages 426–429, commentary on *Sula*.

2811 Ahrold, K. "Critics' choice—Toni Morrison, National Book Critics Circle prize." *Encore Amer. and Worldwide News.* Feb. 6, 1978: 38. For *Song of Solomon*.

2812 Allen, Samuel. *Boston Univ. J.* 26.1 1978: 67–72. Rev. of *Song of Solomon*.

2813 Atlas, Marilyn J. "The darker side of Toni Morrison's *Song of Solomon*." *Society for the Study of Midwestern Lit. Newsletter.* 10.2 1980: 1–13.

2814 Atlas, Marilyn J. "A woman both shiny and brown: feminist strength in Toni Morrison's *Song of Solomon*." *Society for the Study of Midwestern Lit. Newsletter.* 9.3 1979: 8–12.

2815 Atwood, Margaret. *N.Y. Times Book Rev.* Sept. 13, 1987: 1, 49. Rev. of *Beloved*.

2816 Baker-Fletcher, Karen. *Commonweal.* Nov. 6, 1987: 631–633. Rev. of *Beloved*.

2817 Bakerman, Jane. *CLA J.* 21.3 Mar. 1978: 446–448. Rev. of *Song of Solomon*.

2818 Bakerman, Jane. "Failures of love: female initiation in the novels of Toni Morrison." *Amer. Lit.* 52.4 Jan. 1981: 541–563.

2819 Bakerman, Jane. "The seams can't show: an interview with Toni Morrison." *Black Amer. Lit. Forum.* 12.2 Sum. 1978: 56–60.

2820 Banyiwa-Horne, Naana. "The scary face of the self: an analysis of the character of Sula in Toni Morrison's *Sula*." *Sage.* 2.1 Spr. 1985: 28–31.

2821 Barthold, Bonnie J. "Toni Morrison, *Song of Solomon*." In BART: 174–184.

2822 Beaty, Jerome. In BEAT: 661–666. Criticism on *Sula*.

2823 Beaver, Harold. "Blackgothic." *Times (London) Literary Suppl.* Nov. 24, 1978: 1359. Rev. of *Song of Solomon*.

2824 Bell, Pearl K. "Self-seekers." *Commentary.* 72.2 Aug. 1981: 56–58. Rev. of *Tar Baby*.

2825 Bell, Roseann P. *Obsidian.* 2.3 Wint. 1976: 93–95. Rev. of *Sula*.

2826 Bischoff, Joan. "The novels of Toni Morrison: studies in thwarted sensitivity." *Studies in Black Lit.* 6 1976: 21–23.

2827 Blake, Susan L. "Folklore and community in *Song of Solomon.*" *Melus.* 7.3 Fall 1980: 77–82.

2828 Blake, Susan L. "Toni Morrison." In DL33: 187–199. Includes biography and additional bibliography.

2829 Bowman, Diane Kim. "Flying high: the American Icarus in Morrison, Roth, and Updike." *Perspectives on Contemporary Lit.* 8 1982: 10–17.

2830 Brenner, Gerry. "*Song of Solomon:* Morrison's rejection of Rank's monomyth and feminism." *Studies in Amer. Fiction.* 15.1 Spr. 1987: 13–24. The role of the hero in Morrison's novel.

2831 Brown, Rosellen. "Grits and grace." *New York.* Apr. 13, 1981: 42. Rev. of *Tar Baby.*

2832 Brown, Rosellen. "The pleasure of enchantment." *Nation.* Oct. 17, 1987: 418–421. Rev. of *Beloved.*

2833 Bruck, Peter. "Returning to one's roots: the motif of searching and flying in Toni Morrison's *Song of Solomon* (1977)." In BRUC: 289–305.

2834 Butler, Robert James. "Open movement and selfhood in Toni Morrison's *Song of Solomon.*" *Centennial Rev.* 28–29.4–1 Fall 1984–Wint. 1985: 58–75.

2835 Byerman, Keith E. "Beyond realism: the fictions of Gayl Jones and Toni Morrison." In BYER: 171–216.

2836 Byerman, Keith E. "Intense behaviors: the use of the grotesque in *The Bluest Eye* and *Eva's Man.*" *CLA J.* 25.4 June 1982: 447–457.

2837 Campbell, Jane. "Ancestral quests in Toni Morrison's *Song of Solomon* and David Bradley's *The Chaneysville Incident.*" In CAMP: 136–153.

2838 Cary, Meredith. "New roles in old societies." In CARY: 166–176. Criticism on *Sula.*

2839 Charles, Pepsi. "An interview with Toni Morrison." *Nimrod.* 21–22.2–1 1977: 43–51.

2840 Christian, Barbara. "Community and nature: the novels of Toni Morrison." In CHRF: 47–63.

2841 Christian, Barbara. "Community and nature: the novels of Toni Morrison." *Journal of Ethnic Studies.* 7.4 Wint. 1980: 65–78.

2842 Christian, Barbara. "The concept of class in the novels of Toni Morrison." In CHRF: 71–80.

2843 Christian, Barbara. "The contemporary fables of Toni Morrison." In CHRW: 137–179.

2844 Christian, Barbara. "Pass it on." In CHRW: 239–252. Comparative study of Paule Marshall, Morrison, and Alice Walker.

2845 Christian, Barbara. "Testing the strength of the Black cultural bond: review of Toni Morrison's *Tar Baby.*" In CHRF: 65–69.

2846 Clark, Norris B. "Flying Black: Toni Morrison's *The Bluest Eye, Sula, and Song of Solomon.*" *Minority Voices.* 4.2 1980: 51–63.

2847 Clemons, Walter. "A gravestone of memories." *Newsweek.* Sept. 28, 1987: 74–75. Rev. of *Beloved.*

2848 Coleman, James. "The quest for wholeness in Toni Morrison's *Tar Baby.*" *Black Amer. Lit. Forum.* 20.1–2 Spr.–Sum. 1986: 63–73.

2849 Cooper, Grace C. "Imagery in Toni Morrison's novels: the Black perspective." *J. of Mental Imagery.* 19.4 1986: 41–52.

2850 Cooper-Clark, Diana. In COOR: 190–211. An interview.

2851 Crouch, Stanley. "Aunt Medea." *New Republic.* Oct. 19, 1987: 38–43. Rev. of *Beloved.*

2852 Dahlin, R., Ed. "Columbus discovered America?" *Publishers Weekly.* Sept. 20, 1976: 50. Interview.

2853 Davis, Cynthia A. "Self, society, and myth in Toni Morrison's fiction." *Contemporary Lit.* 23.3 Sum. 1982: 323–342.

2854 Davis, Hope Hale. "Casting a strong spell." *New Leader.* Nov. 2, 1987: 20–21. Rev. of *Beloved.*

2855 DeWeever, Jacqueline. "The inverted world of Toni Morrison's *The Bluest Eye* and *Sula.*" *CLA J.* 22.4 June 1979: 402–414.

2856 Dixon, Melvin. "If you surrender to the air . . ." *Callaloo.* 1.4 1978: 170–173. Rev. of *Song of Solomon.*

2857 Edelberg, Cynthia Dubin. "Morrison's voices: formal education, the work ethic, and the Bible." *Amer. Lit.* 58.2 May 1986: 217–237.

2858 Ellman, Mary. "Seven recent novels." *Yale Rev.* 67.4 Sum. 1978: 592–599. Rev. of *Song of Solomon* (and novels by other authors).

2859 Erickson, Peter B. "Images of nurturance in Toni Morrison's *Tar Baby.*" *CLA J.* 28.1 Sept. 1984: 11–32.

2860 Fishman, Charles. "Naming names: three recent novels by women writers." *Names.* 32.1 Mar. 1984: 33–44. *Tar Baby* compared with Alice Walker's *Meridian* and Margaret Atwood's *Life Before Man.*

2861 Frederick, Earl. *Nation.* Nov. 19, 1977: 536. Rev. of *Song of Solomon.*

2862 Frye, Joanne S. "Growing up female: *Lives of Girls and Women* and *The Bluest Eye.*" In FRYE: 97–108. Compares Alice Munro's *Lives of Girls and Women* with Morrison's novel.

2863 Gardiner, Judith Kegan. "The (US)es of (I)dentity: a response to Abel on (E)merging identities." *Signs.* 6.3 Spr. 1981: 436–442. Pages 438–440 commentary on *Sula* in response to Elizabeth Abel's article in the same issue.

2864 Giddings, Paula. "The triumphant song of Toni Morrison." *Encore Amer. and Worldwide News.* Dec. 12, 1977: 26–30. On *Song of Solomon.*

2865 Gillespie, Marcia Ann. "Toni Morrison's *Beloved:* out of slavery's inferno." *Ms.* 16.5 Nov. 1987: 66, 68.

2866 Giovanni, Nikki. *Encore Amer. and Worldwide News.* Nov. 7, 1977: 39–40. Rev. of *Song of Solomon.*

2867 Govan, Sandra Y. *Cresset.* 41.7 May 1978: 26. Rev. of *Song of Solomon.*

2868 Harris, A. Leslie. "Myth as structure in Toni Morrison's *Song of Solomon.*" *Melus.* 7.3 Fall 1980: 69–76.

2869 Harris, Jessica. *Essence.* 8.5 Sept. 1977: 24. Rev. of *Song of Solomon.*

2870 Harris, Norman. "The Black university in contemporary Afro-American fiction." *CLA J.* 30.1 Sept. 1986: 1–13.

2871 Harris, Trudier. "Denial of the ritual: Toni Morrison, *Tar Baby.*" In HARR: 148–162.

2872 Harris, Trudier. "The maid as southern and northern mammy: Charles W. Chesnutt, *The Marrow of Tradition* (1901), Kristin Hunter, *God Bless the Child* (1964), Toni Morrison, *The Bluest Eye* (1970)." In HARS: 35–69.

2873 Hill, L. *Black Enterprise.* 11 July 1981: 13. Rev. of *Tar Baby.*

2874 Holloway, Karla F.C. and Stephanie Demetrakopoulos. *New Dimensions of Spirituality: A Biracial and Bicultural Reading of the Novels of Toni Morrison.* Westport, CT: Greenwood, 1987. Essays on various works of Morrison. Includes some bibliography.

2875 Homans, Margaret. "'Her very own howl': the ambiguities of representation in recent women's fiction." *Signs.* 9.2 Wint. 1983: 191–195.

2876 Horning, Beth. *Off Our Backs.* 11.7 July 1981: 24. On *Tar Baby.*

2877 House, Elizabeth B. "The 'sweet life' in Toni Morrison's fiction." *Amer. Lit.* 56.2 May 1984: 181–202.

2878 House, Elizabeth B. "Toni Morrison." In DY81: 114–119. Includes biography and additional bibliography.

2879 Hovet, Grace Ann and Barbara Lounsberry. "Flying as symbol and legend in Toni Morrison's *The Bluest Eye, Sula,* and *Song of Solomon.*" *CLA J.* 27.2 Dec. 1983: 119–140.

2880 Howard, Maureen. "A novel of exile and home." *New Republic.* 184.12 Mar. 21, 1981: 29–30, 32. On *Tar Baby.*

2881 Hudson-Withers, Glenora. "Toni Morrison's world of topsy-turvydom: a methodological explication of new Black literary criticism." *Western J. of Black Studies.* 10.3 Fall 1986: 132–136.

2882 Iannone, Carol. "Toni Morrison's career." *Commentary.* 84.6 Dec. 1987: 59–63. Criticism on *The Bluest Eye, Sula, Song of Solomon, Tar Baby, Beloved.*

2883 Irving, John. *N.Y. Times Book Rev.* Mar. 29, 1981: 1. Rev. of *Tar Baby.*

2884 Jackson, Marni. *Maclean's.* Apr. 27, 1981: 59–60. Rev. of *Tar Baby.*

2885 Jefferson, Margo. *Newsweek.* Sept. 12, 1977: 93, 96. Rev. of *Song of Solomon.*

2886 Jones, Bessie W. and Audrey L. Vinson. *The World of Toni Morrison: Explorations in Literary Criticism.* Dubuque, IA: Kendall, 1985.

2887 Joyce, Joyce Ann. "Structural and thematic unity in Toni Morrison's *Song of Solomon.*" *CEA Critic.* 49.2–4 Wint. 1986–Sum. 1987: 185–198.

2888 Kellogg, Mary Alice. "The ladies of New Orleans." *Harper's Bazaar.* 116.3256 Mar. 1983: 246, 279. Morrison wrote the script for a musical called *New Orleans,* opening on Broadway in the spring of 1983.

2889 Klotman, Phyllis R. "Dick-and-Jane and the Shirley Temple sensibility in *The Bluest Eye.*" *Black Amer. Lit. Forum.* 13.4 Wint. 1979: 123–125.

2890 Lange, Bonnie Shipman. "Toni Morrison's rainbow code." *Critique.* 24.3 Spr. 1983: 173–181.

2891 Lardner, Susan. *New Yorker.* Nov. 7, 1977: 217. Rev. of *Song of Solomon.*

2892 Lardner, Susan. *New Yorker.* June 15, 1981: 147–151. Rev. of *Tar Baby.*

2893 LeClair, Thomas. "'The language must not sweat': a conversation with Toni Morrison." *New Republic.* Mar. 21, 1981: 25–29.

2894 LeClair, Tom. "An interview with Toni Morrison." In LECL: 252–261.

2895 Lee, Dorothy H. "The quest for self: triumph and failure in the works of Toni Morrison." In EVAN: 346–359.

2896 Lee, Dorothy H. *"Song of Solomon:* to ride the air." *Black Amer. Lit. Forum.* 16.2 Sum. 1982: 64–70.

2897 Lee, Valerie Gray. "Use of folktalk in novels by Black women writers." *CLA J.* 23.3 Mar. 1980: 266–272. On Morrison, Zora Neale Hurston, and Gayl Jones.

2898 Lewis, Vashti Crutcher. "African tradition in Toni Morrison's *Sula*." *Phylon.* 48.1 Mar. 1987: 91–97.

2899 Lounsberry, Barbara and Grace Ann Hovet. "Principles of perception in Toni Morrison's *Sula*." *Black Amer. Lit. Forum.* 13.4 Wint. 1979: 126–129.

2900 Lupton, Mary Jane. "Clothes and closure in three novels by Black women." *Black Amer. Lit. Forum.* 20.4 Wint. 1986: 409–421. Some commentary on *Tar Baby*.

2901 MacKethan, Lucinda H. "Names to bear witness: the theme and tradition of naming in Toni Morrison's *Song of Solomon*." *CEA Critic.* 49.2–4 Wint. 1986–Sum. 1987: 199–207.

2902 Mano, D.K. "How to write two first novels with your knuckles." *Esquire.* 86.6 Dec. 1976: 62, 66. On *Eva's Man* and Gayl Jones' *Corregidora*.

2903 Martin, Odette C. "The novels of Toni Morrison: *Sula*." *First World.* 1 Wint. 1977: 34–44.

2904 McDowell, Edwin. "Behind the best sellers." *N.Y. Times Book Rev.* July 5, 1981: 18. Mentions several of Morrison's novels.

2905 McKay, Nellie. "An interview with Toni Morrison." *Contemporary Lit.* 24.4 Wint. 1983: 413–429.

2906 Medwick, Cathleen. "Oh, Albany! What's Toni Morrison's first play doing at the 'wrong end' of the Hudson?" *Vogue.* 176 Jan. 1986: 56. On *Dreaming Emmett*.

2907 Medwick, Cathleen. "Toni Morrison: a great American author, a spirit of love and rage...." *Vogue.* 171.4 Apr. 1981: 288–289, 330–332.

2908 Mickelson, Anne Z. "Winging upward: Black women: Sarah E. Wright, Toni Morrison, Alice Walker." In MICK: 124–153. On several works.

2909 Middleton, Victoria. *"Sula:* an experimental life." *CLA J.* 28.4 June 1985: 367–381.

2910 Miller, Adam David. "Breedlove, peace and the dead: some observations on the world of Toni Morrison." *Black Scholar.* 9.6 Mar. 1978: 47–50.

2911 Milton, Edith. *Yale Rev.* 71.2 Jan. 1982: 259–260. Rev. of *Tar Baby.*

2912 Miner, Madonne M. "Lady no longer sings the blues: rape, madness, and silence in *The Bluest Eye*." In PRYS: 176–191.

2913 Mitchell, Leatha S. "Toni Morrison, my mother, and me." In BOWL: 58–60.

2914 Mobley, Marilyn E. "Narrative dilemma: Jadine as cultural orphan in Toni Morrison's *Tar Baby*." *Southern Rev.* 23.4 Oct. 1987: 761–770.

2915 Munich, Adrienne. "Notorious signs, feminist criticism and literary tradition." In GREE: 238–259. Includes criticism on *Sula*.

2916 Munro, C. Lynn. "The tattooed heart and the serpentine eye: Morrison's choice of an epigraph for *Sula*." *Black Amer. Lit. Forum.* 18.4 Wint. 1984: 150–154.

2917 Myers, Linda Buck. "Perception and power through naming:

characters in search of a self in the fiction of Toni Morrison." *Explorations in Ethnic Studies.* 7.1 Jan. 1984: 39–55.

2918 Naylor, Gloria and Toni Morrison. "A conversation." *Southern Rev.* 21.3 July 1985: 567–593.

2919 Nodelman, Perry. "The limits of structures: a shorter version of a comparison between Toni Morrison's *Song of Solomon* and Virginia Hamilton's *M.C. Higgins the Great.*" *Children's Lit. Association Q.* 7.3 Fall 1982: 45–48.

2920 O'Meally, Robert G. "'Tar baby, she don' say nothin'.'" *Callaloo.* 4.1–3 Oct.–Feb. 1981: 193–198. Rev. of *Tar Baby.*

2921 Ogunyemi, Chikwenye Okonjo. "Order and disorder in Toni Morrison's *The Bluest Eye.*" *Critique.* 19.1 1977: 112–120.

2922 Ogunyemi, Chikwenye Okonjo. "*Sula:* 'A Nigger joke'." *Black Amer. Lit Forum.* 13.4 Wint. 1979: 130–133.

2923 Ordóñez, Elizabeth J. "Narrative texts by ethnic women: rereading the past, reshaping the future." *Melus.* 9.3 Wint. 1982: 19–28. Commentary on *Sula.*

2924 Parker, Bettye J. "Complexity: Toni Morrison's women — an interview essay." In BELL: 250–257.

2925 Pinckney, Darryl. *N.Y. Rev. of Books.* Apr. 30, 1981: 24–25. Rev. of *Tar Baby.*

2926 Portales, Marco. "Toni Morrison's *The Bluest Eye:* Shirley Temple and Cholly." *Centennial Rev.* 30.4 Fall 1986: 496–506.

2927 Price, Reynolds. *N.Y. Times Book Rev.* Sept. 11, 1977: 1. Rev. of *Song of Solomon.*

2928 Pullin, Faith. "Landscapes of reality: the fiction of contemporary Afro-American women." In LEEE: 173–203. On several works.

2929 Reed, Dennis. *CLA J.* 31.2 Dec. 1987: 256–258. Rev. of *Beloved.*

2930 Reyes, Angelita. "Ancient properties in the new world: the paradox of the 'other' in Toni Morrison's *Tar Baby.*" *Black Scholar.* 17.2 Mar.–Apr. 1986: 19–25.

2931 "Robert Lowell and Toni Morrison — Book Critics Circle Award Winners." *Coda.* 5.4 1978: 13. For *Song of Solomon.*

2932 Rodman, S. *National Rev.* June 26, 1981: 730–732. Rev. of *Tar Baby.*

2933 Rogers, Norma. *Freedomways.* 18.2 1978: 107–109. Rev. of *Song of Solomon.*

2934 Rosenburg, Ruth. "'And the children may know their names': Toni Morrison's *Song of Solomon.*" *Literary Onomastics Studies.* 8 1981: 195–219.

2935 Rosenburg, Ruth. "Seeds in the hard ground: Black girlhood in *The Bluest Eye.*" *Black Amer. Lit. Forum.* 21.4 Wint. 1987: 435–445.

2936 Royster, Philip M. "Milkman's flying: the scapegoat transcended in Toni Morrison's *Song of Solomon.*" *CLA J.* 24.4 June 1981: 419–440.

2937 Royster, Philip M. "The novels of Toni Morrison: *The Bluest Eye.*" *First World.* 1 Wint. 1977: 34–44.

2938 Royster, Philip M. "A priest and a witch against the spiders and the snakes: scapegoating in Toni Morrison's *Sula.*" *Umoja.* 2 1978: 149–168.

2939 Ruas, Charles. In RUAS: 215–243. Interview.

2940 Rubin, H. "Working both sides of the desk: editors who write . . . writers who edit." *Publishers Weekly.* Nov. 7, 1980: 28–31.

2941 Schultz, Elizabeth. "African and Afro-American roots in contemporary Afro-American literature: the difficult search for family origins." *Studies in Amer. Fiction.* 8.2 1980: 127–145. Compares Alex Haley's *Roots* to Morrison's *Song of Solomon.*

2942 Scruggs, Charles. "The nature of desire in Toni Morrison's *Song of Solomon.*" *Arizona Q.* 38 Wint. 1982: 311–335.

2943 Shannon, Anna. "'We was girls together': a study of Toni Morrison's *Sula.*" *Midwestern Miscellany.* 10 1982: 9–22. Edited by Marilyn J. Atlas.

2944 Sheed, Wilfrid. "Improbable assignment." *Atlantic.* 247.4 Apr. 1981: 119–120. Rev. of *Tar Baby.*

2945 Sheppard, R.Z. *Time.* Mar. 16, 1981: 90, 92. Rev. of *Tar Baby.*

2946 Simama, Jabari. "Acute depiction of bourgeois reality." *First World.* 1 Wint. 1977: 45–48. Rev. of *Song of Solomon.*

2947 Skerrett, Joseph T., Jr. "Recitation to the griot: storytelling and learning in Toni Morrison's *Song of Solomon.*" In PRYS: 192–202.

2948 Smith, Amanda. "Toni Morrison." *Publishers Weekly.* Aug. 21, 1987: 50–51. Interview.

2949 Smith, Cynthia J. "Black fiction by Black females." *Cross Currents.* 26.3 Fall 1976: 340–343. Rev. of *Sula.*

2950 Smith, Valerie. "The quest for and discovery of identity in Toni Morrison's *Song of Solomon.*" *Southern Rev.* 21.3 July 1985: 721–732.

2951 Smith, Valerie. "Remembering one's ancient properties." *Sewanee Rev.* 89 Oct. 1981: cxv–cxvii. Rev. of *Tar Baby.*

2952 Smith, Valerie. "Toni Morrison's narratives of community." In SMTV: 122–153. On *Song of Solomon, The Bluest Eye,* and *Sula.*

2953 Spallino, Chiara. "*Song of Solomon:* an adventure in structure." *Callaloo.* 8.3 Fall 1985: 510–524.

2954 Spillers, Hortense J. "A hateful passion, a lost love." *Feminist Studies.* 9.2 Sum. 1983: 293–323. On Morrison's *Sula,* Margaret Walker's *Jubilee* and Zora Neale Hurston's *Their Eyes Were Watching God.*

2955 Stein, Karen. "'I didn't even know his name': name and naming in Toni Morrison's *Sula.*" *Names.* 28.3 Sept. 1980: 226–229.

2956 Stein, Karen. "Toni Morrison's *Sula:* a Black woman's epic." *Black Amer. Lit. Forum.* 18.4 Wint. 1984: 146–150.

2957 Stepto, Robert B. "'Intimate things in place': a conversation with Toni Morrison." In FISH: 167–182.

2958 Stepto, Robert B. "'Intimate things in place': a conversation with Toni Morrison." In HARP: 213–229.

2959 Stepto, Robert B. "'Intimate things in place': a conversation with Toni Morrison." *Massachusetts Rev.* 18.3 Aut. 1977: 473–489.

2960 Tate, Claudia C. *CLA J.* 21.2 Dec. 1977: 327–329. Rev. of *Song of Solomon.*

2961 Thurman, Judith. "A house divided." *New Yorker.* Nov. 2, 1987: 175–180. Rev. of *Beloved.*

2962 Traylor, Eleanor W. "The fabulous world of Toni Morrison: *Tar Baby.*" In BARA: 333–352.

2963 Turner, Darwin T. "Theme, characterization, and style in the works of Toni Morrison." In EVAN: 361–369.

2964 Umeh, Marie A. "A comparative study of the idea of motherhood in two third world novels." *CLA J.* 31.1 Sept. 1987: 31–43. Compares Buchi Emecheta's *The Joys of Motherhood* with Morrison's *The Bluest Eye.*

2965 Wade-Gayles, Gloria. "Giving birth to self: the quests for wholeness of Sula Mae Peace and Meridian Hill." In WADE: 184–215.

2966 Wade-Gayles, Gloria. "The truths of our mothers' lives: mother-daughter relationships in Black women's fiction." *Sage.* 1.2 Fall 1984: 8–12. Morrison's *The Bluest Eye* (1970) compared to Dorothy West's *The Living Is Easy* (1948) and Paule Marshall's *Brown Girl, Brownstones* (1959).

2967 Wagner, Linda W. "Toni Morrison: mastery of narrative." In RAIN: 190–205.

2968 Ward, Geoffrey C. "Telling how it was." *Amer. Heritage.* 38.8 Dec. 1987: 14, 18. Rev. of *Beloved.*

2969 Washington, Elsie E. "Toni Morrison now." *Essence.* 18.6 Oct. 1987: 58, 136–137. Interview.

2970 Watkins, Mel. "Talk with Toni Morrison." *N.Y. Times Book Rev.* Sept. 11, 1977: 48, 50.

2971 Weems, Renita. "Artists without art form: a look at one Black woman's world of unrevered Black women." *Conditions 5.* 2.2 Aut. 1979: 48–58.

2972 Wegs, Joyce M. "Toni Morrison's *Song of Solomon:* a blues song." *Essays in Lit.* 9.2 Fall 1982: 211–223.

2973 Weixlmann, Joe. "Culture clash, survival, and transformation: a study of some innovative Afro-American novels of detection." *Mississippi Q.* 38.1 Wint. 1984/85: 21. On several works.

2974 Werner, Craig H. "Homer's Joyce: John Updike, Ronald Sukenick, Robert Coover, Toni Morrison." In WERN: 88–96.

2975 Wigan, Angela. "Native daughter." *Time.* Sept. 12, 1977: 76. Rev. of *Song of Solomon.*

2976 Willis, Susan. "Eruptions of funk: historicizing Toni Morrison." *Black Amer. Lit. Forum.* 16.1 Spr. 1982: 34–42.

2977 Willis, Susan. "Eruptions of funk: historicizing Toni Morrison." In BEVI: 113–129.

2978 Willis, Susan. "Eruptions of funk: historicizing Toni Morrison." In GATE: 263–283.

2979 Willis, Susan. "Eruptions of funk: historicizing Toni Morrison." In WILL: 83–109.

2980 Wilson, Judith. "A conversation with Toni Morrison." *Essence.* 12.3 July 1981: 84–86, 128, 130.

2981 Winslow, Henry F., Sr. *Crisis.* 85.3 Mar. 1978: 105–106. Rev. of *Song of Solomon.*

2982 Winslow, Henry F., Sr. *Crisis.* 88.5 June 1981: 247–248. Rev. of *Tar Baby.*

Moseka, Aminata *see* **Lincoln, Abbey**

Thylias Moss

Poetry

2983 "Acceptance of the grave." *Indiana Rev.* 7.1 Wint. 1984: 66–67.

2984 "The barren midwife speaks of duty." *North Dakota Q.* 52.2 Spr. 1984: 98.

2985 "A child's been dead a week." *Texas Rev.* 5.1-2 Spr.-Sum. 1984: 138–139.

2986 *Hosiery Seams on a Bowlegged Woman: Poems.* Cleveland: Cleveland State Univ. Poetry Center, 1983.

2987 "The owl in daytime." *Indiana Rev.* 7.1 Wint. 1984: 63.

2988 "Rush hour." *Essence.* 14.8 Dec. 1983: 134.

2989 "Secrets behind the names." *Indiana Rev.* 7.1 Wint. 1984: 68–69.

2990 "Taluca, twenty years later." *Texas Rev.* 5.1-2 Spr.-Sum. 1984: 138.

2991 "The undertaker's daughter (for M. Egolf)." *Indiana Rev.* 7.1 Wint. 1984: 64–65.

Ruby D. Moxley (1934–)

Poetry

2992 "Ol' tim legion." In WETH: 92.

2993 "Saturday night." In WETH: 91.

2994 "Sixth and Walnut Street." In WETH: 93.

Harryette Mullen

Poetry

2995 "Alabama memories." *Southern Exposure.* 9.3 Fall 1981: 73.

2996 "Anatomy." *Nimrod.* 21-22.2-1 1977: 198.

2997 "A basic need." *Negro History Bull.* 39.7 Nov.-Dec. 1976: 638.

2998 "The big one." *Nimrod.* 21-22.2-1 1977: 194.

2999 "A Black woman never faints (for Gertrude Wilks)." *Greenfield Rev.* 7.3-4 Spr.-Sum. 1979: 25.

3000 "Cold storage." *Black Amer. Lit. Forum.* 13.4 Wint. 1979: 149.

3001 "Eyes in the back of her head." *Nimrod.* 21-22.2-1 1977: 195.

3002 "Floorwax mother." *Nimrod.* 21-22.2-1 1977: 196.

3003 "The joy." *Nimrod.* 21-22.2-1 1977: 199.

3004 "Juke box man." *Nimrod.* 21-22.2-1 1977: 194.

3005 "Jump city." *Obsidian.* 3.2 Sum. 1977: 49.

3006 "Madonna." *Greenfield Rev.* 7.3-4 Spr.-Sum. 1979: 25.

3007 "Momma sayings." *Open Places.* 29 Spr. 1980: 14. Rpt. *Open Places,* Aut. 1981, pages 149-150.

3008 "The night we slept on the beach." *Open Places.* 29 Spr. 1980: 10.

3009 "No more arguments, no more anything." *Black Amer. Lit. Forum.* 13.4 Wint. 1979: 149.

3010 "Painting myself a new mirror." *Open Places.* 29 Spr. 1980: 12.

3011 "Recipe." *Callaloo.* 5.2 1979: 31.

3012 "Roadmap." *Greenfield Rev.* 7.3-4 Spr.-Sum. 1979: 24.

3013 "Saturday afternoon, when chores are done." *Essence.* 13.3 July 1982: 17.

3014 "Saturday afternoon, when chores are done." *Open Places.* 29 Spr. 1980: 16.

3015 "Saturday afternoon, when chores are done." *Southern Exposure.* 9.4 Wint. 1981: 4.

3016 "Shedding skin." *Praxis.* 2.4 1978: 134.

3017 "Stirrings." *Nimrod.* 21-22.2-1 1977: 231.

3018 "They are bloated with power." *Negro History Bull.* 39.7 Nov.-Dec. 1976: 638.

3019 "To a woman." *Black Amer. Lit. Forum.* 13.4 Wint. 1979: 149.

3020 "Tree." *Praxis.* 2.4 1978: 318.

3021 *Tree Tall Woman: Poems.* Galveston, TX: Energy Earth Communications, 1981.

3022 "Unable to grasp the meaning." *Third Woman.* 3.1-2 1986: 8.

Pauli Murray (1910-1985)

Autobiography

3023 "The fourth generation of proud shoes." *Southern Exposure.* 4 Wint. 1977: 4-9. Murray's account of her family.

3024 *Song in a Weary Throat: An American Pilgrimage.* NY: Harper, 1987.

Biography

3025 Burgen, Michele. "Lifestyle: Rev. Dr. Pauli Murray." *Ebony.* 34.11 Sept. 1979: 107-108, 110, 112.

3026 Scarupa, Harriet Jackson. "The extraordinary faith of Pauli Murray." *Essence.* 8.8 Dec. 1977: 90-91, 107, 109-110.

Poetry

3027 "Dark testament." In STET: 84-92.

3028 "Inquietude." In STET: 92.

3029 "Prophecy." *Essence.* 16.6 Oct. 1985: 124.

3030 "Song." In STET: 93.

Textual Criticism

3031 Giddings, Paula. "Fighting Jane Crow." *Nation.* May 23, 1987: 689-690. Rev. of *Song in a Weary Throat.*

3032 McHenry, Susan. "The unsinkable Pauli Murray." *Ms.* 15.11 May 1987: 14, 16-17. Rev. of *Song in a Weary Throat.*

3033 McKay, Nellie. "Pauli Murray." In DL41: 248-251. Includes biography and additional bibliography.

3034 Miller, Casey and Kate Swift. "Pauli Murray." *Ms.* 8.8 Mar. 1980: 60, 63-64. Criticism and biography.

3035 Montgomery, N.S. *Christian Century.* Sept. 30, 1987: 828. Rev. of *Song in a Weary Throat.*

3036 Shockley, Ann A. *Women's Rev. of Books.* 4.10-11 July-Aug. 1987: 19. Rev. of *Song in a Weary Throat.*

3037 Williams, Pat. *N.Y. Times Book Rev.* Mar. 29, 1987: 12. Rev. of *Song in a Weary Throat.*

Schaarazetta Natelege

Poetry
3038 "The violin's song." *Obsidian.* 7.1 Spr. 1981: 61.

Gloria Naylor (1950-)

Essay
3039 "Until death do us part. . ." *Essence.* 16.1 May 1985: 133.

Novels
3040 *Linden Hills.* NY: Ticknor & Fields, 1985.
3041 *Mama Day* [Excerpts]. *Southern Rev.* 23.4 Oct. 1987: 836–873. (The novel was published in 1988 by Ticknor & Fields, NY.)
3042 *The Women of Brewster Place.* NY: Viking, 1982.

Short Fiction
3043 "A life on Beekman Place." *Essence.* 10.11 Mar. 1980: 82–83, 91, 93, 94, 96.
3044 "When mama comes to call." *Essence.* 13.4 Aug. 1982: 67–68, 121–122, 124–126.

Textual Criticism and Interviews
3045 Brown, Beth. "A compression of time: three contemporary Black authors reflect." *J. of Black Studies.* 18.1 Sept. 1987: 109–115. Rev. of *Linden Hills* (pages 111–113).
3046 Christian, Barbara. "No more buried lives — the theme of lesbianism in Lorde, Naylor, Shange, Walker." *Feminist Issues.* 5 Spr. 1985: 3–20.
3047 Christian, Barbara. "No more buried lives: the theme of lesbianism in Audre Lorde's *Zami,* Gloria Naylor's *The Women of Brewster Place,* Ntozake Shange's *Sassafras, Cypress and Indigo,* and Alice Walker's *The Color Purple.*" In CHRF: 187–204.
3048 Goldstein, W. "A talk with Gloria Naylor." *Publishers Weekly.* Sept. 9, 1983: 35–36.
3049 Gomez, Jewelle. *Women's Rev. of Books.* 2.11 Aug. 1985: 7–8. Rev. of *Linden Hills.*
3050 Gottlieb, Annie. *N.Y. Times Book Rev.* Aug. 22, 1982: 11. Rev. of *The Women of Brewster Place.*
3051 Hairston, Loyle. *Freedomways.* 23.4 1983: 282–285. Rev. of *The Women of Brewster Place.*
3052 "Hum inside the skull." *N.Y. Times Book Rev.* May 13, 1984: 29. Interview.

3053 Johnson, Joe. *Crisis.* 92.5 May 1985: 13, 47–48. Revs. of *Linden Hills* and *The Women of Brewster Place.*

3054 Jones, R. *Commonweal.* May 3, 1985: 283–285. Rev. of *Linden Hills.*

3055 Kazi-Ferrouillet, Kuumba. *Black Collegian.* 15.1 Nov.–Dec. 1983: 26. Rev. of *The Women of Brewster Place.*

3056 Kendrick, Gerald D. *J. of Black Studies.* 14.3 Mar. 1984: 389–390. Rev. of *The Women of Brewster Place.*

3057 Kulp, Denise. *Off Our Backs.* 13.11 Dec. 1983: 9, 23. Rev. of *The Women of Brewster Place.*

3058 Naylor, Gloria and Toni Morrison. " A conversation." *Southern Rev.* 21.3 July 1985: 567–593.

3059 Watkins, Mel. *N.Y. Times Book Rev.* Mar. 3, 1985: 11. Rev. of *Linden Hills.*

3060 Wickenden, D. *New Republic.* Sept. 6, 1982: 37–38. Rev. of *The Women of Brewster Place.*

3061 Williams, Sherley Anne. "Roots of privilege, new Black fiction." *Ms.* 13.12 June 1985: 69–72. Revs. of Naylor's *Linden Hills,* Andrea Lee's *Sarah Phillips,* and Ntozake Shange's *Betsey Brown.*

Betty H. Neals

Poetry
3062 *Move the Air.* East Orange, NJ: Stonechat, 1985.
3063 *Spirit Weaving.* NY: Sesame, 1977.

Nkabinde, Thulani *see* Davis, Thulani

Njeri Nuru

Poetry
3064 "All Afrikans ain't Afrikan." *Black Amer. Lit. Forum.* 18.1 Spr. 1984: 15–16.

3065 "Atlanta poem number 1." *Black Amer. Lit. Forum.* 18.1 Spr. 1984: 16.

3066 "Atlanta poem number 2." *Black Amer. Lit. Forum.* 18.1 Spr. 1984: 16.

3067 "Bonding." *Black Amer. Lit. Forum.* 18.1 Spr. 1984: 17.

3068 "Little deaths hurt especially." *Black Amer. Lit. Forum.* 18.1 Spr. 1984: 16.

Occomy, Marita B. *see* Bonner (Occomy), Marita

Gloria Oden (1923–)

Autobiography
3069 "The other side of the blanket." *Ms.* 14.2 Aug. 1985: 86.

Essays

3070 "Bonsai." *Negro History Bull.* 40.4 July–Aug. 1977: 716–717. Essay on Black writers.

3071 "Bonsai." *Nimrod.* 21–22.2–1 1977: 200–204.

Poetry

3072 "Girl on a dolphin." *Ark.* 14 1980: 304.

3073 *Resurrections.* Homestead, FL: Olivant, 1978.

3074 "This child is the mother." In STET: 123–127.

3075 *The Tie that Binds.* Homestead, FL: Olivant, 1980.

3076 "The triple mirror." In KONE: 224–225.

3077 "Twenty-three." *Ms.* 11.1–2 July–Aug. 1982: 74.

3078 "The way it is." In ADOF: 227–228.

Textual Criticism

3079 Kessler, Jascha. "Reconsiderations and reviews." *Melus.* 7.3 Fall 1980: 83–87. Radio script, commentary on *Resurrections.*

Brenda Marie Osbey

Poetry

3080 "Another time and farther south." *Southern Rev.* 23.4 Oct. 1987: 804–805.

3081 "The bone step-women." *Southern Rev.* 21.3 July 1985: 831.

3082 *Ceremony for Minneconjoux.* Lexington: Univ. of Kentucky, 1983.

3083 "Ceremony for Minneconjoux." *Southern Exposure.* 12.3 May–June 1984: 48–51.

3084 "Devices of icons." *Southern Rev.* 21.3 July 1985: 834–836.

3085 "Family history." *Essence.* 16.1 May 1985: 188.

3086 "The godchild." *Southern Rev.* 23.4 Oct. 1987: 805–807.

3087 *In These Houses.* Middletown, CT: Wesleyan UP, 1987.

3088 "In these houses of swift easy women." *Southern Rev.* 21.3 July 1985: 830.

3089 "The wastrel-woman poem." *Southern Rev.* 21.3 July 1985: 832–833.

Textual Criticism

3090 Hernton, Calvin. "The tradition." *Parnassus.* 12–13.2–1 Spr.–Sum.–Fall–Wint. 1985: 524–529. Commentary on *Ceremony for Minneconjoux.* Article includes other poets.

3091 Kazi-Ferrouillet, Kuumba. *Black Collegian.* 14.4 Mar.–Apr. 1984: 38. Rev. of *Ceremony for Minneconjoux.*

3092 Wright, Carolyne. "Women poets: seven new voices from small presses." *Northwest Rev.* 23.1 1985: 118–133. Rev. of *Ceremony for Minneconjoux.*

Pat Parker

Essay

3093 "Revolution: it's not neat or pretty or quick." In MORA: 238–242.

Poetry

3094 "For the white person who wants to know how to be my friend." *Heresies*. 4.3 1982: 59.

3095 "From the cavities of bones." In STET: 238.

3096 "Goat child." In CRUG: 68–77.

3097 "I followed a path." In STET: 239.

3098 *Jonestown and Other Madness*. Ithaca, NY: Firebrand, 1985.

3099 *Movement in Black: Collected Poems, 1978–1981*. Trumansburg, NY: Crossing, 1983.

3100 *Movement in Black: The Collected Poetry of Pat Parker, 1961–1978*. Trumansburg, NY: Crossing, 1978.

3101 "There is a woman in this town." *Chrysalis*. 4 1977: 32–33.

3102 "There is a woman in this town." In STET: 240–242.

3103 "Where will you be?" *Conditions 5*. 2.2 Aut. 1979: 128–132.

3104 "Where will you be?" In SMIT: 209–213.

3105 *Womanslaughter*. Oakland, CA: Diana, 1978.

Short Fiction

3106 "Shoes." In GRAH: 176–183.

Textual Criticism

3107 Clarke, Cheryl. *Conditions 6*. 2.3 Sum. 1980: 217–225. Rev. of *Movement in Black*.

3108 Rushin, Kate. "Pat Parker: creating room to speak and grow." *Sojourner*. 11.1 Oct. 1985: 28–29.

3109 Smith, Barbara. "Naming the unnameable: the poetry of Pat Parker." *Conditions 3*. 1.3 1978: 99–103. Revs. of *Child of Myself* (1971) and *Pit Stop* (1973).

Michelle Parkerson

Poetry

3110 "Aftermath (for Vicki)." *Obsidian*. 6.1–2 Spr.–Sum. 1980: 192.

3111 "Dawn in Soweto." *Obsidian*. 6.1–2 Spr.–Sum. 1980: 189.

3112 "Epilogue 3." *Essence*. 10.7 Nov. 1979: 19.

3113 "Epilogue: Romance 3." *Obsidian*. 6.1–2 Spr.–Sum. 1980: 186.

3114 "Evening constitutional." *Obsidian*. 6.1–2 Spr.–Sum. 1980: 188.

3115 "Memo to James Hampton, Builder of the Third Millenium altars." *Obsidian*. 6.1–2 Spr.–Sum. 1980: 191–192.

3116 "(Observations at a poetry reading, Women's Detention Center, Summer '75)." *Conditions 5*. 2.2 Aut. 1979: 68.

3117 "Resumé." *Conditions 5*. 2.2 Aut. 1979: 65–67.

3118 "Resumé." *Obsidian.* 6.1–2 Spr.–Sum. 1980: 192–193.
3119 "Reunion." *Obsidian.* 6.1–2 Spr.–Sum. 1980: 189.
3120 "Then as now…" *Obsidian.* 6.1–2 Spr.–Sum. 1980: 190.
3121 *Waiting Rooms.* Washington, DC: Common Ground, 1983.
3122 "You done us proud." *Obsidian.* 6.1–2 Spr.–Sum. 1980: 187.

Lucille J. Patterson

Poetry
3123 "Black children cry." *Western J. of Black Studies.* 1.3 Sept. 1977: 184.
3124 "Black drummers." *Western J. of Black Studies.* 1.3 Sept. 1977: 185.

Ann Petry (1912–)

Novel
3125 "Mamie." In WASA: 307–343. Excerpt from *The Narrows* (1953).

Short Fiction
3126 "Doby's gone." In FISH: 202–207.

Summary of Novel
3127 Southgate, Robert L. In SOUT: 157–158. Summary of *The Street* (1945).

Textual Criticism and Interviews
3128 Bell, Bernard W. "Ann Lane Petry." In BELA: 178–183. On several works.
3129 Bell, Bernard W. "Ann Petry's demythologizing of American culture and Afro-American character." In PRYS: 105–115.
3130 Bowen, Angela. "The literary traditions of Black women." *Sojourner.* 9.10 June 1984: 21.
3131 Gross, Theodore L. "Ann Petry: the novelist as social critic." In LEEE: 41–53.
3132 Harris, Trudier. "Northern maids: stepping toward militancy: Ann Petry, *The Street* (1946), William Melvin Kelley, *Dem* (1964)." In HARS: 87–109.
3133 Hernton, Calvin C. "The significance of Ann Petry: the fear of Bigger Thomas and the rage of Lutie Johnson." In HERN: 59–88.
3134 Ivy, James W. "Ann Petry talks about first novel." In BELL: 197–200. Petry talks about her 1945 novel, *The Street.*
3135 Lattin, Vernon E. "Ann Petry and the American dream." *Black Amer. Lit. Forum.* 12.2 Sum. 1978: 69–72. On several works.
3136 McDowell, Margaret B. "*The Narrows:* a fuller view of Ann Petry." *Black Amer. Lit. Forum.* 14.4 Wint. 1980: 135–141.
3137 Noble, Jeanne. In NOBL: 175–177. On several works.
3138 Poirier, Suzanne. "Ann Petry: from pharmacist to novelist." *Pharmacy in History.* 28.1 1986: 26–33.

3139 Pryse, Marjorie. "'Pattern against the sky': deism and motherhood in Ann Petry's *The Street.*" In PRYS: 116–131.

3140 Shinn, Thelma J. Wardrop. "Women in the novels of Ann Petry." In SPAC: 108–117.

3141 Washington, Gladys J. "A world made cunningly: a closer look at Ann Petry's short fiction." *CLA J.* 30.1 Sept. 1986: 14–29.

3142 Washington, Mary Helen. "'Infidelity becomes her': the ambivalent woman in the fiction of Ann Petry and Dorothy West." In WASA: 297–306.

3143 Williams, Sherley A. *Ms.* 15.3 Sept. 1986: 23. Rev. of *The Street.*

3144 Yarborough, Richard. "The quest for the American dream in three Afro-American novels: *If He Hollers Let Him Go, The Street,* and *Invisible Man.*" *Melus.* 8.4 Wint. 1981: 33–59. Comments on Petry's *The Street,* pages 41–47.

Linda Piper (1949–)

Poetry
3145 "Missionaries in the jungle." In STET: 184.
3146 "Sweet Ethel." In STET: 183–184.

Ann Plato

Poetry
3147 "The natives of America." In STET: 43–45.
3148 "Reflections, written on visiting the grave of a venerated friend." In STET: 46–47.
3149 "To the first of August." In STET: 45–46.

Carlene Hatcher Polite (1932–)

Summary of Novel
3150 Southgate, Robert L. In SOUT: 70–72. Summary of *The Flagellants* (1967).

Textual Criticism and Interviews
3151 Lottman, Herbert R. In AUTH: 123–126. Interview, biographical information.

3152 Worthington-Smith, Hammett. "Carlene Hatcher Polite." In DL33: 215–218. Biography and bibliography included.

Margaret Porter (1905–1975)

Poetry
3153 "Inflation." In BARA: 264.

3154 "Sugarman." In BARA: 262-263.

3155 "When I write." In BARA: 263-264.

Aishah Rahman

Drama

3156 "The lady and the tramp." In BARA: 284-299.

3157 "The Mojo and the Sayso." *Massachusetts Rev.* 28.4 Wint. 1987: 561-608.

3158 "Transcendental blues." In BARA: 265-284.

3159 "Unfinished women cry in no man's land while a bird dies in a gilded cage." In WILK: 197-237.

Essay

3160 "To be Black, female and a playwright." *Freedomways.* 19.4 1979: 256-260.

Dorothy Randall-Tsuruta

Editing

3161 Lawson, Jennifer Blackman and Dorothy Randall-Tsuruta, Eds. *High Expectations: Poems for Black Women.* Pittsburgh, CA: Los Medans College, 1977.

Poetry

3162 "An African-American in Ghana to visit." *Negro History Bull.* 42.2 Apr.-May-June 1979: 54.

3163 "Bicentennial woman." *Negro History Bull.* 40.3 May-June 1977: 704.

3164 "Bicentennial woman." *Black Scholar.* 11.8 Nov.-Dec. 1980: 78.

3165 "Bicentennial woman II." *Negro History Bull.* 40.3 May-June 1977: 704.

3166 "Bicentennial woman II." *Black Scholar.* 11.8 Nov.-Dec. 1980: 78.

3167 "Grandma." *Negro History Bull.* 42.2 Apr.-May-June 1979: 54.

3168 "'Grandmaw' 1889-1976." *Negro History Bull.* 42.2 Apr.-May-June 1979: 54.

3169 "In Ghana." *Black Scholar.* 11.8 Nov.-Dec. 1980: 78.

3170 "Ready yet unresigned." *Black Scholar.* 11.8 Nov.-Dec. 1980: 79.

3171 "Ready yet unresigned." *Essence.* 15.9 Jan. 1985: 130.

Rashida

Short Fiction

3172 "Jonetta." *Conditions 5.* 2.2 Aut. 1979: 81-85.

Isetta Crawford Rawls (1941–)

Poetry
3173 *Flashbacks.* Detroit: Lotus, 1977.

Henrietta Cordelia Ray (1861–1916)

Poetry
3174 "Antigone and Oedipus." In STET: 40–41.
3175 "The dawn of love." In STET: 39–40.
3176 "Idyl: sunrise." In STET: 37–38.
3177 "Idyl: sunset." In STET: 38.
3178 "Milton." In STET: 39.
3179 "Robert G. Shaw." In STET: 37.
3180 "To my father." In STET: 38–39.

Sarah Carolyn Reese

Poetry
3181 *Songs of Freedom: Poems.* Detroit: Lotus, 1983.

Textual Criticism
3182 Brown, Beth. *CLA J.* 28.1 Sept. 1984: 102–109. Rev. of *Songs of Freedom* (with reviews of other books).

Crystal Rhodes

Drama
3183 "The trip." In OSTR: 207–217.

Jeannette Robinson

Poetry
3184 "Lady dressed in blue." *Obsidian.* 3.1 Spr. 1977: 66.

Louise Robinson

Poetry
3185 *Blacksongs, Series I: Four Poetry Broadsides by Black Women.* Detroit: Lotus, 1977. Includes Jill Boyer's "Sun song," Robinson's "Woman-song," Paulette C. White's "Lost your momma," and Naomi L. Madgett's "Woman with flower."

Carolyn M. Rodgers (1945-)

Essay
3186 "An amen arena." In EVAN: 373-376. On her writing.

Poetry
3187 "Aunt Dolly." In BARA: 313-314.

3188 "A common poem." In ADOF: 140.

3189 "Contemporary / psalm." *Encore Amer. and Worldwide News.* Sept. 18, 1979: 39.

3190 "Folk." In BARA: 314.

3191 "For H.W. Fuller." *Essence.* 12.7 Nov. 1981: 16.

3192 "For muh' dear." In ADOF: 38-39.

3193 "For sapphires." In ADOF: 39.

3194 *The Heart As Ever Green: Poems.* Garden City, NY: Anchor-Doubleday, 1978.

3195 "How I got ovah." In ADOF: 142.

3196 "It is deep." In BELL: 377-378.

3197 "Jesus was crucified or: It must be deep." In STET: 180-182.

3198 "Love." *Ebony.* 38.4 Feb. 1983: 48.

3199 "Mannesahs." In BARA: 312.

3200 "Masquerade." In STET: 178-180.

3201 "No such thing as a witch / just a woman, needing some love." *Ebony.* 36.10 Aug. 1981: 54. Excerpt from *How I Got Ovah* (1975).

3202 "Poem for some Black women." In STET: 176-178.

3203 "Some me of beauty." In ADOF: 141.

3204 "Terra cotta." In ADOF: 143-144.

3205 "Touch, poem 5." In BARA: 313.

3206 "Touch, translation, poem 4." In BARA: 312.

3207 "Translations." *Black Scholar.* 11.5 May-June 1980: 71.

3208 "U name this one." In STET: 183.

3209 "We dance like Ella Riffs." In ADOF: 216-217.

3210 "Wimmin." In BARA: 315.

Textual Criticism
3211 Davis, Jean. "Carolyn Rodgers." In DL41: 287-295. Biography and bibliography included.

3212 Giddings, Paula. "Speaking of freedom." *Encore Amer. and Worldwide News.* Sept. 18, 1978: 38. Rev. of *The Heart As Ever Green.*

3213 Giovanni, Nikki. "A poet's reflections." *Encore Amer. and Worldwide News.* Sept. 18, 1978: 39.

3214 Jamison, Angelene. "Imagery in the women poems: the art of Carolyn Rodgers." In EVAN: 377-392.

3215 Mberi, Antar Sudan Katara. "Reaching for unity and harmony." *Freedomways.* 20.1 1980: 48-49.

3216 McElroy, Hilda Njoki. *Black World.* 25.4 Feb. 1976: 51-52, 79-81. Rev. of *How I Got Ovah.*

3217 Parker-Smith, Bettye J. "Running wild in her soul: the poetry of Carolyn Rodgers." In EVAN: 393-410.

3218 Sales, Estella M. "Contradictions in Black life: recognized and reconciled in *How I Got Ovah.*" *CLA J.* 25.1 Sept. 1981: 74-81.

3219 Ward, Jerry W. *New Orleans Rev.* 5.2 1976: 189-190. Rev. of *How I Got Ovah.*

3220 Winkler, Susan Kathleen. "The city and the prairie." *New Renaissance.* 11 1979: 103-110. Rev. of *The Heart As Ever Green.*

Sandra Rogers

Poetry
3221 "Waiting for her man too long." In BARA: 316.

Charlemae H. Rollins

Biography
3222 Commire, Anne. "Charlemae H. Rollins." In CO26: 171.

Renée Roper (1951-)

Poetry
3223 "Caníbolos de la montaña." In WETH: 109-110.
3224 "Emma in my third eye." In WETH: 107.
3225 "Going home." In WETH: 108-109.

Donna Kate Rushin

Poetry
3226 "The Black back-ups." In SMIT: 60-63.
3227 "The Black goddess." In SMIT: 328-330.
3228 "The bridge poem." In MORA: xxi-xxii.
3229 "The tired poem: last letter from a typical unemployed Black professional woman." *Conditions 5.* 2.2 Aut. 1979: 72-76.
3230 "The tired poem: last letter from a typical unemployed Black professional woman." In SMIT: 255-259.

Sonia Sanchez (1935-)

Children's Stories
3231 *A Sound Investment: Short Stories for Young Readers.* Chicago: Third World, 1980.

Essays

3232 "The poet as a creator of social values." *Black Scholar.* 16.1 Jan.–Feb. 1985: 20–25, 27–28.

3233 "Ruminations / reflections." In EVAN: 415–418. On her writing.

Foreword

3234 Angola, Bibi, Comp. and Ed. *Assata Speaks: And the People Speak on Assata.* Brooklyn, NY: Black News (typography and layout), 1980. Foreword by Sonia Sanchez.

Poetry

3235 "Black magic." *Black Scholar.* 18.1 Jan.–Feb. 1987: 54.

3236 "Blk / rhetoric." *Black Scholar.* 18.1 Jan.–Feb. 1987: 33.

3237 "Depression." *Callaloo.* 5.2 1979: 30.

3238 "Don't wanna be." In ADOF: 98–99.

3239 "Father and daughter." *Essence.* 12.6 Oct. 1981: 18.

3240 "For our lady." In KONE: 182–183.

3241 "For unborn Malcolms." *Steppingstone.* Wint. 1983: 17.

3242 *Generations: Poetry, 1969–1985.* London: Karnak House, 1986.

3243 "Haiku." *Western J. of Black Studies.* 9.3 Fall 1985: 174.

3244 "Haiku and tanka." *Black Scholar.* 10.3–4 Nov.–Dec. 1978: 49.

3245 *Homegirls and Handgrenades: A Collection of Poetry and Prose.* NY: Thunder's Mouth, 1984.

3246 "I have walked a long time." *Callaloo.* 5.2 1979: 19–20.

3247 *I've Been a Woman: New and Selected Poems.* Sausalito, CA: Black Scholar, 1978.

3248 "Indianapolis / summer / 1969 / poem." *Black Scholar.* 18.1 Jan.–Feb. 1987: 34.

3249 "Kwa mama zetu waliotuzaa." *Nimrod.* 21–22.2–1 1977: 245.

3250 "Kwa mama zetu waliotuzaa (For our mothers who gave us birth)." In BARA: 327–329.

3251 "A love poem written for Sterling Brown after reading a *New York Times* article re: a mummy kept preserved for about 3000 years." *Black Scholar.* 8.5 Mar. 1977: 45.

3252 "Love poems II." *Black Scholar.* 8.5 Mar. 1977: 45.

3253 "Malcolm." *Black Scholar.* 18.1 Jan.–Feb. 1987: 32.

3254 "Malcolm." *Steppingstone.* Wint. 1983: 16.

3255 "Memorial." In STET: 242–245.

3256 "Notes from a journal." *Amer. Poetry Rev.* 6.5 Sept.–Oct. 1977: 30.

3257 "Now poem. For us." In ADOF: 26–27.

3258 "Old words." In BARA: 322–325.

3259 "Personal letter No. 2." *Black Scholar.* 18.1 Jan.–Feb. 1987: 31.

3260 "Personal letter No. 3." *Black Scholar.* 18.1 Jan.–Feb. 1987: 31.

3261 "Poem (for DCS 8th graders 1966–67)." *Black Scholar.* 18.1 Jan.–Feb. 1987: 32.

3262 "Poem at thirty." In ADOF: 126.

3263 "Poem at thirty." In STET: 245–246.

3264 "A poem for Jesse Jackson." *Essence.* 15.3 July 1984: 123.

3265 "Poem for my father." *Black Scholar.* 18.1 Jan.–Feb. 1987: 51.

3266 "Poem for my father." *Parnassus.* 12–13.2–1 Spr.–Sum.–Fall–Wint. 1985: 352.

3267 "A poem for Sterling Brown." In BARA: 317–318.

3268 "Poem No. 7." *Nimrod.* 21–22.2–1 1977: 244.

3269 "Poem No. 8 (I've been a woman...)." *Callaloo.* 5.2 1979: 20.

3270 "A poem of praise." *Callaloo.* 5.2 1979: 21–23.

3271 "Present." *Amer. Poetry Rev.* 6.1 Jan.–Feb. 1977: 27.

3272 "Present." In ADOF: 127–128.

3273 "Present." In BARA: 325–326.

3274 "Re death." *Black Scholar.* 9.2 Oct. 1977: 55–57.

3275 "Rebirth." *Amer. Poetry Rev.* 6.1 Jan.–Feb. 1977: 27.

3276 "Six haikus and two tankas." *Beloit Poetry J.* 29.2 Wint. 1978–79: 34–35.

3277 "Small comment." *Black Scholar.* 18.1 Jan.–Feb. 1987: 34.

3278 "So strange." *Callaloo.* 5.2 1979: 21.

3279 "Summer words for a sister addict." In STET: 246.

3280 "Summer words of a sistuh addict." *Black Scholar.* 18.1 Jan.–Feb. 1987: 32.

3281 "Ten fifteen a.m.—April 27, 1969." In BELL: 342.

3282 "To all brothers: from all sisters." *Western J. of Black Studies.* 9.3 Fall 1985: 174.

3283 *Under a Soprano Sky.* NY: Thunder's Mouth, 1986.

Short Fiction

3284 "Just don't never give up on love." In BARA: 318–321.

3285 "Just don't never give up on love." *Parnassus.* 12–13.2–1 Spr.–Sum.–Fall–Wint. 1985: 353–356.

Textual Criticism and Interviews

3286 Cornwell, Anita. "Attuned to the energy: Sonia Sanchez." *Essence.* 10.3 July 1979: 10–11. On Sanchez and her poetry.

3287 Graham, Beryl. *Black Books Bull.* 7.1 1980: 54–55. Rev. of *A Sound Investment.*

3288 Leibowitz, Herbert. "Exploding myths: an interview with Sonia Sanchez." *Parnassus.* 12–13.2–1 Spr.–Sum.–Fall–Wint. 1985: 357–368.

3289 Madhubuti, Haki. "Sonia Sanchez: the bringer of memories." In EVAN: 419–432.

3290 Patterson, Raymond. "What's happening in Black poetry." *Poetry Rev.* 2 Apr. 1985: 7–11.

3291 Salaam, Kalamu ya. "Sonia Sanchez." In DL41: 295–306. Includes biography and additional bibliography.

3292 Salkey, Andrew. *Black Scholar.* 10.8–9 May–June 1979: 84–85. Rev. of *I've Been a Woman.*

3293 Scruggs-Rogers, Emma. *Sepia.* 30.12 Dec. 1981: 78. Rev. of *A Sound Investment.*

3294 Tate, Claudia. "Sonia Sanchez." In TATE: 132–148. Interview.

3295 Walker Alexander, Margaret. *Black Scholar.* 11.3 Jan.–Feb. 1980: 92–93. Rev. of *I've Been a Woman.*

3296 Williams, David. "The poetry of Sonia Sanchez." In EVAN: 433–448.

3297 Williams, John D. "The pain of women, the joy of women, the sadness and depth of women." *Callaloo.* 5.2 1979: 147–149. Rev. of *I've Been a Woman.*

Satiafa (Vivian V. Gordon)

Poetry
  3298 "For dark women and others." *Western J. of Black Studies.* 7.3 Fall 1983: 146–147.
  3299 *For Dark Women and Others: Poems.* Detroit: Lotus, 1982.

Textual Criticism
  3300 Barnes-Harden, Alene. *J. of Black Studies.* 14.2 Dec. 1983: 261–262. Rev. of *For Dark Women and Others.*

Saunders, Ruby C. *see* Allah, Fareedah

Baraka Sele (Pamela Cobb) (1950–)

Poetry
  3301 "Evolution." *Amelia.* 1.2 Oct. 1984: 13.
  3302 "Footsteps." *Amelia.* 1.2 Oct. 1984: 13.
  3303 "Gerald Cheatom, 1970." *Black Amer. Lit. Forum.* 18.1 Spr. 1984: 8.
  3304 "Listen." *Black Amer. Lit. Forum.* 18.1 Spr. 1984: 8.
  3305 "Spirit people." *Black Amer. Lit. Forum.* 18.1 Spr. 1984: 9.
  3306 "Uprising: a day in the history of revolutionary warfare." *Black Amer. Lit. Forum.* 18.1 Spr. 1984: 8.

Assata Shakur (Joanne Chesimard)

Autobiography
  3307 *Assata: An Autobiography.* Westport, CT: L. Hill, 1987.

Biography
  3308 Angola, Bibi, Comp. and Ed. *Assata Speaks: And the People Speak on Assata.* Brooklyn, NY: Black News (typography and layout), 1980. Foreword by Sonia Sanchez.

Essay
  3309 "Women in prison: how we are." *Black Scholar.* 9.7 Apr. 1978: 8–15.

Poetry
    3310 "What is left?" *Heresies.* 1 Jan. 1977: 101.

Ntozake Shange (Paulette L. Williams) (1948–)

Drama
    3311 *A Daughter's Geography.* NY: St. Martin's, 1983. Includes three sections, originally performed separately: "It hasn't always been this way / a choreopoem," "Bocas: a daughter's geography," and "From okra to greens / a different kinda love story."
    3312 *For Colored Girls Who Have Considered Suicide / When the Rainbow Is Enuf: A Choreopoem.* San Lorenzo, CA: Shameless Hussy, 1976.
    3313 *From Okra to Greens: A Different Kinda Love Story: A Play with Music and Dance.* NY: Samuel French, 1985.
    3314 *A Photograph: Lovers in Motion. Poemplay.* NY: Samuel French, 1981.
    3315 "A scene from *Boogie Woogie Landscapes.*" *Ms.* 10.2 Aug. 1981: 70–71, 94. From *Three Pieces.*
    3316 *Spell No. 7: A Theatre Piece in Two Acts.* NY: Samuel French, 1981.
    3317 "Spell No. 7: geechee jibara quik magic trance manual for technologically stressed third world people." In WILK: 239–291.
    3318 *Three Pieces.* NY: St. Martin's, 1981. Includes the short plays *Spell No. 7; A Photograph: Lovers in Motion;* and *Boogie Woogie Landscapes.*

Essays
    3319 *See No Evil: Prefaces, Essays and Accounts, 1976–83.* San Francisco: Momo's, 1984. Includes prefaces to the plays; essays on writers.

Foreword
    3320 *Black Book.* NY: St. Martin's, 1986. Shange wrote the foreword to this book of photographs of Afro-American men.

Novels
    3321 *Betsey Brown.* NY: St. Martin's, 1985.
    3322 "Christmas for Sassafrass, Cypress and Indigo." *Essence.* 13.8 Dec. 1982: 68–70, 116, 119–121. Excerpt from *Sassafrass, Cypress and Indigo.*
    3323 *Sassafrass.* Berkeley, CA: Shameless Hussy, 1976.
    3324 *Sassafrass, Cypress and Indigo: A Novel.* NY: St. Martin's, 1982.

Poetry
    3325 "Black and white two-dimensional planes." *Callaloo.* 5.2 1979: 56–62.
    3326 "Comin to terms." In WASH: 251–254.
    3327 "Cross oceans into my heart." In BRUA: 167–170.
    3328 "Cypress-Sassafras [sic]." In FISH: 281–286.
    3329 "Dark phrases." In STET: 270–272.
    3330 "Frank Albert and Viola Benzena Owens." In STET: 273–276.
    3331 *From Okra to Greens: Poems.* St. Paul: Coffee House, 1984.

3332 "Get it and feel good." *Essence.* 13.1 May 1982: 22.

3333 "Graduation nite." In BRUA: 170–172.

3334 "Gray." *Callaloo.* 5.2 1979: 63.

3335 "Is not so gd to be born a girl." *Black Scholar.* 10.8–9 May–June 1979: 28–29.

3336 "Jonestown or the disco." In DALE: 74–75.

3337 "Like the fog & the sun teasin the rapids." *Mademoiselle.* 82.9 Sept. 1976: 28.

3338 "Memory (for philip wilson, oliver lake, david murray & julius hemphill)." *Mademoiselle.* 82.9 Sept. 1976: 28.

3339 "Moon journey." *Heresies.* 4.2 (No. 14) 1982: 34.

3340 *Nappy Edges.* NY: St. Martin's, 1978.

3341 "Nappy edges (a cross country sojourn)." In STET: 268–269.

3342 "No more love poems no. 1." In STET: 268–269.

3343 "Oh she gotta head fulla hair." *Black Scholar.* 10.3–4 Nov.–Dec. 1978: 13–14.

3344 "On becomin successful." *Mademoiselle.* 82.9 Sept. 1976: 28.

3345 "Otherwise i would think it odd to have rape prevention month." *Black Scholar.* 10.8–9 May–June 1979: 29–30.

3346 "She bleeds." *Essence.* 11.1 May 1980: 103.

3347 *Some Men.* [St. Louis]: 1981. A pamphlet of poems.

3348 "Sue-Jean." *Little Magazine.* 11.1 1977: 26–28.

3349 "Toussaint." In BLIC: 153–157. Excerpt from *For Colored Girls....*

3350 *Tween Itaparica y Itapua.* NY: Basement Editions, 1978. A broadside.

3351 "Unrecovered losses / Black theatre traditions." *Black Scholar.* 10.10 July–Aug. 1979: 7–9.

3352 "We are just kinda that way." *Beloit Poetry J.* 29.2 Wint. 1978–1979: 22.

3353 "With no immediate cause." *Heresies.* 6 1978: 12.

3354 "With no immediate cause." *Radical America.* 13.6 Nov. 1979: 48.

3355 "Wow, yr just like a man!" *Ms.* 7.6 Dec. 1978: 50, 52. From *Nappy Edges.*

3356 "Yo u tu." *Little Magazine.* 10.1 1976: 27–29.

Poetry and Prose

3357 *Natural Disasters and Other Festive Occasions.* San Francisco: Heirs, 1977.

3358 *Ridin' the Moon in Texas: Word Paintings.* NY: St. Martin's, 1987.

Short Fiction

3359 "Aw, babee, you so pretty." *Essence.* 9.12 Apr. 1979: 87, 145–146. In poetic form.

3360 "Aw, babee, you so pretty." In WASH: 87–92. In poetic form.

Textual Criticism and Interviews

3361 Allen, Bonnie. "A home instinct." *Essence.* 11.4 Aug. 1980: 17, 21.

3362 Bailey, A. Peter. *Black Collegian.* 10.3 Dec. 1978–Jan. 1979: 70. Rev. of a production of *Spell No. 7.*

3363 Bambara, Toni Cade. *"For Colored Girls* — and white girls too." *Ms.* 5.3 Sept. 1976: 36, 38.

3364 Bell, Roseann Pope. *"For Colored Girls..." Black Collegian.* 7.5 May–June 1977: 48–49. Rev. of a production of the play on Broadway.

3365 Betsko, Kathleen and Rachel Koenig. In BETS: 365–376. An interview.

3366 Bigsby, C.W.E. In BIGC: 411–415. Criticism on *For Colored Girls...*, *Spell No. 7,* and *Boogie Woogie Landscapes.*

3367 Birtha, Becky. *Off Our Backs.* 13.4 Apr. 1983: 17. Rev. of *Sassafrass, Cypress and Indigo.*

3368 Blackwell, Henry. "An interview with Ntozake Shange." *Black Amer. Lit. Forum.* 13.4 Wint. 1979: 134–138.

3369 Bond, Jean Carey. *Freedomways.* 16.2 1976: 187–191. Rev. of a production of *For Colored Girls....*

3370 Brown, Elizabeth. "Ntozake Shange." In DL38: 240–250. Includes biography and additional bibliography.

3371 Brown, Janet. "For colored girls who have considered suicide / when the rainbow is enuf." In BROW: 114–132.

3372 Christ, Carol P. "'i found god in myself ... & i loved her fiercely': Ntozake Shange." In CHRA: 97–117.

3373 Christian, Barbara. "No more buried lives: the theme of lesbianism in Lorde, Naylor, Shange, Walker." *Feminist Issues.* 5 Spr. 1985: 3–20.

3374 Christian, Barbara. "No more buried lives: the theme of lesbianism in Audre Lorde's *Zami,* Gloria Naylor's *The Women of Brewster Place,* Ntozake Shange's *Sassafras [sic], Cypress and Indigo,* and Alice Walker's *The Color Purple.*" In CHRF: 187–204.

3375 Clarke, Cheryl. *Conditions 5.* 2.2 Aut. 1979: 159–164. Rev. of *Nappy Edges.*

3376 Clurman, Harold. *Nation.* May 1, 1976: 542. Rev. of *For Colored Girls....*

3377 Cohen, Esther. "Three sisters." *Progressive.* 47.1 Jan. 1983: 56. Rev. of *Sassafrass, Cypress and Indigo.*

3378 Daniels, Bonnie. *"For Colored Girls* ... a catharsis." *Black Scholar.* 10.8–9 May–June 1979: 61–62.

3379 Dong, Stella. "PW interviews." *Publishers Weekly.* May 3, 1985: 227.

3380 El 'Zabar, Kai. *Black Books Bull.* 6.4 1980: 75–76. Rev. of *Nappy Edges.*

3381 Elliot, Jeffrey M. "Ntozake Shange: genesis of a choreopoem." *Negro History Bull.* 41.1 Jan.–Feb. 1978: 798–800. An interview.

3382 Fleming, Robert. "A conversation with the author." *Encore Amer. and Worldwide News.* 9.6 June 1980: 35–37. An interview.

3383 Flowers, Sandra Hollin. *"Colored Girls:* textbook for the eighties." *Black Amer. Lit. Forum.* 15.2 Sum. 1981: 51–54.

3384 Gillespie, Marcia Ann. "Ntozake Shange talks with Marcia Ann Gillespie." *Essence.* 16.1 May 1985: 122–124, 203, 205.

3385 Glastonbury, Marion. *New Statesman.* Oct. 4, 1985: 28–29. Rev. of *Betsey Brown.*

3386 Harper, Michael S. *N.Y. Times Book Rev.* Oct. 21, 1979: 18. Rev. of *Nappy Edges.*

3387 Harris, Jessica. *Essence.* 9.7 Nov. 1978: 16. Rev. of *Nappy Edges.*

3388 Harris, Jessica. *"For Colored Girls Who Have Considered Suicide / When the Rainbow Is Enuf*—the women who are the rainbow." *Essence.* 7.7 Nov. 1976: 87–89, 102–104, 120–122, 147.

3389 Isaacs, Susan. *N.Y. Times Book Rev.* Sept. 12, 1982: 12–13. Rev. of *Sassafrass, Cypress and Indigo.*

3390 Johnson, Joe. *Crisis.* 92.8 Oct. 1985: 10, 55–56. Rev. of *Betsey Brown.*

3391 Jones, Terry. "The need to go beyond stereotypes." *Black Scholar.* 10.8–9 May–June 1979: 48–49.

3392 Kalem, T.E. "He done her wrong." *Time.* June 14, 1976: 74. Rev. of *For Colored Girls....*

3393 Kazi, Kuumba na. *Black Collegian.* 13.4 Feb.-Mar. 1983: 132, 134. Rev. of *Sassafrass, Cypress and Indigo.*

3394 Kelly, Janis. *Off Our Backs.* 7.10 Dec. 1977: 17. Rev. of *For Colored Girls....*

3395 Latour, Martine. "Ntozake Shange: driven poet / playwright." *Mademoiselle.* 82.9 Sept. 1976: 182, 226. An interview.

3396 Lewis, Barbara. *"For Colored Girls Who Have Considered Suicide / When the Rainbow Is Enuf*—the poet." *Essence.* 7.7 Nov. 1976: 86, 119–120.

3397 Mitchell, Carolyn. "'A laying on of hands': transcending the city in Ntozake Shange's *For Colored Girls Who Have Considered Suicide / When the Rainbow Is Enuf.*" In SQUI: 230–248.

3398 "Ntozake Shange: playwright." *Ebony.* 32.10 Aug. 1977: 136.

3399 Peters, Erskine. "Some tragic propensities of ourselves: the occasion of Nzotake Shange's *For Colored Girls Who Have Considered Suicide / When the Rainbow Is Enuf.*" *J. of Ethnic Studies.* 6.1 Spr. 1978: 79–85.

3400 Rhys, Jean. "Ntozake Shange: interviews." *New Yorker.* Aug. 2, 1976: 17–19. In the column "Talk of the Town."

3401 Ribowsky, Mark. "A poetess scores a hit with play on 'what's wrong with black men'." *Sepia.* 25.12 Dec. 1976: 42–46, 48. On *For Colored Girls....*

3402 Richards, Sandra L. "Conflicting impulses in the plays of Ntozake Shange." *Black Amer. Lit. Forum.* 17.2 Sum. 1983: 73–78.

3403 Rushing, Andrea Benton. "For colored girls, suicide or struggle." *Massachusetts Rev.* 22.3 Aut. 1981: 539–550.

3404 Schindehette, Susan. *Saturday Rev.* 11.3 May–June 1985: 74–75. Rev. of *Betsey Brown.*

3405 Shange, Ntozake. "Ntozake Shange interviews herself." *Ms.* 6.6 Dec. 1977: 35, 70, 72.

3406 Smith, Yvonne. "Ntozake Shange: a 'colored girl' considers success." *Essence.* 12.10 Feb. 1982: 12, 14.

3407 Talbert, Linda Lee. "Ntozake Shange: scarlet woman and witch / poet." *Umoja.* 4 1980: 5–10.

3408 Valentine, Dean. *New Leader.* Jan. 2, 1978: 29. On a presentation of her play *A Photograph: A Study in Cruelty.*

3409 Vallely, Jean. "Trying to be nice." *Time.* July 19, 1976: 44–45. An interview.

3410 Webster, Ivan. "Ntozake Shange's bold Brechtian gamble." *Encore Amer. and Worldwide News.* 9.6 June 1980: 34. On her adaptation of Brecht's play *Mother Courage and Her Children.*

3411 Wheatley, Patchy. *Times (London) Literary Supplement.* Dec. 6, 1985: 1406. Rev. of *Betsey Brown.*

3412 White, Evelyn C. *Women's Rev. of Books.* 3.2 Nov. 1985: 11. Rev. of *Betsey Brown.*

3413 Willard, Nancy. *N.Y. Times Book Rev.* May 12, 1985: 12. Rev. of *Betsey Brown.*

3414 Williams, Sherley A. "Roots of privilege, new Black fiction." *Ms.* 13.12 June 1985: 69-72. Revs. of Gloria Naylor's *Linden Hills,* Andrea Lee's *Sarah Phillips,* and Shange's *Betsey Brown.*

Saundra Sharp (1942-)

Poetry
3415 "Long distance." *Essence.* 17.11 Mar. 1987: 132.
3416 *Soft Song.* Los Angeles: Poets Pay Rent, Too, 1978.
3417 "Thirty and a half." *Essence.* 17.6 Oct. 1986: 123.
3418 "This last piece of paper." *Essence.* 17.10 Feb. 1987: 116.

Ann Allen Shockley (1927-)

Bibliography
3419 Dandridge, Rita B. "Gathering pieces: a selected bibliography of Ann Allen Shockley." *Black Amer. Lit. Forum.* 21.1-2 Spr.-Sum. 1987: 133-146. Includes fiction, essays, newspaper columns, letters, reviews by Shockley, and biographical and critical articles about her and her work.

3420 Dandridge, Rita B., Comp. *Ann Allen Shockley: An Annotated Primary and Secondary Bibliography.* Westport, CT: Greenwood, 1987.

Editing
3421 Josey, E.J. and Ann Allen Shockley, Comps. and Eds. *Handbook of Black Librarianship.* Littleton, CO: Libraries Unlimited, 1977.

Essays
3422 "The Black lesbian in American literature: an overview." *Conditions 5.* 2.2 Aut. 1979: 133-142.

3423 "Oral history: a research tool." *Negro History Bull.* 41.1 Jan.-Feb. 1978: 787-789.

3424 "The salsa soul sisters." *Off Our Backs.* 9 Nov. 1979: 13.

Novel
3425 *Say Jesus and Come to Me.* NY: Avon, 1982.

Short Fiction

3426 "A birthday remembered." In KOPB: 286–293. With biographical headnote.

3427 *The Black and White of It.* Tallahassee, FL: Naiad, 1980.

3428 "A case of telemania." *Azalea.* 1.3 Fall 1978: 1–5.

3429 "A case of telemania." In BULK: 138–143.

3430 "A meeting of the Sapphic Daughters." *Sinister Wisdom.* 9 Spr. 1979: 54–59.

3431 "The more things change." *Essence.* 8.6 Oct. 1977: 78–79, 93–94, 97, 99.

3432 "The world of Rosie Polk." *Black Amer. Lit. Forum.* 21.1–2 Spr.–Sum. 1987: 113–132.

Textual Criticism

3433 Clark, Terri. *Off Our Backs.* 9 Nov. 1979: 21. Rev. of *Loving Her* (novel, 1974).

3434 Houston, Helen R. "Ann Allen Shockley." In DL33: 232–236. Includes biography and additional bibliography.

3435 Morris, Debra. *Off Our Backs.* 11 Oct. 1981: 16. Rev. of *The Black and White of It.*

3436 Reynolds, Lynne. *Conditions 7.* 3.1 Spr. 1981: 152–158. Rev. of *The Black and White of It.*

Judy Dothard Simmons (1944–)

Poetry

3437 "Alabama." In ADOF: 45.

3438 "The clock turns backwards." *Essence.* 17.12 Apr. 1987: 118.

3439 "Courage (for Jane Cortez)." *Essence.* 11.12 Apr. 1981: 19.

3440 *Decent Intentions.* Bronx, NY: Blind Beggar, 1983.

3441 "Don't blame him (for Thelonius Monk)." *Steppingstone.* 1 Sum. 1982: 33.

3442 "Equal opportunity." In BARA: 331–332.

3443 "Fragments of myself / the women." *Conditions 5.* 2.2 Aut. 1979: 95.

3444 "Generations." In ADOF: 16–17.

3445 "It's comforting." In ADOF: 138–139.

3446 "Linseed oil and dreams." In BARA: 332.

3447 "Minority." *Conditions 5.* 2.2 Aut. 1979: 93–94.

3448 "Minority." In BARA: 330.

3449 "Survivor." In ADOF: 137–138.

Verta Mae Smart-Grosvenor (1939–)

Interview

3450 *Publishers Weekly.* In AUTH: 292–294. On Smart-Grosvenor's book *Vibration Cooking* (1970).

Poetry
3451 "Nothin but a feelin." *Essence.* 7.10 Feb. 1977: 62.

Short Fiction
3452 "Don't cry for me, Carolina." *Essence.* 13.3 July 1982: 70–72, 74, 128, 132, 135.

3453 "Skillet blond." In BARA: 124–130.

Barbara Smith (1946–)

Editing
3454 *Home Girls: A Black Feminist Anthology.* NY: Kitchen Table: Women of Color, 1983.

3455 Hull, Gloria T.; Patricia Bell Scott; Barbara Smith, Eds. *All the Women Are White, All the Blacks Are Men, but Some of Us Are Brave: Black Women's Studies.* Old Westbury, NY: Feminist, 1982.

3456 Smith, Barbara and Lorraine Bethel, Eds. *The Black Women's Issue.* Brooklyn, NY: Conditions, 1979. Special issue of *Conditions,* No. 5, Vol. 2, No. 2, Aut. 1979.

Essays
3457 "Barbara Smith on Black feminism." *Sojourner.* 10.4 Dec. 1984: 13–14.

3458 "Doing research on Black women." *Radical Teacher.* 3 Nov. 1976: 25–27. Presents thematic reading lists, including one on Black lesbian writers.

3459 "Homophobia: why bring it up?" *Interracial Books for Children Bull.* 14.3-4 1983: 7–8. A discussion of misconceptions about homosexuals.

3460 "Notes for yet another paper on Black feminism, or will the real enemy please stand up." *Conditions 5.* 2.2 Aut. 1979: 123–127.

3461 "Racism and women's studies." In HULL: 48–51.

3462 "A rock and a hard place: relationships between Black and Jewish women." *Women's Studies Q.* 11.3 Fall 1983: 7–9.

3463 Smith, Barbara and Beverly Smith. "'I am not meant to be alone and without you who understand': letters from Black feminists, 1972–1978." *Conditions 4.* 2.1 Wint. 1979: 62–77.

3464 Smith, Barbara with Beverly Smith, *et al.* "Face-to-face, day-to-day — racism CR [consciousness raising]." *Heresies.* 4.3 1982: 66–67.

3465 Smith, Barbara with Beverly Smith, *et al.* "Face-to-face, day-to-day — racism CR [consciousness raising]." In HULL: 52–56.

3466 "Toward a Black feminist criticism." *Conditions 2.* 1.2 Oct. 1977: 25–44.

3467 "Toward a Black feminist criticism." In BOWL: 32–40.

3468 "Toward a Black feminist criticism." In NEWT: 3–18.

3469 "Toward a Black feminist criticism." In SHOW: 168–185.

3470 "Toward a Black feminist criticism." *Radical Teacher.* 7 Mar. 1978: 20–27.

Foreword

3471 *The Combahee River Collective Statement: Black Feminist Organizing in the Seventies and Eighties.* NY: Kitchen Table: Women of Color, 1986. Foreword by Barbara Smith.

3472 Roberts, J.R., Comp. *Black Lesbians: An Annotated Bibliography.* Tallahassee, FL: Naiad, 1981. Smith's foreword is on pages ix–x.

Non-Fiction

3473 Smith, Barbara, with Elly Bulkin and Minnie Bruce. *Yours in Struggle: Three Feminist Perspectives on Anti-Semitism and Racism.* Brooklyn, NY: Long Haul, 1984. Contains Smith's essay "Between a rock and a hard place: relationships between Black and Jewish women," pages 65–87.

3474 *Toward a Black Feminist Criticism.* Brooklyn, NY: Out and Out Books, 1977. On Black women authors and on lesbianism.

Poetry

3475 "The bowl." In HOFF: 136–138.

3476 "Poem for my sister, No. 1, Birmingham, 1963." *Southern Voices.*

3477 "Spoilage." *Abatis.* 1 1983: 8.

3478 "Theft (for Angelina Weld Grimké)." *Chrysalis.* 10 1980: 91.

Short Fiction

3479 "Except for the fire." *Sojourner.* 11.2 Oct. 1985: 21.

3480 "Home." *Conditions 8.* 3.2 Spr. 1982: 100–105.

3481 "Home." In SMIT: 64–69.

Textual Criticism and Interviews

3482 Cenen and Barbara Smith. "The blood—yes, the blood: a conversation." In SMIT: 31–51.

3483 "'Keeping Black women at the center': a conversation between Gloria T. Hull and Barbara Smith." *Off Our Backs.* 12.5 May 1982: 22–23.

3484 Moraga, Cherríe and Barbara Smith. "Lesbian literature: a third world feminist perspective." In CRUI: 55–65.

3485 Moraga, Cherríe and Gloria Anzaldúa. "Across the kitchen table: a sister-to-sister dialogue." *Sinister Wisdom.* 18 1981: 63–75. Conversation between the authors and sisters Barbara and Beverly Smith.

3486 Parkerson, Michelle. "Some place that's our own: an interview with Barbara Smith." *Off Our Backs.* 14.4 Apr. 1984: 10–12, 26.

3487 Sorrel, Lorraine. "This bridge moves feminists." *Off Our Backs.* 12.4 Apr. 1982: 4–5, 11. Interview of Smith and of Cherríe Moraga.

3488 Streeter, Caroline A. *Off Our Backs.* 14.8 Aug.–Sept. 1984: 10–11. Rev. of *Home Girls.*

3489 Walker, Alice. "Breaking chains and encouraging life." *Ms.* 8.10 Apr. 1980: 35–36, 38, 40–41. Rev. of *Conditions: Five: The Black Women's Issue,* ed. by Lorraine Bethel and Barbara Smith.

Beverly Smith (1946–)

Essays

3490 Smith, Barbara and Beverly Smith. "'I am not meant to be alone and without you who understand': letters from Black feminists." *Conditions 4*. 2.1 Wint. 1979: 62–77.

3491 Smith, Beverly with Barbara Smith, *et al*. "Face-to-face, day-to-day—racism CR [consciousness raising]." *Heresies*. 4.3 1982: 66–67.

3492 Smith, Beverly with Barbara Smith, *et al*. "Face-to-face, day-to-day—racism CR [consciousness raising]." In HULL: 52–56.

3493 Smith, Beverly with Judith Stein and Priscilla Golding. "'The possibility of life between us': a dialogue between Black and Jewish women." *Conditions 7*. 3.1 Spr. 1981: 25–46.

Journal Writing

3494 "Diane." *Common Lives, Lesbian Lives*. 1 Fall 1981: 59–67.

3495 "The wedding." *Conditions 5*. 2.2 Aut. 1979: 103–108.

3496 "The wedding." In SMIT: 171–176.

Poetry

3497 "If you be a flower." *Sojourner*. 11.2 Oct. 1985: 32.

3498 "Sun, you are my lover." *Sojourner*. 9.10 June 1984: 27.

3499 "Wash days." *Sojourner*. 9.10 June 1984: 27.

Mary Carter Smith

Biography

3500 Beckles, Frances N. In BECK: 108–114.

Poetry

3501 *Heart to Heart*. Columbia, MD: C.H. Fairfax, 1980.

3502 *Town Child*. Columbia, MD: Nordika, 1976.

Short Fiction

3503 "The lions and the rabbits: a fable." *Crisis*. 85.3 Mar. 1978: 104–105.

Ellease Southerland (1943–)

Novel

3504 *Let the Lion Eat Straw*. NY: Scribner, 1979.

Textual Criticism

3505 Brookhart, Mary Hughes. "Ellease Southerland." In DL33: 239–244. Includes biography and additional bibliography.

3506 Fuller, Hoyt W., Angela Jackson, and James C. Kilgore. "Two views: *Let the Lion Eat Straw*." *First World*. 2.3 1979: 49–52.

3507 Stetson, Erlene. "Black female experience as it is." *Obsidian.* 7.2–3 Sum.–Wint. 1981: 224–225. Rev. of *Let the Lion Eat Straw.*

3508 Watkins, Mel. *N.Y. Times Book Rev.* June 3, 1979: 14. Rev. of *Let the Lion Eat Straw.*

3509 Webster, Ivan. *Encore Amer. and Worldwide News.* May 21, 1979: 51. Rev. of *Let the Lion Eat Straw.*

3510 Wilson, Judith. *Essence.* 10.6 Oct. 1979: 15. Rev. of *Let the Lion Eat Straw.*

Anne Spencer (1882–1975)

Poetry
3511 "At the carnival." In STET: 68–69.
3512 "Before the feast of Shushan." In STET: 69–70.
3513 "Lady, lady." In STET: 72.
3514 "Letter to my sister." In STET: 70–71.
3515 "Substitution." In STET: 71.

Textual Criticism
3516 Dean, Sharon G. "Anne Spencer." In DL54: 420–427. Biographical information and bibliography included.

3517 Greene, J. Lee. "Anne Spencer." In DL51: 252–259. Biography and bibliography included.

3518 Greene, J. Lee. *Time's Unfading Garden: Anne Spencer's Life and Poetry.* Baton Rouge: Louisiana State Univ., 1977. Forty-two of Spencer's fifty extant poems are reprinted on pages 175–197.

3519 Perry, Margaret. "Anne Spencer." In PERH: 134–135. On several works.

3520 Perry, Margaret. In PERM: 157–160. On several works.

3521 Stetson, Erlene. "Anne Spencer." *CLA J.* 21.3 Mar. 1978: 400–409. On several works.

Hortense J. Spillers

Editing
3522 Pryse, Marjorie and Hortense J. Spillers, Eds. *Conjuring: Black Women, Fiction, and Literary Tradition.* Bloomington: Indiana UP, 1985.

Essays
3523 "Kinship and resemblances: women on women (a review essay)." *Feminist Studies.* 11 Spr. 1985: 111–125. On Stetson's *Black Sister* and Christian's *Black Women Novelists.*

3524 "The politics of intimacy: a discussion." In BELL: 87–106. On James Baldwin's *If Beale Street Could Talk,* in which a woman is the central character.

3525 "'Turning the century': notes on women and difference." *Tulsa Studies* *in Women's Lit.* 3 Spr.–Fall 1984: 178–185. On Tate's *Black Women Writers at Work* and Smith's *Home Girls.*

Short Fiction
3526 "Isom." *Essence.* 11.1 May 1980: 88–91, 116, 119–120, 123–124, 126, 128.
3527 "A lament." *Black Scholar.* 8.5 Mar. 1977: 12–16.

Shirley O. Steele

Short Fiction
3528 "Shoes are made for walking." In SMIT: 260–269.

Thelma J. Stiles

Drama
3529 "No one man show." In OSTR: 243–260.

Elma Stuckey (1907–)

Poetry
3530 "Reprobate." *Black Amer. Lit. Forum.* 17.4 Wint. 1983: 171.
3531 Stuckey, Elma. *Collected Poems of Elma Stuckey.* Chicago: Precedent, 1987.

Textual Criticism and Interviews
3532 Roediger, David. "Elma Stuckey: a poet laureate of Black history." *Negro History Bull.* 40.2 Mar.–Apr. 1977: 690–691.
3533 Roediger, David. "An interview with Elma Stuckey." *Black Amer. Lit. Forum.* 11.4 Wint. 1977: 151–153.

Pat Suncircle

Short Fiction
3534 "A day's growth." *Christopher Street.* 1.8 Feb. 1977: 23–27.
3535 "Mariam." *Sinister Wisdom.* 7 Fall 1978: 34–39.
3536 "When the time came." *Christopher Street.* 2.6 Apr. 1978: 30–35.

Lynn Suruma

Poetry
3537 "Turning corners." In BELL: 367.

Eleanora E. Tate (1948-)

Children's Stories
3538 *Just an Overnight Guest.* NY: Dial, 1980.
3539 *The Secret of Gumbo Grove.* NY: F. Watts, 1987.

Textual Criticism
3540 Banfield, Beryle. *Interracial Books for Children Bull.* 12.2 1981: 21-22.
Rev. of *Just an Overnight Guest.*

Mildred D. Taylor (1943-)

Children's Stories
3541 *The Friendship.* NY: Dial, 1987.
3542 *The Gold Cadillac.* NY: Dial, 1987.
3543 *Let the Circle Be Unbroken.* NY: Dial, 1981. Sequel to *Roll of Thunder, Hear My Cry.*
3544 *Roll of Thunder, Hear My Cry.* NY: Dial, 1976. Sequel to *Song of the Trees* (1975).
3545 *Roll of Thunder, Hear My Cry* [Excerpt]. In ABBO: 568-585.

Miscellaneous
3546 Taylor, Mildred D. "Newbery Award acceptance speech." *Horn Book.* 53.4 Aug. 1977: 401-409. Given at the American Library Association meeting in Detroit, 1977, for *Roll of Thunder, Hear My Cry.*

Textual Criticism
3547 Commire, Anne. "Mildred D. Taylor." In CO15: 275-277. Biographical and bibliographical information included.
3548 Cooper, Ilene. *Booklist.* Dec. 15, 1987: 713. Rev. of *The Friendship.*
3549 Dussel, Sharon L. "Profile: Mildred D. Taylor." *Language Arts.* 58.5 May 1981: 599-604. Some biographical information and bibliography.
3550 Eiger, Melanie. *Best Sellers.* 41.11 Feb. 1982: 444. Rev. of *Let the Circle Be Unbroken.*
3551 *Encore Amer. and Worldwide News.* 6.7 Apr. 4, 1977: 44. Rev. of *Roll of Thunder, Hear My Cry.*
3552 Fisher, Margery. *Growing Point.* 16.9 Apr. 1978: 3286-3287. Rev. of *Roll of Thunder, Hear My Cry.*
3553 Fisher, Margery. *Growing Point.* 20.6 Mar. 1982: 4033. Rev. of *Let the Circle Be Unbroken.*
3554 Fogelman, Phyllis J. "Mildred D. Taylor." *Horn Book.* 53.4 Aug. 1977: 410-414. Biography and criticism.
3555 Fritz, Jean. *N.Y. Times Book Rev.* Nov. 21, 1976: 62. Rev. of *Roll of Thunder, Hear My Cry.*
3556 Hannabuss, Stuart. "Beyond the formula: Part II." *Junior Bookshelf.* 46.5 Oct. 1982: 173-176. Rev. of *Roll of Thunder, Hear My Cry.*

3557 Heins, Ethel L. *Horn Book.* 58.2 Apr. 1982: 173–174. Rev. of *Let the Circle Be Unbroken.*

3558 Hobbs, M. *Junior Bookshelf.* 46.3 June 1982: 112. Rev. of *Let the Circle Be Unbroken.*

3559 Holtze, Sally Holmes. *Horn Book.* 52.6 Dec. 1976: 627. Rev. of *Roll of Thunder, Hear My Cry.*

3560 Holtze, Sally Holmes. In HOLT: 307–309. Some biographical and bibliographical information.

3561 Jordan, June. "Mississippi in the thirties." *N.Y. Times Book Rev.* Nov. 15, 1981: 55, 58. Rev. of *Let the Circle Be Unbroken.*

3562 Martin, Ruby. *J. of Reading.* 20.5 Feb. 1977: 433–435. Rev. of *Song of the Trees.*

3563 Moore, Emily R. *Interracial Books for Children Bull.* 7.7 1976: 18. Rev. of *Roll of Thunder, Hear My Cry.*

3564 Rees, David. "The color of skin: Mildred Taylor." In REEM: 104–113. On several works.

3565 Taxel, Joel. "The Black experience in children's fiction: controversies surrounding award winning books." *Curriculum Inquiry.* 16.3 Fall 1986: 245–281. Compares two historical novels, Ouida Sebestyen's *Words by Heart* and Paula Fox's *The Slave Dancer,* with Taylor's *Roll of Thunder, Hear My Cry.*

Luisah Teish

Essay
3566 "Women's spirituality: a household act." In SMIT: 331–351. Excerpt from a work in progress on spiritual traditions and practices among women in the South.

Folklore
3567 *Jambalaya: The Natural Woman's Book of Personal Charms and Practical Rituals.* San Francisco: Harper, 1985. A practical book based on the author's beliefs about voodoo.

Short Fiction
3568 "Ole Black Emelda." *Southern Exposure.* 10.4 July–Aug. 1982: 22–23.

Textual Criticism and Interviews
3569 Anzaldúa, Gloria. "O.K., Momma, who the hell am I?: an interview with Luisah Teish..." In MORA: 221–231. On feminist spirituality.

3570 Oliver, D.S. "Leading a charmed life." *Women's Rev. of Books.* 3.11 Aug. 1986: 11–12. Rev. of *Jambalaya.*

Lucy Terry (1730–1821)

Poetry
3571 "Bars fight, August 28, 1746." In STET: 12.

Ianthe Thomas (1951–)

Children's Stories

3572 *Eliza's Daddy.* NY: Harcourt, Brace, Jovanovich, 1976.
3573 *Hi, Mrs. Mallory!* NY: Harper: 1979.
3574 *My Street's a Morning Cool Street.* NY: Harper, 1976.
3575 *Willie Blows a Mean Horn.* NY: Harper, 1981.

Textual Criticism

3576 Blank, Annette C. *Children's Book Rev. Service.* 7.11 June 1979: 105. Rev. of *Hi, Mrs. Mallory!*

3577 Elleman, Barbara. *Booklist.* Apr. 1, 1981: 1109. Rev. of *Willie Blows a Mean Horn.*

3578 Haskins, James S. *Children's Book Rev. Service.* 9.7 Feb. 1981: 55. Rev. of *Willie Blows a Mean Horn.*

3579 Kaye, Marilyn. *Booklist.* July 15, 1979: 1631. Rev. of *Hi, Mrs. Mallory!*

3580 Lewis, Marjorie. *School Library J.* 25.9 May 1979: 68. Rev. of *Hi, Mrs. Mallory!*

3581 Moore, Emily R. *Interracial Books for Children Bull.* 7.5 1976: 12. Rev. of *My Street's a Morning Cool Street.*

3582 Pennington, Jane. *Interracial Books for Children Bull.* 11.6 1980: 16–17. Rev. of *Hi, Mrs. Mallory!*

3583 Rose, Karel. *School Library J.* 23.6 Feb. 1977: 58. Rev. of *My Street's a Morning Cool Street.*

3584 Schroeder, Melinda. *School Library J.* 23.6 Feb. 1977: 58. Rev. of *Eliza's Daddy.*

3585 Spence, Patricia. *Children's Book Rev. Service.* 4.11 June 1976: 91. Rev. of *My Street's a Morning Cool Street.*

3586 Sutherland, Zena. *Bull. of the Center for Children's Books.* 32.11 July–Aug. 1979: 203. Rev. of *Hi, Mrs. Mallory!*

3587 Sutherland, Zena. *Bull. of the Center for Children's Books.* 34.11 July–Aug. 1981: 221. Rev. of *Willie Blows a Mean Horn.*

3588 Taylor, Mary Agnes. *Reading Teacher.* 30.8 May 1977: 947. Rev. of *My Street's a Morning Cool Street.*

3589 Weller, Joan. *School Library J.* 27.8 Apr. 1981: 118–119. Rev. of *Willie Blows a Mean Horn.*

3590 Wilms, Denise M. *Booklist.* Sept. 1, 1976: 43. Rev. of *My Street's a Morning Cool Street.*

3591 Wilson, Geraldine L. *Interracial Books for Children Bull.* 13.4–5 1982: 26–27. Rev. of *Willie Blows a Mean Horn.*

Joyce Carol Thomas (1938–)

Children's Stories

3592 *Bright Shadow.* NY: Avon, 1983. Sequel to *Marked by Fire.*
3593 *The Golden Pasture.* NY: Scholastic, 1986.

3594 *Marked by Fire.* NY: Avon, 1982.
3595 *Water Girl.* NY: Avon, 1986.

Poetry

3596 "Aretha." *Black Scholar.* 12.6 Nov.–Dec. 1981: 34. Rpt. from *Black Scholar* 7.8 (May 1976): 59.
3597 *Black Child.* NY: Zamani, 1981.
3598 "Church poem." In ADOF: 51–53.
3599 "Hide the children." *Amer. Poetry Rev.* 6.1 Jan.–Feb. 1977: 28.
3600 "I know a lady." In ADOF: 37–38.
3601 *Inside the Rainbow: Poems.* Palo Alto, CA: Penny/Zikawuna, 1982.
3602 "The MJQ." In ADOF: 165.
3603 "Poem for Otis Redding." In ADOF: 164–165.
3604 "Where is the Black Community." In ADOF: 64–65.

Short Fiction

3605 "Lubelle Berries." *Black Scholar.* 10.3–4 Nov.–Dec. 1978: 18–21.

Textual Criticism and Interviews

3606 Banfield, Beryle. *Interracial Books for Children Bull.* 13.4–5 1982: 28. Rev. of *Black Child.*
3607 Childress, Alice. *N.Y. Times Book Rev.* Apr. 18, 1982: 38. Rev. of *Marked by Fire.*
3608 Commire, Anne. "Joyce Carol Thomas." In CO40: 208–209. Some biographical information and additional bibliography.
3609 Griffith, Susan C. *New Directions for Women.* 13 Jan.–Feb. 1984: 18. Rev. of *Bright Shadow.*
3610 Middlebrook, Thomas and Diane W. Middlebrook. "Joyce Carol Thomas." In YALO: 30–39. An interview.
3611 Randall-Tsuruta, Dorothy. *Black Scholar.* 13.4–5 Sum. 1982: 48. Rev. of *Marked by Fire.*
3612 Wilson, Geraldine L. *Freedomways.* 23.4 1983: 289–290. Rev. of *Marked by Fire.*

Clara Ann Thompson

Poetry

3613 "His answer." In STET: 42. From her collection *Songs from the Wayside* (1908).
3614 "Mrs. Johnson objects." In STET: 42–43. From her collection *Songs from the Wayside* (1908).

Thulani *see* Davis, Thulani

Sojourner Truth (1797–1883)

Speech

3615 "Ain't I a woman?" In STET: 24–25. Poeticized adaptation (by Erlene Stetson) of a speech given at the Women's Rights Convention, Akron, Ohio, 1852.

Gladys T. Turner (1935–)

Children's Stories

3616 *Autobiography of Tammy: A Life Full of Love and Fun.* Dayton, OH: Challenge, 1978.

3617 *Bus Ride to Alabama: A Children's Story.* Dayton, OH: Challenge, 1980.

3618 *Papa Babe's Stamp Collection.* Smithtown, NY: Exposition, 1983.

Mary Elizabeth Vroman (1923–1967)

Short Fiction

3619 "See how they run." In BLIC: 125–140. Made into a movie, *Bright Road* (1953).

Summary of Children's Story

3620 Southgate, Robert L. In SOUT: 79–81. Summary of *Harlem Summer* (1967).

Textual Criticism

3621 Blicksilver, Edith. "Mary Elizabeth Vroman." In DL33: 255–258. Provides biographical information and additional bibliography.

Gloria Wade-Gayles

Essays

3622 "She who is Black and mother: in sociology and fiction, 1940–1970." In RODG: 89–106.

3623 "The truths of our mothers' lives: mother-daughter relationships in Black women's fiction." *Sage.* 1.2 Fall 1984: 8–12.

Non-Fiction

3624 *No Crystal Stair: Visions of Race and Sex in Black Women's Fiction.* NY: Pilgrim, 1984.

Poetry

3625 "Cracked." In BELL: 361–362.

3626 "Love's name." *Essence.* 7.5 Sept. 1976: 16.

3627 "Parade." In BELL: 365–366.
3628 "Sometimes as women only." In BELL: 363–364.

Alice Walker (1944–)

Bibliography
3629 Fifer, Elizabeth. "A bibliography of writings by Alice Walker." In RAIN: 165–171. Lists entries from 1966 to 1983.

Children's Stories
3630 *To Hell with Dying.* San Diego: Harcourt, 1987.

Editing
3631 *I Love Myself When I Am Laughing . . . And Then Again When I Am Looking Mean and Impressive: A Zora Neale Hurston Reader.* Old Westbury, NY: Feminist, 1979. Introduction by Mary Helen Washington.

Essays
3632 "Am I blue?" *Ms.* 15.1 July 1986: 29–30. On the feelings of animals.
3633 "Anaïs Nin: 1903–1977." *Ms.* 5.10 Apr. 1977: 46.
3634 "China: a poet takes snapshots in her mind, meets trees and relatives, and learns that she writes in Chinese." *Ms.* 13.9 Mar. 1985: 51–52, 54, 106–107.
3635 "Embracing the dark and the light." *Essence.* 13.3 July 1982: 67, 114, 117–118, 121. Rpt. in *In Search of Our Mothers' Gardens: Womanist Prose* as "If the present looks like the past, what does the future look like?"
3636 "Father: for what you were." *Essence.* 16.1 May 1985: 93–94, 96.
3637 "Finding Celie's voice." *Ms.* 14.6 Dec. 1985: 71–72, 96.
3638 "If the present looks like the past, what does the future look like? . . ." *Heresies.* 4.3 1982: 56–59.
3639 *In Search of Our Mothers' Gardens: Womanist Prose.* NY: Harcourt, 1983.
3640 "In search of our mothers' gardens." In GILN: 2374–2382.
3641 "In search of our mothers' gardens." In RUDD: 92–102.
3642 "In search of our mothers' gardens." *Southern Exposure.* 4.4 1976: 60–64.
3643 "In the closet of the soul: a letter to an African-American friend." *Ms.* 15.5 Nov. 1986: 32–35. The representation of the character "Mister" in *The Color Purple.*
3644 "Letters forum: anti-Semitism." *Ms.* 11.8 Feb. 1983: 13, 15–16.
3645 "Looking for Zora." In ASCH: 430–447.
3646 "Looking for Zora." In HARP: 377–392.
3647 "Lulls—a native daughter returns to the South." *Ms.* 5.7 Jan. 1977: 58–61, 89–90.
3648 "My father's country is the poor." *Black Scholar.* 8.8–10 Sum. 1977: 41–43. Rpt. in *In Search of Our Mothers' Gardens;* also, in *Ms,* Sept. 1977, as "Secrets of the new Cuba."
3649 "Nuclear exorcism: beyond cursing the day we were born." *Mother Jones.* 7.8 Sept.–Oct. 1982: 20–21. Rpt. in *In Search of Our Mothers' Gardens* as "Only

justice can stop a curse." Speech given at a San Francisco nuclear arms rally, March 1982.

3650 "On 'Anaïs Nin: 1903–1977'." *Ms.* 6.2 Aug. 1977: 8. Reply to letter of Lani M. Nolan.

3651 *"One* child of one's own." *Ms.* 8.2 Aug. 1979: 47–50, 72–75. On childbirth and creativity.

3652 *"One* child of one's own: a meaningful digression within the work(s)." In STER: 121–140.

3653 "Only justice can stop a curse." In MCAL: 262–265.

3654 "Only justice can stop a curse." In SMIT: 352–355.

3655 "Other voices, other moods." *Ms.* 7.8 Feb. 1979: 50–51, 70. Rpt. in *In Search of Our Mothers' Gardens* as "Looking to the side and back."

3656 "Saving the life that is your own: the importance of models in the artist's life." In FISH: 151–158. Also appears in *Women's Center Reid Lectureship: Papers by Alice Walker and June Jordan,* NY: Barnard College Women's Center, 1976. A speech given at the Modern Language Association meeting, San Francisco, 1975.

3657 "Secrets of the new Cuba." *Ms.* 6.3 Sept. 1977: 71–72, 74, 96–99.

3658 "'Silver writes.'" *Perspectives: The Civil Rights Quarterly.* 14.2 Sum. 1982: 22–23. On the term "civil rights." Rpt. in *In Search of Our Mothers' Gardens.*

3659 "Uncle Remus, no friend of mine." *Southern Exposure.* 9.2 Sum. 1981: 29–31.

3660 "When a tree falls. . ." *Ms.* 12.7 Jan. 1984: 48, 52–53, 55.

3661 "When the other dancer is the self." *Ms.* 11.11 May 1983: 70, 72, 142–143.

3662 "Writing *The Color Purple.*" In EVAN: 453–456. Also appears in *In Search of Our Mothers' Gardens.*

Foreword

3663 Hemenway, Robert. *Zora Neale Hurston: A Literary Biography.* Urbana: Univ. of Illinois, 1977. Walker's foreword is entitled "Zora Neale Hurston — a cautionary tale and a partisan view," pages xi–xviii.

3664 Smedley, Agnes. *Daughter of Earth.* NY: Feminist, 1987. Walker wrote the foreword to Smedley's novel, originally published in 1929.

Novels

3665 *The Color Purple.* NY: Harcourt, 1982.

3666 *Meridian.* NY: Harcourt, 1978.

3667 *Meridian* [Excerpt]. *Essence.* 7.3 July 1976: 73–78.

Poetry

3668 "Beyond what." In FER3: 550.

3669 "Burial." In FISH: 294–296.

3670 "Burial." In FORK: 325–328.

3671 "Each one, pull one." In BARA: 356–359.

3672 "Early losses: a requiem." In STET: 223–228.

3673 "Every morning." *Ladies' Home J.* 102.5 May 1985: 103.

3674 "Family of." In BARA: 354–356.

3675 "Forgive me if my praises." *Black Scholar.* 10.3–4 Nov.–Dec. 1978: 46.

3676 *Good Night, Willie Lee, I'll See You in the Morning: Poems.* NY: Dial, 1979.

3677 "Good night, Willie Lee, I'll see you in the morning." *Nimrod.* 21–22.2–1 1977: 298.

3678 *Horses Make a Landscape Look More Beautiful: Poems.* NY: Harcourt, 1984.

3679 "I find my own small person." *Amer. Poetry Rev.* 6.1 Jan.–Feb. 1977: 28–29.

3680 "I said to poetry." In BARA: 353–354.

3681 "I'm really very fond." In BARA: 359–360.

3682 "I'm really very fond." *Ms.* 7.10 Apr. 1979: 21.

3683 "If those people like you." *Ms.* 7.10 Apr. 1979: 21.

3684 "The instant of our parting." *Nimrod.* 21–22.2–1 1977: 297.

3685 "Light baggage (for Zora, Nella, Jean)." *Amer. Poetry Rev.* 6.1 Jan.–Feb. 1977: 28.

3686 "Light baggage (for Zora, Nella, Jean)." In GAES: 151.

3687 "My daughter is coming." *Callaloo.* 2.2 1979: 33.

3688 "New face." *Essence.* 14.7 Nov. 1983: 122.

3689 "On crying in public (for June, sister of mercy)." *Amer. Poetry Rev.* 6.1 Jan.–Feb. 1977: 29.

3690 "On stripping bark from myself (for Jane, who said trees die from it)." *Amer. Poetry Rev.* 6.1 Jan.–Feb. 1977: 28.

3691 "On stripping bark from myself (for Jane, who said trees die from it)." In GAES: 150–151.

3692 "Once." In STET: 213–223.

3693 "Overnights." *Callaloo.* 2.2 1979: 109.

3694 "Poem at thirty-nine." *Ms.* 11.12 June 1983: 101.

3695 "Representing the universe." In BARA: 360.

3696 "Revolutionary petunias." In STET: 212.

3697 "Talking to my grandmother who died poor some years ago (while listening to Richard Nixon declare 'I am not a crook')." *Black Scholar.* 12.6 Nov.–Dec. 1981: 25.

3698 "Threatened." In GAES: 152.

3699 "When Golda Meir was in Africa." *Black Scholar.* 10.6–7 Mar.–Apr. 1979: 8.

3700 "When Golda Meir was in Africa." *Ms.* 7.10 Apr. 1979: 21.

3701 "When we held our marriage." *Nimrod.* 21–22.2–1 1977: 296.

3702 "Women." *Essence.* 11.1 May 1980: 102.

3703 "Women." In BANK: 376.

3704 "Women." In FISH: 297.

3705 "Women." In HOFF: 201–203.

3706 "Women." In HULL: xiii.

3707 "Women." In REIT: 102.

3708 "Your soul shines." *Nimrod.* 21–22.2–1 1977: 295.

Prose Checklist

3709 Kirschner, Susan. "Alice Walker's nonfictional prose: a checklist, 1966–1984." *Black Amer. Lit. Forum.* 18.4 Wint. 1984: 162–163.

Short Fiction

3710 "The abortion." In ABRA: 127–137.

3711 "The abortion." *Mother Jones.* 5.7 Aug. 1980: 30–33, 61.

3712 "Advancing Luna—and Ida B. Wells." In WASH: 63–81.

3713 "Advancing Luna—and Ida B. Wells." *Ms.* 6.1 July 1977: 75–79, 93–94, 97.

3714 "Coming apart." In KOPO: 323–334.

3715 "Coming apart." In LEDE: 95–104. Appeared in *Ms,* Feb. 1980, as "When women confront porn at home."

3716 "Cuddling." *Essence.* 16.3 July 1985: 74–76.

3717 "Everyday use." In BLIC: 267–272.

3718 "Everyday use." In GILN: 2366–2374.

3719 "Everyday use." In KOPB: 230–239.

3720 "Everyday use." In SPIN: 70–81.

3721 "Her sweet Jerome." In FER2: 204–210.

3722 "How did I get away with killing one of the biggest lawyers in the state? It was easy." *Ms.* 9.5 Nov. 1980: 72, 75.

3723 "Kindred spirits." *Esquire.* 104.2 Aug. 1985: 106–111.

3724 "Laurel." In WASH: 48–59.

3725 "Laurel." *Ms.* 7.5 Nov. 1978: 64–66, 83–84.

3726 "A letter of the times." *Ms.* 10.4 Oct. 1981: 62–64.

3727 "The lover." *Essence.* 11.12 Apr. 1981: 87, 132, 135, 137–138. From *You Can't Keep a Good Woman Down.*

3728 "Nineteen fifty-five, or, You can't keep a good woman down." *Ms.* 9.9 Mar. 1981: 54, 57, 85–87.

3729 "Olive oil." *Ms.* 14.2 Aug. 1985: 35–36, 78.

3730 "Petunias." *Conditions 3.* 1.3 Spr. 1978: 41.

3731 "The revenge of Hannah Kemhuff." In FISH: 184–195.

3732 "A sudden trip home in the spring." In FANN: 163–172. Also appears in *You Can't Keep a Good Woman Down.*

3733 "To hell with dying." In LONG: 714–719.

3734 "To hell with dying." *Reader's Digest.* 123.738 Oct. 1983: 110–114. From her collection *In Love and Trouble* (1973).

3735 "When women confront porn at home." *Ms.* 8.7 Feb. 1980: 67, 69–70, 75–76. Published elsewhere as "Coming apart."

3736 *You Can't Keep a Good Woman Down: Stories.* NY: Harcourt, 1981.

Summary of Novel

3737 Southgate, Robert L. In SOUT: 167–168. Summary of *The Third Life of Grange Copeland* (1970).

Textual Criticism and Interviews

3738 Allen, Bruce. *Smithsonian.* 14.10 Jan. 1984: 133–134. Rev. of *In Search of Our Mothers' Gardens.*

3739 Anello, R. "Characters in search of a book." *Newsweek.* June 21, 1982: 67. On *The Color Purple.*

3740 Babb, Valerie. "*The Color Purple:* writing to undo what writing has done." *Phylon.* 47.2 June 1986: 107–116.

3741 Baker, Houston A., Jr. and Charlotte Pierce-Baker. "Patches: quilts and community in Alice Walker's 'Everyday use'." *Southern Rev.* 21.3 July 1985: 706–720.

3742 Bartelme, Elizabeth. "Victory over bitterness." *Commonweal.* Feb. 11, 1983: 93–94. Rev. of *The Color Purple.*

3743 Bell, Bernard W. "Alice Walker." In BELA: 259–269. On several works.

3744 Bell, Carolyn Wilkerson. In MA84: 368–373. On *In Search of Our Mothers' Gardens.*

3745 Blount, Marcellus. "A woman speaks." *Callaloo.* 6.1 1983: 118–122. On *The Color Purple.*

3746 Bradley, Jane. *Woman of Power.* 1 Spr. 1984: 106: Rev. of *In Search of Our Mothers' Gardens.*

3747 Brewer, Krista. "Writing to survive: an interview with Alice Walker." *Southern Exposure.* 9.2 Sum. 1981: 12–15.

3748 Brown, Beth. *CLA J.* 27.3 Mar. 1984: 348–352. On *In Search of Our Mothers' Gardens.*

3749 Buncombe, Marie H. "Androgyny as metaphor in Alice Walker's novels." *CLA J.* 30.4 June 1987: 419–427.

3750 Burnside, Gordon. *Commonweal.* Apr. 29, 1977: 281–284. Rev. of *Meridian.*

3751 Byerman, Keith E. "Women's blues: the fiction of Toni Cade Bambara and Alice Walker." In AYER: 104–170.

3752 Byrd, Rudolph P. "Sound advice from a friend: words and thoughts from the higher ground of Alice Walker." *Callaloo.* 6.1 1983: 123–129. On *In Search of Our Mothers' Gardens.*

3753 Chambers, Kimberly R. "Right on time: history and religion in Alice Walker's *The Color Purple.*" *CLA J.* 31.1 Sept. 1987: 44–62.

3754 Christian, Barbara. "Alice Walker." In DL33: 258–271. Biographical information and additional bibliography included.

3755 Christian, Barbara. "Alice Walker: the Black woman artist as wayward." In CHRF: 81–101.

3756 Christian, Barbara. "Alice Walker: the Black woman artist as wayward." In EVAN: 457–477.

3757 Christian, Barbara. "An angle of seeing: motherhood in Buchi Emecheta's *The Joys of Motherhood* and Alice Walker's *Meridian.*" In CHRF: 211–252.

3758 Christian, Barbara. "The contrary women of Alice Walker: a study of *In Love and Trouble.*" *Black Scholar.* 12.2 Mar.–Apr. 1981: 21–30, 70–71.

3759 Christian, Barbara. "The contrary women of Alice Walker: a study of female protagonists in *In Love and Trouble.*" In CHRF: 31–46.

3760 Christian, Barbara. "No more buried lives: the theme of lesbianism in Lorde, Naylor, Shange, Walker." *Feminist Issues.* 5.1 Spr. 1985: 3–20.

3761 Christian, Barbara. "No more buried lives: the theme of lesbianism in Audre Lorde's *Zami,* Gloria Naylor's *The Women of Brewster Place,* Ntozake Shange's *Sassafrass, Cypress and Indigo,* and Alice Walker's *The Color Purple.*" In CHRF: 187–204.

3762 Christian, Barbara. "Novels for everyday use: the novels of Alice Walker." In CHRW: 180–238.

3763 Christian, Barbara. "Pass it on." In CHRW: 239–252. Comparative study of Marshall, Morrison, and Walker.

3764 Christian, Barbara. "The short story in process." *Callaloo*. 5.1–2 1982: 195–198. Rev. of *You Can't Keep a Good Woman Down*.

3765 Christian, Barbara. "We are the ones that we have been waiting for: political content in Alice Walker's novels." *Women's Studies International Forum*. 9.4 1986: 421–426.

3766 Coleman, Viralene J. "Miss Celie's song." *Publications of the Arkansas Philological Assoc*. 11.1 Spr. 1985: 27–34. On *The Color Purple*.

3767 Commire, Anne. "Alice Walker." In CO31: 177–179. Biographical information included.

3768 Cooke, Michael G. "Intimacy: the interpenetration of the one and the all in Robert Hayden and Alice Walker." In COOK: 133–176. On the short story "The abortion" and on the novel *Meridian*.

3769 Cooke, Michael G. "Recent novels: women bearing violence." *Yale Rev*. 66.1 Oct. 1976: 146–155. On *Meridian*.

3770 Copeland, Hazel. "*Langston Hughes, American Poet:* a review." *Black Books Bull*. 4.1 Spr. 1976: 56. Rev. of Walker's book for children, written in 1974.

3771 "Creative woman: success requires talent and drive." *Ebony*. 32.10 Aug. 1977: 135.

3772 Davidon, Ann Morrissett. "Beacons." *Progressive*. 48.2 Feb. 1984: 42–43. Rev. of *In Search of Our Mothers' Gardens*.

3773 Davis, Thadious M. "Alice Walker." In DL06: 350–358. Includes biography and additional bibliography.

3774 Davis, Thadious M. "Alice Walker's celebration of self in southern generations." In PREN: 38–53.

3775 Davis, Thadious M. "Alice Walker's celebration of self in southern generations." *Southern Q*. 31.4 Sum. 1983: 39–53. Has commentaries on the short stories "Elethia" and "Petunias."

3776 DeLong, Nancy. *Sojourner*. 9.7 Mar. 1984: 24. Rev. of *In Search of Our Mothers' Gardens*.

3777 Dirda, Michael. "In praise of poetry." *Book World (Washington Post)*. Dec. 9, 1979: 11. Rev. of *Good Night, Willie Lee....*

3778 Dworkin, Susan. "The strange and wonderful story of the making of *The Color Purple*." *Ms*. 14.6 Dec. 1985: 66–70, 94–95.

3779 El Saffar, Ruth. "Alice Walker's *The Color Purple*." *International Fiction Rev*. 12.1 Wint. 1985: 11–17.

3780 Ensslen, Klaus. "Collective experience and individual responsibility: Alice Walker's *The Third Life of Grange Copeland*." In BRUC: 189–218.

3781 Erickson, Peter. "'Cast out alone / to heal / and re-create / ourselves': family-based identity in the work of Alice Walker." *CLA J*. 23.1 Sept. 1979: 71–94. On *The Third Life of Grange Copeland*, "A sudden trip home in the spring," and *Meridian*.

3782 Farwell, Marilyn R. *Northwest Rev*. 21.1 1983: 167–176. On *The Color Purple*.

3783 Fifer, Elizabeth. "Alice Walker: the dialect and letters of *The Color Purple*." In RAIN: 155–171.

3784 Fifer, Elizabeth. "The dialect and letters of *The Color Purple*." In RAIN: 154–165.

3785 Fishman, Charles. "Naming names: three recent novels by women writers." *Names*. 32.1 Mar. 1984: 33–44. Compares Walker's *Meridian* with Toni Morrison's *Tar Baby* and Margaret Atwood's *Life Before Man*.

3786 Fleming, Robert. *Encore Amer. and Worldwide News*. Apr. 2, 1979: 50. Rev. of *Good Night, Willie Lee*. . . .

3787 Fontenot, Chester J. "Alice Walker: 'The diary of an African nun' and DuBois' double consciousness." In BELL: 150–156.

3788 Fontenot, Chester J. "Alice Walker: 'The diary of an African nun' and DuBois' double consciousness." *J. of Afro-Amer. Issues*. 5.2 Spr. 1977: 192–196. On Walker's short story.

3789 Fontenot, Chester J. "Modern Black fiction: from tragedy to romance." *Cornell Rev*. 3 Spr. 1978: 115–123. On "Diary of an African nun."

3790 Freeman, Alma S. "Zora Neale Hurston and Alice Walker: a spiritual kinship." *Sage*. 2.1 Spr. 1985: 37–40. Criticism on Walker's *Meridian* and *In Love and Trouble* and on Hurston's *Their Eyes Were Watching God*.

3791 Gaston, Karen C. "Women in the lives of Grange Copeland." *CLA J*. 24.3 Mar. 1981: 276–286.

3792 Gay, Clifford. *Times (London) Literary Suppl*. Aug. 19, 1977: 1014. Rev. of *Meridian*.

3793 Gernes, Sonia. *America*. Feb. 2, 1985: 93–94. Rev. of *Horses Make a Landscape Look More Beautiful*.

3794 Goldstein, William. "Alice Walker on the set of *The Color Purple*." *Publishers Weekly*. Sept. 6, 1985: 46–48.

3795 Graham, Maryemma. *Freedomways*. 23.4 1983: 278–280. Rev. of *The Color Purple*.

3796 Guy-Sheftall, Beverly. "Literary profile: Alice Walker, you can go home again." *Black Southerner*. 1 June 1984: 9.

3797 Hairston, Loyle. "Alice in the mainstream, an essay review." *Freedomways*. 24.3 1984: 182–190. On *In Search of Our Mothers' Gardens*.

3798 Harris, Jessica. "An interview with Alice Walker." *Essence*. 7.3 July 1976: 33.

3799 Harris, Trudier. "*The Color Purple* as the culmination of Alice Walker's portrayal of Black women." *Studies in Amer. Fiction*. 14 Spr. 1986: 1–17.

3800 Harris, Trudier. "Folklore in the fiction of Alice Walker: a perpetuation of historical and literary traditions." *Black Amer. Lit. Forum*. 11.1 Spr. 1977: 3–8.

3801 Harris, Trudier. "On *The Color Purple*, stereotypes, and silence." *Black Amer. Lit. Forum*. 18.4 Wint. 1984: 155–161.

3802 Harris, Trudier. "Three Black women writers and humanism: a folk perspective." In MILL: 50–74. On Sarah Wright's *This Child's Gonna Live*, Alice Walker's *The Third Life of Grange Copeland*, and Paule Marshall's *The Chosen Place, The Timeless People*.

3803 Harris, Trudier. "Tiptoeing through taboo, incest in 'The child who favored daughter'." *Modern Fiction Studies.* 28.3 Aut. 1982: 494–505. On Walker's short story.

3804 Hellenbrand, Harold. "Speech, after silence: Alice Walker's *The Third Life of Grange Copeland.*" *Black Amer. Lit. Forum.* 20.1-2 Spr.-Sum. 1986: 113–128.

3805 Henderson, Mae G. "*The Color Purple:* revisions and redefinitions." *Sage.* 2.1 Spr. 1985: 14–18. Comments on the format of the novel.

3806 Hernton, Calvin C. "Who's afraid of Alice Walker? *The Color Purple* as slave narrative." In HERN: 1–36.

3807 Hiers, John T. "Creation theology in Alice Walker's *The Color Purple.*" *Notes on Contemporary Lit.* 14.4 Sept. 1984: 2–3.

3808 Higgins, Chester A., Sr. "Pulitzer beginning to do something right." *Crisis.* 90.6 June–July 1983: 49. On *The Color Purple.*

3809 Hogue, W. Lawrence. "History, the feminist discourse, and Alice Walker's *The Third Life of Grange Copeland.*" *Melus.* 12.2 Sum. 1985: 45–62.

3810 "Hum inside the skull." *N.Y. Times Book Rev.* May 13, 1984: 1, 28. Interview.

3811 Kane, Patricia. "The prodigal daughter in Alice Walker's 'Everyday use'." *Notes on Contemporary Lit.* 15.2 Mar. 1985: 7.

3812 Kelly, Ernece B. *CLA J.* 27.1 Sept. 1983: 91–96. Rev. of *The Color Purple.*

3813 Krauth, Leland. "Mark Twain, Alice Walker, and the aesthetics of joy." *Proteus.* 1.2 Fall 1984: 9–14.

3814 Lee, Dorothy. "Three Black plays: alienation and paths to recovery." *Modern Drama.* 19.4 Dec. 1976: 397–404. Criticism on plays by Alice Walker, Elder, and Gordone.

3815 Lenhart, Georgann. "Inspired purple?" *Notes on Contemporary Lit.* 14.3 May 1984: 2–3. *The Color Purple* compared to Evelyn Tooley Hunt's 'Taught me purple.'

3816 "Letters to God are postmarked with a Pulitzer." *People Weekly.* Dec. 26, 1983–Jan. 2, 1984: 85, 87. On *The Color Purple.*

3817 Lowe, Cynthia. *Black Books Bull.* 4.4 Wint. 1976: 60–61. Rev. of *Meridian.*

3818 Lupton, Mary Jane. "Clothes and closure in three novels by Black women." *Black Amer. Lit. Forum.* 20.4 Wint. 1986: 409–421. Includes criticism on *The Color Purple.*

3819 Marcus, Greil. *New Yorker.* June 7, 1976: 133–136. Rev. of *Meridian.*

3820 Marcus, Greil. *Rolling Stone.* Jan. 26, 1978: 55. Rev. of *The Third Life of Grange Copeland.*

3821 McDowell, Deborah E. "The self in bloom: Alice Walker's *Meridian.*" *CLA J.* 24.3 Mar. 1981: 262–275.

3822 McFadden, Margaret. In MA83: 139–143. On *The Color Purple.*

3823 McGowan, Martha J. "Atonement and release in Alice Walker's *Meridian.*" *Critique.* 23.1 1981: 25–36.

3824 Mickelson, Anne Z. "Winging upward: Black women: Sarah E. Wright, Toni Morrison, Alice Walker." In MICK: 154–174. On "In love and trouble" and *Meridian.*

3825 Moore, Opal. *Iowa J. of Literary Studies.* 5 1984: 107–110. On *In Search of Our Mothers' Gardens.*

3826 Mootry-Ikerionwu, Maria K. *CLA J.* 27.3 Mar. 1984: 345–348. Rev. of *The Color Purple.*

3827 Morris, Deb. *Off Our Backs.* 13.4 Apr. 1983: 16. On *You Can't Keep a Good Woman Down* and *The Color Purple.*

3828 Mort, Jo-Ann. *Commonweal.* June 1, 1984: 345. Rev. of *In Search of Our Mothers' Gardens.*

3829 Murray, G.E. *Fiction International.* 6–7 1976: 171–172. Rev. of *Meridian.*

3830 Naylor, Carolyn. *Black Scholar.* 13.2–3 Spr. 1982: 84–85. Rev. of *You Can't Keep a Good Woman Down.*

3831 Nedelhaft, Ruth. "Domestic violence in literature: a preliminary study." *Mosaic.* 17.2 Spr. 1984: 242–259. On *The Color Purple.*

3832 Norment, Lynn. "*The Color Purple:* controversial prize-winning book becomes an equally controversial movie." *Ebony.* 41.4 Feb. 1986: 146, 148, 150, 155.

3833 Nowak, Hanna. "Alice Walker: poetry celebrating life." In HASL: 111–125.

3834 Nowik, Nan. "Mixing art and politics: the writings of Adrienne Rich, Marge Piercy, and Alice Walker." *Centennial Rev.* 30.2 Spr. 1986: 208–218.

3835 Parker-Smith, Bettye J. "Alice Walker's women: in search of some peace of mind." In EVAN: 478–493. On several works.

3836 Piercy, Marge. "The little nuances of history." *Book World (Washington Post).* May 31, 1981: 11. Rev. of *You Can't Keep a Good Woman Down.*

3837 Piercy, Marge. *N.Y. Times Book Rev.* May 23, 1976: 5, 12. Rev. of *Meridian.*

3838 Pinckney, Darryl. "Black victims, Black villains." *N.Y. Rev. of Books.* Jan. 29, 1987: 17–20. On *The Color Purple.*

3839 Pollitt, Katha. "Stretching the short story." *N.Y. Times Book Rev.* May 24, 1981: 9, 15. Rev. of *You Can't Keep a Good Woman Down.*

3840 Prescott, Peter S. "A long road to liberation." *Newsweek.* June 21, 1982: 67–68. Rev. of *The Color Purple.*

3841 Pryse, Marjorie. "Zora Neale Hurston, Alice Walker, and the 'ancient power' of Black women." In PRYS: 1–24. On the influence of Black women fiction writers on women's literary criticism.

3842 Randall-Tsuruta, Dorothy. *Black Scholar.* 14.3–4 Sum. 1983: 54–55. Rev. of *The Color Purple.*

3843 Rhodes, Jewell Parker. *America.* Feb. 25, 1984: 137–138. Rev. of *In Search of Our Mothers' Gardens.*

3844 Rogers, Norma. *Freedomways.* 16.2 1976: 120–122. Rev. of *Meridian.*

3845 Rose, Pat. "Growing books at Wild Trees Press." *Small Press.* 4.2 Nov.-Dec. 1986: 30–35. The success of Walker and Robert Allen on the small press they established in California.

3846 Rosenberg, L.M. *N.Y. Times Book Rev.* Apr. 7, 1985: 12. Rev. of *Horses Make a Landscape Look More Beautiful.*

3847 Royster, Philip M. "In search of our fathers' arms: Alice Walker's persona of the alienated darling." *Black Amer. Lit. Forum.* 20.4 Wint. 1986: 347–370.

3848 Rumens, Carol. "Heirs to the dream." *Times (London) Literary Suppl.* June 18, 1982: 676. Revs. of *Meridian* and *You Can't Keep a Good Woman Down.*

3849 Sadoff, Dianne F. "Black matrilineage: the case of Alice Walker and Zora Neale Hurston." *Signs.* 11.1 Aut. 1985: 4–26.

3850 Shelton, Frank W. "Alienation and integration in Alice Walker's *The Color Purple.*" *CLA J.* 28.4 June 1985: 382–392.

3851 Smith, Barbara. "Sexual oppression unmasked." *Callaloo.* 7.3 1984: 170–176. On *The Color Purple.*

3852 Smith, Cynthia J. "Black fiction by Black females." *Cross Currents.* 26.3 Fall 1976: 340–343. Has a rev. of *Meridian.*

3853 Smith, Dinitia. "'Celie, you a tree'." *Nation.* Sept. 4, 1982: 181–183. Rev. of *The Color Purple.*

3854 Stade, George. "Womanist fiction and male characters." *Partisan Rev.* 52.3 1985: 264–270. On *The Color Purple.*

3855 Stein, Karen F. "*Meridian:* Alice Walker's critique of revolution." *Black Amer. Lit. Forum.* 20.1–2 Spr.–Sum. 1986: 129–141.

3856 Steinem, Gloria. "Do you know this woman? She knows you: a profile of Alice Walker." *Ms.* 10.12 June 1982: 35, 37, 89–90, 92–94.

3857 Tate, Claudia. "Alice Walker." In TATE: 175–187. On several works.

3858 Tavormina, M. Teresa. "Dressing the spirit: clothworking and language in *The Color Purple.*" *J. of Narrative Technique.* 16 1986: 220–230.

3859 Towers, Robert. "Good men are hard to find." *N.Y. Rev. of Books.* Aug. 12, 1982: 35–36. On *Meridian* and *The Color Purple.*

3860 Turner, Darwin. "A spectrum of Blackness." *Parnassus.* 4.2 Spr.–Sum. 1976: 202–218. Compares Walker's *Revolutionary Petunias* with two works by Ishmael Reed.

3861 Twum-Akwaboah, Edward. In MA82: 976–980. On *You Can't Keep a Good Woman Down.*

3862 Vigderman, Patricia. "From rags to rage to art." *Nation.* Dec. 17, 1983: 635, 637–638. Rev. of *In Search of Our Mothers' Gardens.*

3863 Wade-Gayles, Gloria. "Giving birth to self: the quests for wholeness of Sula Mae Peace and Meridian Hill." In WADE: 184–215.

3864 Walker, Cam. *Southern Exposure.* 5.1 Spr. 1977: 102–103. On *Meridian* and *The Third Life of Grange Copeland.*

3865 Walker, Robbie J. "Coping strategies of the women in Alice Walker's novels: implications for survival." *CLA J.* 30.4 June 1987: 401–418.

3866 Walsh, Margaret. "The enchanted world of *The Color Purple.*" *Southern Q.* 25 1987: 89–101.

3867 Washington, Mary Helen. "An essay on Alice Walker." In BELL: 133–149. On the short stories "The child who favored daughter," "A sudden trip home in the spring," and the poem "For my sister Molly who in the fifties."

3868 Washington, Mary Helen. "Her mother's gifts." *Ms.* 10.12 June 1982: 38. On Walker's relationship with her mother.

3869 Washington, Mary Helen. "I sign my mother's name: Alice Walker, Dorothy West, Paule Marshall." In PERR: 144–150. On several works.

3870 Watkins, Mel. "Some letters went to God." *N.Y. Times Book Rev.* July 25, 1982: 7. Rev. of *The Color Purple.*

3871 Wesley, Richard. "*The Color Purple:* debate, reading between the lines." *Ms.* 15.3 Sept. 1986: 62, 90–92. On the movie version.

3872 Williamson, Alan. "In a middle style." *Poetry.* 135.6 Mar. 1980: 353–354. On *Good Night, Willie Lee. . . .*

3873 Willis, Susan. "Alice Walker's women." In WILL: 110–128. On *Meridian, The Third Life of Grange Copeland,* and *The Color Purple.*

3874 Willis, Susan. "Alice Walker's women." *New Orleans Rev.* 12.1 Spr. 1985: 33–41.

3875 Wilson, Geraldine L. "Another look at *The Color Purple.*" *Interracial Books for Children Bull.* 17.2 1986: 20–21. On the movie version.

3876 Wilson, Judith. *Essence.* 10.8 Dec. 1979: 16. Rev. of *Good Night, Willie Lee. . . .*

3877 Wilson, Judith. *Essence.* 12.3 July 1981: 17. Rev. of *You Can't Keep a Good Woman Down.*

3878 Winchell, Mark Royden. "Fetching the doctor: shamanistic house calls in Alice Walker's 'Strong horse tea'." *Mississippi Folklore Register.* 15.2 Fall 1981: 97–101.

3879 Worthington, P. "Writing a rationale for a controversial common reading book: Alice Walker's *The Color Purple.*" *English J.* 74.1 Jan. 1985: 48–52.

Margaret Walker (Alexander) (1915–)

Essays
3880 "On being female, Black, and free." In STER: 95–106.

3881 "Some aspects of the Black aesthetic." *Freedomways.* 16.2 1976: 95–102.

Non-Fiction
3882 *Richard Wright, Daemonic Genius: A Portrait of the Man, a Critical Look at His Work.* NY: Amistad, 1985.

Novel
3883 "*Jubilee* [Excerpt]." In ABBO: 599–614. *Jubilee* was published in 1966.

Poetry
3884 "Ballad of the hoppy-toad." In STET: 98–99.

3885 "Birmingham 1963." *Southern Rev.* 21.3 July 1985: 829.

3886 "Black paramour." *Southern Rev.* 21.3 July 1985: 828–829.

3887 "Childhood." In LONG: 438.

3888 "Fanfare, coda, and finale." In BARA: 372–373.

3889 "Five Black men." In BARA: 363–368.

3890 "For Gwen—1969." In FISH: 249–250.

3891 "For Malcolm X." In ADOF: 181–182.

3892 "For my people." *Ebony.* 35.11 Sept. 1980: 151. Originally written in 1937.

3893 "For my people." In ADOF: 248–250.

3894 "For my people." In BLIC: 272–274.

3895 "Girl held without bail." In ADOF: 194–195.
3896 "Girl held without bail." In HOFF: 201.
3897 "I hear a rumbling." *Great Lakes Rev.* 8–9.2–1 Fall 1982–Spr. 1983: 96–98.
3898 "I hear a rumbling." In BARA: 369–371.
3899 "I want to write." In FISH: 249.
3900 "Inflation blues." *Black Scholar.* 11.5 May–June 1980: 74.
3901 "Kissie Lee." In STET: 95–96.
3902 "Lineage." In ADOF: 26.
3903 "Lineage." In BELL: 339.
3904 "Lineage." In HOFF: 50.
3905 "Lineage." In STET: 94.
3906 "Memory." In LONG: 437.
3907 "Molly Means." In STET: 96–97.
3908 "My Mississippi spring." *Southern Rev.* 21.3 July 1985: 827.
3909 "My truth and my flame." In BARA: 361.
3910 "Southern song." In LONG: 437.
3911 "Street demonstration." In ADOF: 194.
3912 "They have put us on hold." *Black Scholar.* 12.5 Sept.–Oct. 1981: 25.
3913 "This is my century . . . Black synthesis of time." In BARA: 361–363.
3914 "Tribute to Robert Hayden, February 1980." *Black Scholar.* 11.4 Mar.–Apr. 1980: 75.
3915 "We have been believers." In LONG: 438–439.

Summary of Novel

3916 Southgate, Robert L. In SOUT: 103–104. Summary of *Jubilee* (1966).

Textual Criticism and Interviews

3917 Barksdale, Richard K. "Margaret Walker: folk orature and historical prophecy." In MILP: 104–117.
3918 Bell, Bernard W. "Margaret Abigail Walker." In BELL: 285–290.
3919 Cary, Meredith. "Ethnic alternatives." In CARY: 120–132. Criticism on *Jubilee.*
3920 Collier, Eugenia. "Fields watered with blood: myth and ritual in the poetry of Margaret Walker." In EVAN: 499–510.
3921 Egejuru, Phanuel and Robert Elliot Fox. "An interview with Margaret Walker." *Callaloo.* 2.2 1979: 29–35.
3922 Freibert, Lucy M. "Southern song: an interview with Margaret Walker." *Frontiers.* 9.3 1987: 50–56.
3923 Gwin, Minrose C. "*Jubilee:* the Black woman's celebration of human community." In GWIN: 151–170. Expanded version of the article that appears in anthology PRYS (see next citation).
3924 Gwin, Minrose C. "*Jubilee:* the Black woman's celebration of human community." In PRYS: 132–150.
3925 Klotman, Phyllis Rauch. "'Oh freedom'—women and history in Margaret Walker's *Jubilee.*" *Black Amer. Lit. Forum.* 11.4 Wint. 1977: 139–145.
3926 Miller, R. Baxter. "The 'etched flame' of Margaret Walker: biblical and literary re-creation in southern history." In ENSO: 157–172.

3927 Miller, R. Baxter. "The 'intricate design' of Margaret Walker: literary and biblical re-creation in southern history." In MILP: 118–135.

3928 "A Mississippi 'jubilee' for Margaret Walker Alexander." *Ebony.* 35.11 Sept. 1980: 146–148, 150–151. Mostly photographs.

3929 Noble, Jeanne. In NOBL: 177–179. On several works.

3930 Powell, Bertie J. "The Black experience in Margaret Walker's *Jubilee* and Lorraine Hansberry's *The Drinking Gourd.*" *CLA J.* 21.2 Dec. 1977: 304–311.

3931 Scarupa, Harriet Jackson. "Margaret Walker Alexander." *Amer. Visions.* 1.2 Mar.–Apr. 1986: 48–52. About her life and writings.

3932 Spillers, Hortense J. "A hateful passion, a lost love." *Feminist Studies.* 9.2 Sum. 1983: 293–323. On Toni Morrison's *Sula,* Margaret Walker's *Jubilee,* and Zora Neale Hurston's *Their Eyes Were Watching God.*

3933 Traylor, Eleanor. "Music as theme: the blues mode in the works of Margaret Walker." In EVAN: 511–525.

Michele Wallace (1952–)

Biographical Essay
3934 "Baby Faith." *Ms.* 16.1–2 July–Aug. 1987: 154, 156, 216.

Non-Fiction
3935 *Black Macho and the Myth of the Superwoman.* NY: Dial, 1978.

Short Fiction
3936 "The envelope." *Essence.* 14.4 Aug. 1983: 93–94.

3937 "The envelope." In BARA: 374–377.

3938 "The storyteller." *Essence.* 14.8 Dec. 1983: 72–74, 134.

Textual Criticism and Interviews
3939 Boorstein, Karen. "Beyond *Black Macho:* an interview with Michele Wallace." *Black Amer. Lit. Forum.* 18.4 Wint. 1984: 163–167.

3940 Gillespie, Marcia Ann. "Macho myths and Michele Wallace." *Essence.* 10.4 Aug. 1979: 76–77, 99–100, 102.

3941 Jordan, June. *N.Y. Times Book Rev.* Mar. 18, 1979: 15. Rev. of *Black Macho and the Myth of the Superwoman.*

3942 Powell, Linda C. *Conditions 5.* 2.2 Aut. 1979: 165–172. Rev. of *Black Macho and the Myth of the Superwoman.*

3943 Thomas, Arthur E. In THOM: 115–127. An interview.

Mildred Pitts Walter

Children's Stories
3944 *Because We Are.* NY: Lothrop, Lee and Shepard, 1983.

3945 *Brother to the Wind.* NY: Lothrop, Lee and Shepard, 1985.

3946 *The Girl on the Outside.* NY: Lothrop, Lee and Shepard, 1982.

3947 *Justin and the Best Biscuits in the World.* NY: Lothrop, Lee and Shepard, 1986.

3948 *My Mama Needs Me.* NY: Lothrop, Lee and Shepard, 1983.

3949 *Trouble's Child.* NY: Lothrop, Lee and Shepard, 1985.

3950 *TY's One-Man Band.* NY: Four Winds, 1980.

Textual Criticism

3951 Carothers, Suzanne C. *Interracial Books for Children Bull.* 15.3 1984: 19. Rev. of *Because We Are.*

3952 Draper, Charlotte W. *Horn Book.* 61.3 May–June 1985: 446. Rev. of *Brother to the Wind.*

3953 Draper, Charlotte W. *Horn Book.* 61.6 Nov.–Dec. 1985: 744. Rev. of *Trouble's Child.*

3954 Wilson, Geraldine L. *Interracial Books for Children Bull.* 14.3-4 1983: 36-37. Rev. of *The Girl on the Outside.*

3955 Wilson, Geraldine L. *Interracial Books for Children Bull.* 14.5 1983: 26-27. Rev. of *My Mama Needs Me.*

Marilyn Nelson Waniek (1946–)

Children's Poetry

3956 Espeland, Pamela and Marilyn Waniek. *The Cat Walked Through the Casserole and Other Poems for Children.* Minneapolis: Carolrhoda, 1984.

Poetry

3957 "Animals who remember." *Georgia Rev.* 32.4 Wint. 1978: 866.

3958 "The century quilt." *Southern Rev.* 21.3 July 1985: 825-826.

3959 "Dinosaur spring." In SMTD: 743-745.

3960 "The dream lover." *Essence.* 14.10 Feb. 1984: 139.

3961 *For the Body: Poems.* Baton Rouge: Louisiana State Univ., 1978.

3962 "For the dead one." *Crisis.* 83.5 May 1976: 148.

3963 "Friday night." *Portland Rev.* 30.1 1984: 154. Translation of a poem by Ralf Thenior.

3964 "The goose invited all the pigs." *Carleton Miscellany.* 18.2 Sum. 1980: 5.

3965 "Herbs in the attic." *Georgia Rev.* 33.4 Wint. 1979: 898.

3966 "Herbs in the attic." In SMTD: 745-746.

3967 "I decide not to have children." *Georgia Rev.* 32.1 Spr. 1978: 44.

3968 "I imagine driving across country." *Hudson Rev.* 31.1 Spr. 1978: 114.

3969 "I send mama home." *Southern Rev.* 21.3 July 1985: 823-825.

3970 "It's all in your head." *Georgia Rev.* 37.4 Wint. 1983: 787-789.

3971 "Light under the door." In SMTD: 740-742.

3972 "Light under the door." *Ohio Rev.* 28 1982: 46-47.

3973 "Like a forgotten dream." *Crisis.* 87.4 Apr. 1980: 151.

3974 "Little Cloud." *Carleton Miscellany.* 18.2 Sum. 1980: 5.

3975 "Mama's promise." *Southern Rev.* 21.3 July 1985: 821-823.

3976 *Mama's Promises: Poems.* Baton Rouge, Louisiana State Univ., 1985.

3977 "My Grandfather walks in the woods." *Hudson Rev.* 31.1 Spr. 1978: 115.
3978 "Naming the animal." *Carleton Miscellany.* 17.2–3 Spr. 1979: 174.
3979 "Night harvest." *Carleton Miscellany.* 17.2–3 Spr. 1979: 175.
3980 "Old bibles." In SMTD: 739–740.
3981 "Other women's children." *Georgia Rev.* 32.1 Spr. 1978: 45.
3982 "Poem with sixteen names." *Crisis.* 85.9 Nov. 1978: 310.
3983 "Poor old blue Monday." *Carleton Miscellany.* 18.2 Sum. 1980: 6.
3984 "A strange beautiful woman." *Crisis.* 87.4 Apr. 1980: 151.
3985 "To my father." *Crisis.* 83.5 May 1976: 148.
3986 "The winter's cold in Norway." *Carleton Miscellany.* 18.2 Sum. 1980: 5.
3987 "Women's locker room." In SMTD: 742–743.

Textual Criticism
3988 Mberi, A.S.K. *Freedomways.* 19.2 1979: 107–108. Rev. of *For the Body: Poems.*

Translation
3989 Waniek, Marilyn N. and Pamela Espeland, Trans. *Hundreds of Hens and Other Poems for Children: Translations from the Works of Danish Poet Halfdan Wedel Rasmussen.* Minneapolis: Black Willow, 1982.

Watkins, Gloria *see* Hooks, Bell

Leona N. Welch (1942–)

Drama
3990 "Hands in the mirror." In OSTR: 267–273.

Kariamu Welsh (Carole Kariamu Welsh)

Autobiography
3991 "I'm not that strong." *Essence.* 9.10 Feb. 1979: 39.

Editing
3992 Asante, Molefi Kete and Kariamu Welsh Asante, Eds. *African Culture: The Rhythms of Unity.* Westport, CT: Greenwood, 1985. Articles by twelve well-known scholars on the intellectual history of people of African heritage.

Poetry
3993 "Sudeka 1." *Obsidian.* 5.3 Wint. 1979: 101.
3994 "Sudeka 2." *Obsidian.* 5.3 Wint. 1979: 102.
3995 "Sudeka 3." *Obsidian.* 5.3 Wint. 1979: 102–103.
3996 "Sudeka 4." *Obsidian.* 5.3 Wint. 1979: 103–104.
3997 "Textured women." *Obsidian.* 5.3 Wint. 1979: 104–105.
3998 *Textured Women, Cowrie Shells and Beetle Sticks: Poems.* Buffalo: Amulefi, 1978.

Short Fiction
3999 "God bless the cook." *Essence.* 12.1 May 1981: 106, 170.
4000 "She was Linda before she was Ayesha." *Essence.* 11.6 Oct. 1980: 106, 167, 171.

Dorothy West

Essay
4001 "My mother, Rachel West." In WASA: 381–384.

Novel
4002 "Cleo." In WASA: 354–380. Excerpt from her novel *The Living Is Easy* (1948).

Summary of Novel
4003 Southgate, Robert L. In SOUT: 108–109. Summary of *The Living Is Easy*.

Textual Criticism
4004 Bowen, Angela. "The literary traditions of Black women." *Sojourner.* 9.10 June 1984: 21.
4005 Perry, Margaret. In PERM: 130–134. On several works.
4006 Wade-Gayles, Gloria. "The truths of our mothers' lives: mother-daughter relationships in Black women's fiction." *Sage.* 1.2 Fall 1984: 8–12. West's *The Living Is Easy* compared to Paule Marshall's *Brown Girl, Brownstones* and Toni Morrison's *The Bluest Eye.*
4007 Washington, Mary Helen. "I sign my mother's name: Alice Walker, Dorothy West, Paule Marshall." In PERR: 144–150.
4008 Washington, Mary Helen. "I sign my mother's name: maternal power in Dorothy West's novel, *The Living Is Easy.*" In WASA: 344–353.
4009 Washington, Mary Helen. "'Infidelity becomes her': the ambivalent woman in the fiction of Ann Petry and Dorothy West." In WASA: 297–306.

Phillis Wheatley (1753–1784)

Bibliography
4010 Inge, M. Thomas, *et al.* In INGE: 6–15. Bibliographical essays, including sections on editions, manuscripts and letters, biography, and criticism.
4011 Robinson, William H. *Phillis Wheatley: A Bio-Bibliography.* Boston: G.K. Hall, 1981.

Biography
4012 Richmond, Merle. *Phillis Wheatley.* NY: Chelsea House, 1987. Children's book. Has bibliography, chronology, and index.

Miscellaneous

4013 Jensen, Marilyn. *Phillis Wheatley: Negro Slave of Mr. John Wheatley.* Scarsdale, NY: Lion, 1987. A biographical novel based on Wheatley's life.

Poetry

4014 "Liberty and peace, a poem." In STET: 13.

4015 "On being brought from Africa to America." In GILN: 133.

4016 "On being brought from Africa to America." In LONG: 18.

4017 "On imagination." In LONG: 15–16.

4018 "On imagination." In STET: 16–17.

4019 "To a gentleman and lady on the death of the lady's brother and sister, and a child of the name Avis, aged one year." In STET: 14–15.

4020 "To S.M. a young African painter, on seeing his work." In STET: 15–16.

4021 "To the Right Honorable William, Earl of Dartmouth, His Majesty's Principal Secretary of State for North America, etc." In GILN: 134–135.

4022 "To the University of Cambridge, in New England." In LONG: 17–18.

Textual Criticism

4023 Gates, Henry Louis, Jr. "Phillis Wheatley and the nature of the Negro." In GATP: 61–79.

4024 Isani, Mukhtar Ali. "Early versions of some works by Phillis Wheatley." *Early Amer. Lit.* 14.2 Fall 1979: 149–155.

4025 Isani, Mukhtar Ali. "'An elegy on leaving ----': a new poem by Phillis Wheatley." *Amer. Lit.* 58.4 Dec. 1986: 609–613.

4026 Isani, Mukhtar Ali. "The first proposed edition of *Poems on Various Subjects* and the Phillis Wheatley Canon." *Amer. Lit.* 49.1 Mar. 1977: 97–103.

4027 Isani, Mukhtar Ali. "'Gambia on my soul': Africa and the African in the writings of Phillis Wheatley." *Melus.* 6.1 Spr. 1979: 64–72.

4028 Isani, Mukhtar Ali. "The Methodist connection: new variants of some Phillis Wheatley poems." *Early Amer. Lit.* 22.1 Spr. 1987: 108–113.

4029 Isani, Mukhtar Ali. "The original version of Wheatley's 'On the death of Dr. Samuel Marshall'." *Studies in Black Lit.* 7.3 Aut. 1976: 20.

4030 Jordan, June. "The difficult miracle of Black poetry in America or something like a sonnet for Phillis Wheatley." *Massachusetts Rev.* 27.2 Sum. 1986: 252–262.

4031 Lapsansky, Phil. "'Deism'—an unpublished poem by Phillis Wheatley." *New England Q.* 50.3 Sept. 1977: 517–520. Commentary on the poem, which is reprinted in the article.

4032 Levernier, James A. "On her poem 'On being brought from Africa to America'." *Explicator.* 40.1 Fall 1981: 25–26.

4033 Nielsen, A.L. "Patterns of subversion in the works of Phillis Wheatley and Jupiter Hammon." *Western J. of Black Studies.* 6.4 Wint. 1982: 212–219.

4034 Noble, Jeanne. In NOBL: 150–153. Biography and general criticism.

4035 O'Neale, Sondra. "A slave's subtle war: Phillis Wheatley's use of biblical myth and symbol." *Early Amer. Lit.* 21.2 Fall 1986: 144–165.

4036 Ogunyemi, Chikwenye Okonjo. "Phillis Wheatley: the modest beginning." *Studies in Black Lit.* 7.3 Aut. 1976: 16-19.

4037 Robinson, William H., Ed. *Critical Essays on Phillis Wheatley.* Boston: G.K. Hall, 1982.

4038 Robinson, William H. In ROBI: 26-62. On several works.

4039 Robinson, William H. *Phillis Wheatley and Her Writings.* NY: Garland, 1984.

4040 Robinson, William H. "Phillis Wheatley in London." *CLA J.* 21.2 Dec. 1977: 187-201.

4041 Rogal, Samuel J. "Phillis Wheatley's Methodist connection." *Black Amer. Lit. Forum.* 21.1-2 Spr.-Sum. 1987: 85-95.

4042 Scheick, William J. "Phillis Wheatley and Oliver Goldsmith: a fugitive satire." *Early Amer. Lit.* 19.1 Spr. 1984: 82-84.

4043 Shields, John C. "Phillis Wheatley and Mather Byles." *CLA J.* 23.4 June 1980: 377-390.

4044 Shields, John C. "Phillis Wheatley's use of classicism." *Amer. Lit.* 52.1 Mar. 1980: 97-111.

4045 Sistrunk, Albertha. "Phillis Wheatley: an eighteenth-century Black American poet revisited." *CLA J.* 23.4 June 1980: 391-398.

4046 Steele, Thomas J., S.J. "The figure of Columbia: Phillis Wheatley plus George Washington." *New England Q.* 54.2 1981: 264-266.

Paulette Childress White (1948-)

Poetry
4047 "Big Maybelle." In SIMC: 99.
4048 "Humbled rocks." In SIMC: 98.
4049 *Lost Your Mama.* Detroit: Lotus, 1977. Blacksongs Series 1.
4050 "Say that I am." In SIMC: 68.
4051 *The Watermelon Dress: Portrait of a Woman: Poems and Illustrations.* Detroit: Lotus, 1984.

Short Fiction
4052 "Alice." *Essence.* 7.9 Jan. 1977: 68-69.
4053 "Alice." In BELL: 352-354.
4054 "Alice." In WASH: 8-11.
4055 "The bird cage." In WASH: 33-41.
4056 "The bird cage." *Redbook.* 151.2 June 1978: 114-115.
4057 "Paper man." *Michigan Q. Rev.* 25.2 Spr. 1986: 329-332. Excerpt from a work in progress.

Textual Criticism
4058 Brown, Beth. *CLA J.* 29.2 Dec. 1985: 250-252. Rev. of *The Watermelon Dress.*

Electa Wiley

Poetry
    4059 "The week." *New Orleans Rev.* 5.1 1976: 58.

Brenda Wilkinson (1946–)

Children's Stories
    4060 *Ludell and Willie.* NY: Harper, 1977.
    4061 *Ludell's New York Time.* NY: Harper, 1980.
    4062 *Not Separate, Not Equal.* NY: Harper, 1987.

Textual Criticism
    4063 Commire, Anne. In CO14: 250–252. Biographical information included.
    4064 Holtze, Sally Holmes. In HOLT: 324–325. Biographical information included.
    4065 King, Cynthia. *N.Y. Times Book Rev.* Feb. 22, 1976: 16, 18. Rev. of *Ludell* (1975).
    4066 McHargue, Georgess. *N.Y. Times Book Rev.* May 22, 1977: 29. Rev. of *Ludell and Willie.*
    4067 Spence, Patricia Ann. *Interracial Books for Children Bull.* 7.1 1976: 14–15. Rev. of *Ludell.*
    4068 Wilson, Geraldine L. *Interracial Books for Children Bull.* 12.2 1981: 18–19. Rev. of *Ludell's New York Time.*

Anita J. Williams

Drama
    4069 "A Christmas story." In OSTR: 303–309.

Elsie Arrington Williams

Poetry
    4070 "Academic evaporation." *Obsidian.* 7.2–3 Sum.–Wint. 1981: 204.
    4071 "A lady." *Obsidian.* 7.2–3 Sum.–Wint. 1981: 205.
    4072 "Suburbia spoke to us last night." *Obsidian.* 7.2–3 Sum.–Wint. 1981: 205.
    4073 "The teacher will come." *Obsidian.* 7.2–3 Sum.–Wint. 1981: 204.

June Vanleer Williams

Poetry
    4074 *Will the Real You Please Stand Up?: Poetry.* Bryn Mawr, PA: Dorrance, 1983.

Lorna V. Williams

Short Fiction
4075 *Jamaica Mento.* St. Clair, Trinidad and Tobago: Publishing Associates, 1978.
4076 "The word is love." In BELL: 322-327.

Lucy Ariel Williams (1905-)

Poetry
4077 "Northboun'." In STET: 57.

Williams, Paulette L. *see* Shange, Ntozake

Regina Williams

Poetry
4078 "Asylum." In BARA: 378-379.
4079 "For our life is a matter of faith." In BARA: 379-380.
4080 "I am not my sister's keeper: I am my sister." In BARA: 381-382.
4081 "Uncle Henry's conjugal visits." *Black Amer. Lit. Forum.* 14.4 Wint. 1980: 171.

Sherley Anne Williams (1944-)

Drama
4082 "Letters from a New England Negro." *Callaloo.* 5.2 1979: 1-16.
4083 "Letters from a New England Negro." *Iowa Rev.* 11.4 1980: 149-188.

Essays
4084 "Anonymous in America." *Boundary 2.* 6.2 Wint. 1978: 435-442.
4085 "The blues roots of contemporary Afro-American poetry." In FISS: 72-87.
4086 "The blues roots of contemporary Afro-American poetry." In HARP: 123-135.
4087 "The blues roots of contemporary Afro-American poetry." *Massachusetts Rev.* 18.3 Aut. 1977: 542-554. With comments by Lucille Clifton, pages 551-554.
4088 "Papa Dick and Sister-Woman: reflections on women in the fiction of Richard Wright." In FLEI: 394-415.

Foreword
4089 Hurston, Zora Neale. *Their Eyes Were Watching God.* Urbana: Univ. of Illinois, 1978. Foreword appears on pages v-xv.

Novel
4090 *Dessa Rose.* NY: Morrow, 1986.

Poetry
4091 "Any woman's blues." In FISH: 289–290.

4092 "Becky start the stories." *Nimrod.* 21–22.2–1 1977: 308.

4093 "The collateral adjective." In FISH: 290.

4094 "Driving wheel." In STET: 260–264.

4095 "The empress brand trim: Ruby reminisces." In STET: 253–254.

4096 "Generations." In FISH: 291–293.

4097 "Generations." *Nimrod.* 21–22.2–1 1977: 305.

4098 "The house of desire." *Essence.* 14.9 Jan. 1984: 112.

4099 "The house of desire." In STET: 255–260.

4100 "I contemplate insanity." *Nimrod.* 21–22.2–1 1977: 306.

4101 "I want Aretha to set this to music." *Second Coming.* 11.1–2 1983: 221.

4102 "The iconography of childhood [excerpts]." In BARA: 383–386.

4103 "Juneteenth: the bicentennial poem." *Black Scholar.* 8.5 Mar. 1977: 36–39.

4104 "Miss Abinetha." *Partisan Rev.* 43.1 1976: 84.

4105 "More straight talk from plain women." *Nimrod.* 21–22.2–1 1977: 307.

4106 "Oral history project." *Callaloo.* 9.1 Wint. 1986: 127–129.

4107 "A record for my friends." In BARA: 388–390.

4108 "Say hello to John." In FISH: 291.

4109 "Say hello to John." In STET: 254–255.

4110 *Some One Sweet Angel Chile.* NY: Morrow, 1982.

4111 "Someone sweet angel child." In HARP: 117–122.

4112 "Someone sweet angel child." *Massachusetts Rev.* 18.3 Aut. 1977: 567–572.

4113 "Soul saga." *Amer. Poetry Rev.* 7.3 May–June 1978: 16–18.

4114 "Straight talk from plain women." *Essence.* 14.6 Oct. 1983: 89.

4115 "Straight talk from plain women." *Nimrod.* 21–22.2–1 1977: 307.

4116 "Tellin the hundred." *Nimrod.* 21–22.2–1 1977: 308.

4117 "This city-light." In BARA: 390–391.

4118 "The wishon line." In BARA: 392–393.

4119 "You were never Miss Brown to me." In BARA: 386–387.

Short Fiction
4120 "The Lawd don't like ugly." In KOPB: 242–264.

4121 "Meditations on history." In WASH: 200–248. Has biographical headnote.

Textual Criticism and Interviews
4122 Bass, George H. *Langston Hughes Rev.* 5.2 1986: 41–44. Rev. of *Dessa Rose.*

4123 Bradley, D. *N.Y. Times Book Rev.* Aug. 3, 1986: 7. Rev. of *Dessa Rose.*

4124 Brown, Beth. *CLA J.* 25.3 Mar. 1982: 365–367. Rev. of *Some One Sweet Angel Chile.*

4125 Davenport, Doris. *Black Amer. Lit. Forum.* 20.3 Fall 1986: 335–340. Rev. of *Dessa Rose.*

4126 Foster, Frances Smith. "The line converges here." *Callaloo.* 5.2 1979: 151–152. Rev. of *The Peacock Poems* (1975).

4127 Gillespie, Marcia. "The seraglio, the plantation—intrigue and survival." *Ms.* 15.3 Sept. 1986: 20–21. Rev. of *Dessa Rose.*

4128 Holt, Elvin. In MA87: 207–211. Rev. of *Dessa Rose.*

4129 Howard, Lillie. "Sherley Anne Williams." In DL41: 343–350. Some biographical information and additional bibliography included.

4130 Kelly, Ernece B. *CLA J.* 30.4 June 1987: 515–518. Rev. of *Dessa Rose.*

4131 Tate, Claudia. "Sherley Anne Williams." In TATE: 205–213. An interview.

4132 Wallace, Michele. *Women's Rev. of Books.* 4.1 Oct. 1986: 1, 3–4. Rev. of *Dessa Rose.*

Geraldine L. Wilson

Non-Fiction

4133 *An Annotated Bibliography of Children's Picture Books: An Introduction to the Literature of Head Start's Children.* Washington: U.S. Department of Health, Education, and Welfare, Office of Human Development Services, 1978.

Poetry

4134 "Love rising." *Essence.* 14.6 Oct. 1983: 88.

4135 "Our children are our children." In BARA: 394–395.

4136 "Refugee mother." In BARA: 394.

Harriet E. Wilson (1828–1863)

Autobiographical Novel

4137 *Our Nig* [Excerpt]. In GILN: 835–839. The work was published originally in 1859.

Textual Criticism

4138 Bell, Bernard W. "Harriet E. Wilson." In BELA: 45–50. On *Our Nig.*

4139 Foster, Frances Smith. "Adding color and contour to early American self-portraitures: autobiographical writings of Afro-American women." In PRYS: 25–38.

4140 Gates, Henry Louis, Jr. "Parallel discursive universes: fictions of the self in Harriet E. Wilson's *Our Nig.*" In GATP: 125–163. Pages 150–163 contain an extensive plot summary of the work with a concurrent chronological biography of the author (prepared by David A. Curtis).

4141 Jefferson, Margo. *Ms.* 12.2 Aug. 1983: 34–35. Rev. of a reissue of *Our Nig; Or, Sketches from the Life of a Free Black, in a Two-Story White House, North. Showing That Slavery's Shadows Fall Even There,* by *"Our Nig."* (Henry Louis Gates, Jr., Ed., NY: Vintage, 1983.)

4142 Jefferson, Margo. *Nation.* May 28, 1983: 675–677. Rev. of the 1983 reissue of *Our Nig.*
4143 Wansley, Joyce. "Pages." *People Weekly.* Sept. 12, 1983: 115–116. Rev. of the reissue of *Our Nig.*

Betty Winston

Novel
4144 *The Africans.* Wayne, PA: Banbury, 1983.
4145 *The Africans* [Excerpt]. *Essence.* 14.6 Oct. 1983: 79–80, 165–166.

Witherspoon, Jill *see* Boyer, Jill Witherspoon

Witherspoon, Naomi Long *see* Madgett, Naomi Long

Barbara Woods

Textual Criticism
4146 Harris, Trudier. "The militants: Barbara Woods, "The Final Supper" (1970), Ted Shine, *Contribution* (1968), Ed Bullins, *The Gentleman Caller* (1969)." In HARS: 155–179. "The Final Supper" appears in *Ten Times Black: Stories from the Black Experience* (Julian Mayfield, Ed. NY: Bantam, 1972), pages 104–105.

Sarah E. Wright (1928–)

Essay
4147 "Black writers' views of America." *Freedomways.* 19.3 1979: 161–162.

Novel
4148 *This Child's Gonna Live* [Excerpt]. *Black Scholar.* 18.4–5 July–Aug.–Sept.–Oct. 1987: 2–9.

Summary of Novel
4149 Southgate, Robert L. In SOUT: 168–170. Summary of *This Child's Gonna Live* (1969).

Textual Criticism
4150 Guilford, Virginia B. "Sarah Elizabeth Wright." In DL33: 293–300. Includes biographical information and additional bibliography.
4151 Harris, Trudier. "Three Black women writers and humanism: a folk perspective." In MILL: 50–74. On Wright's *This Child's Gonna Live,* Alice Walker's *The Third Life of Grange Copeland,* and Paule Marshall's *The Chosen Place, the Timeless People.*

4152 Mickelson, Anne Z. "Winging upward: Black women: Sarah E. Wright, Toni Morrison, Alice Walker." In MICK: 112-124. Contains commentary on *This Child's Gonna Live.*

4153 Redmond, Eugene. In REDM: 335-336. On several works.

Camille Yarbrough

Biography
4154 McCray, Chirlayne. "Camille Yarbrough." *Essence.* 9.5 Sept. 1978: 14. In the column "Essence women."

Children's Stories
4155 *Cornrows.* NY: Putnam, 1979.

4156 *The Little Tree Growin' in the Shade.* NY: Putnam, 1987.

Textual Criticism
4157 Gilbert, Gwen. *Black Books Bull.* 6.4 1980: 86-87. Rev. of *Cornrows.*

4158 Julian, Bea. *Encore Amer. and Worldwide News.* 9.9 Dec. 1981: 37. Rev. of *Cornrows.*

4159 Wilson, Geraldine L. *Interracial Books for Children Bull.* 10.8 1979: 19. Rev. of *Cornrows.*

Yvonne (Y.W. Easton)

Poetry
4160 "Aunt Martha: severance pay." In FISH: 273-275.

4161 "Before the riots." *Ms.* 5.1 July 1976: 57.

4162 "Deborah Lee." In ADOF: 90-91.

4163 "Eastwick: five houses." *Ms.* 6.5 Nov. 1977: 72-73.

4164 "Emma." In ADOF: 91-93.

4165 "Encounter No. 2." *Images.* 8.2 1982: 11.

4166 *Iwilla.* Bronx, NY: Sunbury, 1982.

4167 *Iwilla / Soil.* Bronx, NY: Chameleon, 1985.

4168 *Iwilla Scourge.* Bronx, NY: Chameleon, 1986.

4169 "Junk mail, coupons, something." *Images.* 8.2 1982: 11.

4170 "Nineteen forty-six." *Obsidian.* 2.2 Sum. 1976: 49-50.

4171 "Nineteen thirty-six." In FISH: 275-277.

4172 "Premonition: a contour drawing." *Obsidian.* 2.2 Sum. 1976: 51-52.

4173 "Receive this white garment." *Ms.* 16.1-2 July-Aug. 1987: 52.

4174 "Returning." *Aphra.* 6.3-4 Spr.-Sum. 1976: 73.

4175 "Severance pay." *Ms.* 9.7 Jan. 1981: 33-35.

4176 "The tearing of the skin." In DALE: 62-66.

4177 "The tearing of the skin (Part I)." *Ms.* 7.7 Jan. 1979: 63.

4178 "The welcome." In BARA: 103-104. Published under the name "Y.W. (Yvonne Watkins) Easton."

4179 "Where she was not born." In ADOF: 139-140.

Textual Criticism
   4180 Murray, Joan. *Ms.* 14.9 Mar. 1986: 76. Rev. of *Iwilla / Soil.*

Nzadi Zimele-Keita (Michelle McMichael)

Poetry
   4181 "Birds of paradise." In BARA: 396–398.
   4182 "Long road rhythm." In BARA: 398.
   4183 "What we know." In BARA: 399.

Appendix A:
Works About Black Women Writers

Autobiography

4184 Blackburn, Regina. "In search of the Black female self: African-American women's autobiographies and ethnicity." In JELI: 133–148.

4185 Burgher, Mary. "Images of self and race in the autobiographies of Black women." In BELL: 107–122.

4186 Foster, Frances Smith. "Adding color and contour to early American self-portraitures: autobiographical writings of Afro-American women." In PRYS: 25–38.

Black Women Writers in General

4187 Baraka, Amiri and Amina Baraka. *Confirmation: An Anthology of African-American Women.* NY: Quill, 1983.

4188 Beard, Linda Susan. "The Black Woman Writer and the Diaspora, October 27–30, 1985, Michigan State University, East Lansing, Michigan." *Sage.* 3 Fall 1986: 70–71. Conference report.

4189 Bell, Roseann P., Bettye J. Parker, Beverly Guy-Sheftall. *Sturdy Black Bridges: Visions of Black Women in Literature.* Garden City, NY: Anchor-Doubleday, 1979.

4190 Bethel, Lorraine and Barbara Smith, Eds. *Conditions: Five, The Black Women's Issue.* Brooklyn: Conditions, Fall 1979. Issue of the periodical *Conditions* containing writings by Black women.

4191 Birtha, Becky. "Recovering a literary heritage: Black women's books." *Off Our Backs.* 9.6 June 1979: 14.

4192 Bowles, Juliette, Ed. *In the Memory and Spirit of Frances, Zora, and Lorraine: Essays and Interviews on Black Women and Writing.* Washington, DC: Institute for the Arts and the Humanities, Howard Univ., 1979.

4193 Brown, Martha H. "A listing of non-print materials on Black women." In HULL: 307–326.

4194 Christian, Barbara. *Black Feminist Criticism: Perspectives on Black Women Writers.* NY: Pergamon, 1985.

4195 Christian, Barbara. *From the Inside Out: Afro-American Women's Literature and the State.* Minneapolis: Center for Humanistic Studies, Univ. of Minnesota, 1987.

4196 Christian, Barbara. "Images of Black women in Afro-American literature: from stereotype to character." In CHRF: 1–30.

4197 Collins, Patricia Hill. "The emerging theory and pedagogy of Black women's studies." *Feminist Issues.* 6.1 Spr. 1986: 3–17.

4198 Dance, Daryl C. "Black Eve or Madonna? A study of the antithetical views of the mother in Black American literature." In BELL: 123–132.

4199 Evans, Mari. *Black Women Writers (1950–1980): A Critical Evaluation.* NY: Anchor-Doubleday, 1984.

4200 Finney, Nikky. "Doing write at last." *Essence.* 16.9 Jan. 1986: 128.

4201 Fisher, Dexter, Ed. *The Third Woman: Minority Women Writers of the United States.* Boston: Houghton-Mifflin, 1980.

4202 Gates, Henry Louis, Jr., Ed. "The Black person in art: how should s/he be portrayed? (Part 1)." *Black Amer. Lit. Forum.* 21.1–2 Spr.–Sum. 1987: 3–24. Gates' views on several Black women writers and on the portrayal of women in literature.

4203 Harris, Trudier. "Black writers in a changed landscape, since 1950." In RUBI: 566–577.

4204 Hernton, Calvin. "The sexual mountain and Black women writers." *Black Amer. Lit. Forum.* 18.4 Wint. 1984: 139–145.

4205 Hernton, Calvin. "The sexual mountain and Black women writers." *Black Scholar.* 16.4 July–Aug. 1985: 2–11.

4206 Hernton, Calvin C. *The Sexual Mountain and Black Women Writers: Adventures in Sex, Literature and Real Life.* NY: Anchor-Doubleday, 1987.

4207 Homans, Margaret. "Her very own howl." *Signs.* 9 1983: 186–205.

4208 Hooks, Bell. "Black women writing: creating more space." *Sage.* 2.1 Spr. 1985: 44–46.

4209 Hull, Gloria T. "The Black Woman Writer and the Diaspora." *Black Scholar.* 17.2 Mar.–Apr. 1986: 2–4. Closing address for the conference in East Lansing, 1985. (See Beard entry above.)

4210 Hull, Gloria T. "Rewriting Afro-American literature: a case for Black women writers." *Radical Teacher.* 6 Dec. 1977: 10–14.

4211 Hull, Gloria T., Patricia Bell Scott, Barbara Smith, Eds. *All the Women Are White, All the Blacks Are Men, but Some of Us Are Brave: Black Women's Studies.* Old Westbury, NY: Feminist, 1982.

4212 Lee, Dorothy. "Black voices in Detroit." *Michigan Q. Rev.* 25.2 Spr. 1986: 313–328. Many women authors are mentioned in the article.

4213 Lynch, Acklyn. "Notes on Black women writers of the past two decades." In BOWL: 45–52.

4214 Moraga, Cherríe and Gloria Anzaldúa, Eds. *This Bridge Called My Back: Writings by Radical Women of Color.* Watertown, MA: Persephone, 1981. Black women and other minorities are represented.

4215 O'Neale, Sondra. "Speaking for ourselves: Black women writers of the '80's." *Southern Exposure.* 9.2 Sum. 1981: 16–19.

4216 Rushing, Andrea Benton. "An annotated bibliography of images of Black women in Black literature." *CLA J.* 25.2 Dec. 1981: 234–262.

4217 Sims-Wood, Janet. "African-American women writers: a selected listing of Master's theses and doctoral dissertations." *Sage.* 2.1 Spr. 1985: 69–70.

4218 Spillers, Hortense J. "Kinship and resemblances." *Feminist Studies.* 11.1 Spr. 1985: 111–125.

4219 Spillers, Hortense J. "Review essay: 'Turning the century': notes on women and difference." *Tulsa Studies in Women's Lit.* 3.1–2 Spr.–Fall 1984: 178–185.

4220 Stetson, Erlene. "Black women in and out of print." In MESS: 87–107.

4221 Stetson, Erlene. "Silence: access and aspiration." In ASCH: 236–251.

4222 Tate, Claudia, Ed. *Black Women Writers at Work.* NY: Continuum, 1983.

4223 Tate, Claudia. "In their own write." *Essence.* 14.6 Oct. 1983: 24, 27. Excerpt from Tate's *Black Women Writers at Work.*

4224 Tate, Claudia. "On Black literary women and the evolution of critical discourse." *Tulsa Studies in Women's Lit.* 5.1 Spr. 1986: 111–123.

4225 Wade-Gayles, Gloria. "She who is Black and mother: in sociology and fiction, 1940–1970." In RODG: 89–106.

4226 Walker, Melissa. "The verbal arsenal of Black women writers in America." In BARK: 118–130. Article covers the '70's.

4227 Wallace, Michele. *Black Macho and the Myth of the Superwoman.* NY: Dial, 1979. Controversial and much-quoted book on Black women in America.

4228 Ward, Jerry. "Bridges and deep water." In BELL: 184–190.

4229 Washington, Mary Helen. "'The darkened eye restored': notes toward a literary history of Black women." In WASA: xv–xxxi. Introduction to Washington's book.

4230 Washington, Mary Helen. "New lives and new letters: Black women writers at the end of the seventies." *College English.* 43.1 Jan. 1981: 1–16.

4231 Washington, Mary Helen. "Teaching *Black-Eyed Susans:* an approach to the study of Black women writers." In HULL: 208–217.

4232 Willis, Susan. "Black women writers: taking a critical perspective." In GREE: 211–237.

4233 Willis, Susan. "Envisioning the future." In WILL: 159–168. Images of the future in Black women's writing.

4234 Willis, Susan. "Histories, communities, and sometimes Utopia." In WILL: 3–25.

Drama

4235 Miller, Jeanne-Marie A. "Black women playwrights from Grimké to Shange: selected synopses of their works." In HULL: 280–296. Includes biographical information.

4236 Miller, Jeanne-Marie A. "Images of Black women in plays by Black playwrights." *CLA J.* 20.4 June 1977: 494–507.

4237 Molette, Barbara J. "Black heroes and Afrocentric values in theatre." *J. of Black Studies.* 15.4 June 1985: 447–462. Includes criticism of women playwrights.

4238 Molette, Barbara J. "They speak. Who listens? Black women playwrights." *Black World.* 25.6 Apr. 1976: 28–34. Historical viewpoint.

4239 Wilkerson, Margaret B. *Nine Plays by Black Women.* NY: New American Library, 1986.

Feminism

4240 Brown, Linda. "Dark horse: a view of writing and publishing by dark lesbians." *Sinister Wisdom.* 13 Spr. 1980: 45–50. Survey starts in 1975. Includes a list of publications and self-published writers.

4241 Bulkin, Elly. "Racism and writing: some implications for white lesbian critics." *Sinister Wisdom.* 13 Spr. 1980: 3–22.

4242 Combahee River Collective. *Combahee River Collective Statement.* In SMIT: 272–282. Statement of a Black feminist group founded in Boston in 1974 that Black feminism is a political movement.

4243 Cornwell, Anita. *Black Lesbian in White America.* Tallahassee, FL: Naiad, 1983. Addresses, essays, lectures.

4244 Gomez, Jewelle. "A cultural legacy denied and discovered: Black lesbians in fiction by women." In SMIT: 110–123.

4245 Hammonds, Evelyn. "Toward a Black feminist aesthetic." *Sojourner.* Oct. 1980: 7. Discussion of limitations faced by Black feminist critics.

4246 Hooks, Bell. *Ain't I a Woman: Black Women and Feminism.* Boston: South End, 1981. History of Black women's attitudes toward feminism from 1950 on.

4247 Hooks, Bell. *Feminist Theory: From Margin to Center.* Boston: South End, 1984.

4248 Joseph, Gloria I. and Jill Lewis. *Common Differences: Conflicts in Black and White Feminist Perspectives.* NY: Doubleday, 1981.

4249 McDowell, Deborah E. "New directions for Black feminist criticism." *Black Amer. Lit Forum.* 14.4 Wint. 1980: 153–159.

4250 McDowell, Deborah E. "New directions for Black feminist criticism." In SHOW: 186–199.

4251 Rich, Adrienne. "'Disloyal to civilization': feminism, racism, and gynephobia." *Chrysalis.* 7 1979: 9–27. Racism in feminist writings.

4252 Roberts, J.R. *Black Lesbians: An Annotated Bibliography.* Tallahassee, FL: Naiad, 1981. Over 300 citations of writings by Black women. Foreword by Barbara Smith.

4253 Shockley, Ann Allen. "The Black lesbian in American literature: an overview." *Conditions 5.* 2.2 Aut. 1979: 133–142. Also appears in SMIT: 83–93.

4254 Smith, Barbara. *Home Girls: A Black Feminist Anthology.* NY: Kitchen Table: Women of Color, 1983.

4255 Smith, Barbara. "Toward a Black feminist criticism." *Conditions 2.* 1.2 Oct. 1977: 25–44. See main entry "Barbara Smith" for more articles on Black feminism.

4256 Welsing, Frances; June Jordan; Acklyn Lynch; Barbara Smith. "'Black women writers and feminism' panel: question and answer session." In BOWL: 53–57.

Fiction

4257 "Black women novelists: new generation raises provocative issues." *Ebony.* 40.1 Nov. 1984: 59–60, 62, 64.

4258 Carby, Hazel V. *Reconstructing Womanhood: The Emergence of the Afro-American Woman Novelist.* NY: Oxford, 1987.

4259 Christian, Barbara. *Black Women Novelists: The Development of a Tradition, 1892–1976.* Westport, CT: Greenwood, 1980.

4260 Christian, Barbara. "Trajectories of self-definition: placing contemporary Afro-American women's fiction." In CHRF: 171–186. Also in PRYS: 233–248.

4261 Dandridge, Rita B. "Male critics / Black women's novels." *CLA J.* 23.1 Sept. 1979: 1–11.

4262 Dandridge, Rita B. "On the novels written by selected Black American women: a bibliographical essay." In HULL: 261–279. Includes biographies, letters, articles, interviews, dissertations, and general and individual criticism of Brooks, Fauset, Hurston, Larsen, Marshall, Petry, Morrison, and A. Walker.

4263 Guy-Sheftall, Beverly. In WADE: xiii–xviii. Introduction to Wade-Gayles' *No Crystal Stair.*

4264 Lee, Valerie Gray. "The use of folktalk in novels by Black women writers." *CLA J.* 23.3 Mar. 1980: 266–272.

4265 LeSeur, Geta. "One mother, two daughters: the Afro-American and the Afro-Caribbean female 'Bildungsroman'." *Black Scholar.* 17.2 Mar.–Apr. 1986: 26–33.

4266 McDowell, Deborah E. "'The changing same': generational connections and Black women novelists." *New Literary History.* 18.2 Wint. 1987: 281–302.

4267 Naylor, Carolyn A. "Cross-gender significance of the journey motif in selected Afro-American fiction." *Colby Library Q.* 18.1 1982: 26–38.

4268 O'Neale, Sondra. "Race, sex and self: aspects of 'Bildung' in select novels by Black American women novelists." *Melus.* 9.4 Winter 1982: 25–37. On Harper, Fauset, Hurston, Brooks, K. Hunter, G. Jones, etc.

4269 Pryse, Marjorie and Hortense J. Spillers, Eds. *Conjuring: Black Women, Fiction, and Literary Tradition.* Bloomington: Indiana UP, 1985.

4270 Pullin, Faith. "Landscapes of reality: the fiction of contemporary Afro-American women." In LEEE: 173–203.

4271 Ramsey, Priscilla. "A study of Black identity in 'passing' novels of the nineteenth and early twentieth centuries." *Studies in Black Lit.* 7.2 1976: 1–7.

4272 Schultz, Elizabeth. "Out of the woods and into the world: a study of interracial friendships between women in American novels." In PRYS: 67–85.

4273 Spillers, Hortense J. "Cross-currents, discontinuities: Black women's fiction." In PRYS: 249–261.

4274 Wade-Gayles, Gloria. *No Crystal Stair: Visions of Race and Sex in Black Women's Fiction.* NY: Pilgrim, 1984. Covers 1946 to 1976.

4275 Wade-Gayles, Gloria. "She who is Black and mother: in sociology and fiction, 1940–1970." In RODG: 89–106.

4276 Wade-Gayles, Gloria. "The truths of our mothers' lives: mother-daughter relationships in Black women's fiction." *Sage.* 1.2 Fall 1984: 8–12.

4277 Washington, Mary Helen. *Invented Lives: Narratives of Black Women 1860–1960.* Garden City, NY: Doubleday, 1987.

4278 Washington, Mary Helen. *Midnight Birds: Stories of Contemporary Black Women Writers.* NY: Anchor-Doubleday, 1980.

4279 Watson, Carole McAlpine. *Prologue: The Novels of Black American Women, 1891–1965.* Westport, CT: Greenwood, 1985. Has a chronological list of novels and stories published from 1859 to 1964 and a 22-page section of novels annotated.

4280 Willis, Susan. *Specifying: Black Women Writing the American Experience.* Madison: Univ. of Wisconsin, 1987.

Poetry

4281 Chapman, Dorothy H., Comp. *Index to Poetry by Black American Women.* Westport, CT: Greenwood, 1986. Has indexes by author, subject, title, and first line.

4282 Christian, Barbara. "Afro-American women poets: a historical introduction." In CHRF: 119–125.

4283 Clarke, Cheryl. *Narratives: Poems in the Tradition of Black Women.* New Brunswick, NJ: Sister Books, 1982.

4284 Hernton, Calvin C. "Black women poets: the oral narrative tradition." In HERN: 119–155. Has criticism of Derricotte, Osbey, T. Davis, McElroy, C. Clarke, Dove.

4285 Hull, Gloria T. "Afro-American women poets: a bio-critical survey." In GILS: 165–182.

4286 Hull, Gloria T. "Black women poets from Wheatley to Walker." In BELL: 69–86.

4287 Koolish, Lynda. "The bones of this body say, dance: self-empowerment in contemporary poetry by women of color." In HARQ: 1–56.

4288 Lobo-Cobb, Angela, Ed. *Winter Nest: A Poetry Anthology of Midwestern Women Poets of Color.* Madison, WI: Blue Reed, 1987.

4289 Rushing, Andrea Benton. "Images of Black women in Afro-American poetry." In HARL: 74–84.

4290 Sherman, Joan R. "Afro-American women poets of the nineteenth century: a guide to research and bio-bibliographies of the poets." In HULL: 245–260. Includes books, periodicals, and manuscripts.

4291 Stetson, Erlene. *Black Sister: Poetry by Black American Women, 1746–1980.* Bloomington: Indiana UP, 1981.

Publishing

4292 Berry, Faith. "A question of publishers and a question of audience." *Black Scholar.* 17.2 Mar.–Apr. 1986: 41–49. Describes the history of publishing by Black women.

4293 Bowen, Angela. "*Sage:* a journal that fills a long unmet need." *Sojourner.* 9.8 Apr. 1984: 19. On a scholarly journal that publishes articles on Black women.

4294 Boyd, Melba Joyce. "Out of the poetry ghetto: the life/art struggle of small Black publishing houses." *Black Scholar.* 16.4 July–Aug. 1985: 12–24.

4295 Hernton, Calvin. "The tradition." *Parnassus.* 12–13.2–1 Wint. 1985: 518–550. Publishing by Black women in general and reviews of recent books of poetry by Derricotte, Osbey, T. Davis, McElroy, C. Clarke, Dove.

4296 Rhodes, Jane. "Heard at last: Black female voices." *Utne Reader.* 22 July–Aug. 1987: 118–121, 123. Survey article on publishing by Black women.

Appendix B: Authors by Genre

Autobiography

Angelou, Maya
Brooks, Gwendolyn
Golden, Marita
Jacobs, Harriet
Kennedy, Adrienne
Lorde, Audre
Murray, Pauli
Shakur, Assata
Wilson, Harriet E.

Children's Literature

Boyd, Candy Dawson
Caines, Jeannette
Childress, Alice
Clifton, Lucille
DeVeaux, Alexis
Dionetti, Michelle
Evans, Mari
Feelings, Muriel
Giovanni, Nikki
Greenfield, Eloise
Grimes, Nikki
Guy, Rosa
Hamilton, Virginia
Hunter, Kristin
Jordan, June
Mahiri, Jabari
Mathis, Sharon Bell
Miller, May
Rollins, Charlemae H.
Sanchez, Sonia
Tate, Eleanora E.
Taylor, Mildred D.
Thomas, Ianthe
Thomas, Joyce Carol
Turner, Gladys T.

Vroman, Mary Elizabeth
Walker, Alice
Walter, Mildred Pitts
Waniek, Marilyn Nelson
Wilkinson, Brenda
Yarbrough, Camille

Drama

Baraka, Amina
Bonner (Occomy), Marita
Burrill, Mary
Carroll, Vinette
Childress, Alice
Collins, Kathleen
Cooper, J. California
DeVeaux, Alexis
DuBois, Shirley Graham
Gibson, P.J.
Grimké, Angelina Weld
Hansberry, Lorraine
Houston, Diane
Hunkins, Lee
Jackson, Cherry
Jackson, Elaine
Johnson, Georgia Douglas
Jones, Gayl
Kennedy, Adrienne
Livingston, Myrtle Smith
Martin, Sharon Stockard
Mason, Judi Ann
Miller, May
Molette, Barbara J.
Rahman, Aisha
Rhodes, Crystal
Shange, Ntozake
Stiles, Thelma J.
Welch, Leona N.
Williams, Anita J.
Williams, Sherley Anne

Folklore

Dance, Daryl Cumber
Hurston, Zora Neale
Teish, Luisah

Novels

Bambara, Toni Cade
Brooks, Gwendolyn
Chase-Riboud, Barbara
Childress, Alice
Cliff, Michelle
Fauset, Jessie Redmon
Glass, Frankcina
Golden, Marita
Guy, Rosa
Harper, Frances E.W.
Harrison, Deloris
Hopkins, Pauline E.
Hunter, Kristin
Hurston, Zora Neale
Jones, Gayl
Jourdain, Rose
Kincaid, Jamaica
Larsen, Nella
Lee, Andrea
Lee, Audrey
Marshall, Paule
McMillan, Terry
Meriwether, Louise
Millican, Arthenia J. Bates
Morrison, Toni
Naylor, Gloria
Petry, Ann
Polite, Carlene Hatcher
Shange, Ntozake
Shockley, Ann Allen
Southerland, Ellease
Walker, Alice
Walker (Alexander), Margaret
West, Dorothy
Williams, Sherley Anne
Winston, Betty
Wright, Sarah E.

Poetry

Ada
Adams, Janus

Adams, Jeanette
Adrine-Robinson, Kenyette
Afif, Fatimah
Ai
Alba, Nanina
Allah, Fareedah
Allegra, Donna
Ama, Fayola Kamaria
Amini, Johari M.
Anderson, Kathy Elaine
Angelou, Maya
Armstrong, Denise Carreathers
Banks, Carol Tillery
Baraka, Amina
Barras-Abney, Jonetta Rose
Bennett, Gwendolyn B.
Bethel, Lorraine
Bird, Bessie Calhoun
Birtha, Becky
Blackdykewomon, Lou
Blackwomon, Julie
Bogus, S. Diane
Bourke, Sharon
Boyd, Melba Joyce
Boyer, Jill Witherspoon
Bragg, Linda Brown
Braxton, Joanne M.
Brooks, Gwendolyn
Brown, Beth
Brown, Linda J.
Brown, Wilmette
Burroughs, Margaret T.G.
Burt, Della
Byrd, Stephanie
Capdeville, Annetta Elam
Carpenter, Pandoura
Christian, Robin
Clarke, Cheryl
Cliff, Michelle
Clifford, Carrie Williams
Clifton, Lucille
Clinton, Michelle T.
Cloud, Flyin' Thunda
Cobb, Alice S.
Coleman, Wanda
Coleman, Willie M.
Collier, Eugenia W.
Collins, June L.
Connor-Bey, Brenda
Cooper, Afua Pam
Cortez, Jayne

Cowdery, Mae V.
Crews, Stella
Cumbo, Kattie M.
Damali, Nia
Danner, Margaret Esse
Davenport, Doris Diosa
Davis, Gloria
Davis, Thadious M.
Davis, Thulani
Dee, Ruby
Derricotte, Toi
DeVeaux, Alexis
Diara, Schavi Mali
Dove, Rita
Dunbar-Nelson, Alice M.
Emeruwa, Leatrice W.
Eshe, Aisha
Evans, Mari
Ewart, Audrey
Fabio, Sarah Webster
Farmer, Ruth
Fatisha
Fauset, Jessie Redmon
Faust, Naomi F.
Fields, Julia
Finney, Nikky
Flowers, Yvonne A.
Freeman, Carol
Fuller, Stephany Inua
Garnett, Ruth M.
Gee, Lethonia
Gibbs, Joan
Gibbs, Michele
Giovanni, Nikki
Gomez, Jewelle
Gossett, Hattie
Green, Jaki Shelton
Gregory, Carole Clemmons
Griffith, Lois Elaine
Grimes, Nikki
Grimké, Angelina Weld
Grimké, Charlotte Forten
Hall-Evans, Jo Ann
Hansberry, Lorraine
Harper, Frances E.W.
Henderson, Safiya
Hooks, Bell
Hope, Akua Lezli
Hopkins, Lea
Howard, Mariah Britton
Hull, Gloria T.

Hunter, Jacquelyn Furgus
Hunter, Kristin
Hyman, Lateifa-Ramona L.
Ingrum, Adrienne
Ismaili, Rashidah
Jackson, Angela
Jackson, Mae
Jackson, Patti-Gayle
Jackson-Opoku, Sandra J.
Jefferson, Annetta
Jessye, Eva
Jewell, Terri L.
Jimason, Joanne
Johnson, Eloise McKinney
Johnson, Georgia Douglas
Johnson, Helene
Jonas, Rosalie
Jones, Cheryl
Jones, Gayl
Jones, Patricia
Jordan, Anasa
Jordan, June
Kein, Sybil
Kendrick, Dolores
Kgositsile, Aneb
Lane, Pinkie Gordon
Lawson, Jennifer Blackman
Lee, Audrey
Lights, Rikki
Lincoln, Abbey
Livingston, Myrtle Smith
Loftin, Elouise
Lomax, Pearl Cleage
Lorde, Audre
Louise, Esther
Loving, Oyoko
Madgett, Naomi Long
Mahone, Barbara J.
Major, Deborah
Malveaux, Julianne
M'Buzi, Malkia
McClaurin, Irma
McCray, Chirlane
McElroy, Colleen J.
Mealy, Rosemari
Miller, May
Millican, Arthenia J. Bates
Mitchell, Karen L.
Moore, Cynthia B.
Moore, Opal
Mootry, Maria K.

Moss, Thylias
Moxley, Ruby D.
Mullen, Harryette
Murray, Pauli
Natelege, Schaarazetta
Neals, Betty H.
Nuru, Njeri
Oden, Gloria
Osbey, Brenda Marie
Parker, Pat
Parkerson, Michelle
Patterson, Lucille J.
Piper, Linda
Plato, Ann
Porter, Margaret
Randall-Tsuruta, Dorothy
Rawls, Isetta Crawford
Ray, Henrietta Cordelia
Reese, Sarah Carolyn
Robinson, Jeannette
Robinson, Louise
Rodgers, Carolyn M.
Rogers, Sandra
Roper, Renée
Rushin, Donna Kate
Sanchez, Sonia
Satiafa
Sele, Baraka
Shakur, Assata
Shange, Ntozake
Sharp, Saundra
Simmons, Judy Dothard
Smart-Grosvenor, Verta Mae
Smith, Barbara
Smith, Beverly
Smith, Mary Carter
Spencer, Anne
Stuckey, Elma
Suruma, Lynn
Terry, Lucy
Thomas, Joyce Carol
Thompson, Clara Ann
Wade-Gayles, Gloria
Walker, Alice
Walker (Alexander), Margaret
Waniek, Marilyn Nelson
Welch, Leona N.
Welsh, Kariamu
Wheatley, Phillis
White, Paulette Childress
Wiley, Electa

Williams, Elsie Arrington
Williams, June Vanleer
Williams, Lucy Ariel
Williams, Regina
Williams, Sherley Anne
Wilson, Geraldine L.
Yvonne
Zimele-Keita, Nzadi

Science Fiction

Butler, Octavia E.

Short Fiction

Allegra, Donna
Anderson, Kathy Elaine
Anderson, Mignon Holland
Angelou, Maya
Arobateau, Red
Bambara, Toni Cade
Banks, Barbara
Barras-Abney, Jonetta Rose
Birtha, Becky
Blackwomon, Julie
Bogus, S. Diane
Boyer, Jill Witherspoon
Brown, Beth
Brown, Linda J.
Clarke, Cheryl
Cooper, J. California
DeRamus, Betty
DeVeaux, Alexis
Dove, Rita
Gomez, Jewelle
Griffith, Lois Elaine
Harper, Frances E.W.
Harrison, Deloris
Hodges, Frenchy
Hopkins, Pauline E.
Hunter, Kristin
Hurston, Zora Neale
Jackson, Angela
Jackson, Mae
Jackson-Opoku, Sandra J.
Jones, Gayl
Jones, Lucille
Jones, Muriel
Kincaid, Jamaica

Lawson, Jennifer Blackman
Lee, Andrea
Lee, Audrey
Lights, Rikki
Lorde, Audre
Marshall, Paule
Mason, Judi Ann
Mays, Raymina
McElroy, Colleen J.
Meriwether, Louise
Millican, Arthenia J. Bates
Moore, Opal
Morrison, Toni
Naylor, Gloria
Parker, Pat
Petry, Ann
Rashida
Sanchez, Sonia

Shockley, Ann Allen
Smart-Grosvenor, Verta Mae
Smith, Barbara
Smith, Mary Carter
Spillers, Hortense J.
Steele, Shirley O.
Suncircle, Pat
Teish, Luisah
Thomas, Joyce Carol
Vroman, Mary Elizabeth
Walker, Alice
Wallace, Michele
Welsh, Kariamu
White, Paulette Childress
Williams, Lorna V.
Williams, Sherley Anne
Woods, Barbara

List of Abbreviations

General Abbreviations

Amer.	American
Assoc.	Association
Assoc. Ed.	Associate Editor
Aut.	Autumn
Bull.	Bulletin
Comp(s).	Compiler(s)
Ed(s).	Editor(s)
Educ.	Education
J.	Journal
Lit.	Literature
Pr.	Press
Q.	Quarterly
Rev. ed.	Revised edition
Rev(s).	Review(s)
Rpt.	Reprinted
Spr.	Spring
Sum.	Summer
Suppl.	Supplement
Univ.	University
UP	University Press
Vol(s).	Volume(s)
Wint.	Winter

Abbreviations for Books Indexed

ABBO   Abbott, Dorothy, Ed. *Mississippi Writers: Reflections of Childhood and Youth. Vol. 1: Fiction.* Jackson: UP of Mississippi, 1985.

ABEL   Abel, Elizabeth; Marianne Hirsch; Elizabeth Langland, Eds. *The Voyage In: Fictions of Female Development.* Hanover NH: UP of New England, 1983.

ABRA   Abrahams, William, Ed. *Prize Stories 1981: The O. Henry Awards.* Garden City NY: Anchor-Doubleday, 1981.

ADOF   Adoff, Arnold, Comp. and Ed. *Celebrations: A New Anthology of Black American Poetry.* Chicago: Follett, 1977.

ARAT   Arata, Esther Spring and Nicholas John Rotoli. *Black American Playwrights, 1800 to the Present: A Bibliography.* Metuchen NJ: Scarecrow, 1976.

ASCH   Ascher, Carol; Louise DeSalvo; Sara Ruddick, Eds. *Between Women: Biographers, Novelists, Critics, Teachers and Artists Write About Their Work on Women.* Boston: Beacon, 1984.

AUTH   Publishers Weekly, Editors and Contributors. *The Author Speaks: Selected PW Interviews, 1967–1976.* NY: Bowker, 1977.

AUTN   Nykoruk, Barbara, Ed. *Authors in the News.* Detroit: Gale, 1976.

BANK   Bankier, Joanna and Deirdre Lashgari, Eds. *Women Poets of the World.* NY: Macmillan, 1983.

BARA   Baraka, Amiri (LeRoi Jones) and Amina Baraka. *Confirmation: An Anthology of African-American Women.* NY: Quill, 1983.

BARK   Barker, Francis; Peter Hulme; Margaret Iverson. *Confronting the Crisis: War, Politics, and Culture in the Eighties.* Colchester: Univ. of Essex, 1984.

BART   Barthold, Bonnie J. *Black Time: Fiction of Africa, the Caribbean, and the United States.* New Haven: Yale UP, 1981.

BEAT   Beaty, Jerome, Comp. *Norton Introduction to Fiction.* NY: Norton, 1981.

BECK   Beckles, Frances N. *Twenty Black Women: A Profile of Contemporary Black Maryland Women.* Baltimore: Gateway, 1978.

BELA   Bell, Bernard W. *The Afro-American Novel and Its Tradition.* Amherst: Univ. of Massachusetts, 1987.

BELL   Bell, Roseann P.; Bettye J. Parker; Beverly Guy-Sheftall, Eds. *Sturdy Black Bridges: Visions of Black Women in Literature.* Garden City NY: Anchor-Doubleday, 1979.

BETS   Betsko, Kathleen and Rachel Koenig. *Interviews with Contemporary Women Playwrights.* NY: Beech Tree, 1987.

BEVI   Bevilacqua, Winifred F., Ed. *Fiction by American Women: Recent Views.* Port Washington NY: Associated Faculty, 1983.

BIGC   Bigsby, C.W.E. *A Critical Introduction to Twentieth-Century Drama. (Vol. 3).* Cambridge, Eng.: Cambridge UP, 1985.

BIGS   Bigsby, C.W.E. *The Second Black Renaissance: Essays in Black Literature.* Westport CT: Greenwood, 1980.

BLIC   Blicksilver, Edith. *The Ethnic American Woman: Problems, Protests, Lifestyle.* Dubuque IA: Kendall-Hunt, 1979.

BLOO   Bloom, Harold, Ed. *American Women Poets.* NY: Chelsea House, 1986.

BOCK   Bock, Hedwig and Albert Wertheim, Eds. *Essays on Contemporary American Drama.* Munich: Max Hueber, 1981.

BOWL   Bowles, Juliette, Ed. *In the Memory and Spirit of Frances, Zora, and Lorraine: Essays and Interviews on Black Women and Writing.* Washington DC: Institute for the Arts and the Humanities, Howard Univ., 1979.

BROW   Brown, Janet. *Feminist Drama: Definition and Critical Analysis.* Metuchen NJ: Scarecrow, 1979.

BRUA   Bruchac, Joseph, Ed. *The Next World: Poems by Thirty-Two Third World Americans.* Trumansburg NY: Crossing, 1978.

BRUC   Bruck, Peter and Wolfgang Karrer. *The Afro-American Novel Since 1960.* Amsterdam: Gruner, 1982.

BULK   Bulkin, Elly and Joan Larkin, Eds. *Lesbian Fiction: An Anthology.* Watertown MA: Persephone, 1981.

BYER   Byerman, Keith E. *Fingering the Jagged Grain: Tradition and Form in Recent Black Fiction.* Athens: Univ. of Georgia, 1985.

CAMP   Campbell, Jane. *Mythic Black Fiction: The Transformation of History.* Knoxville: Univ. of Tennessee, 1986.

CARB   Carby, Hazel V. *Reconstructing Womanhood: The Emergence of the Afro-American Woman Novelist.* NY: Oxford, 1987.

CARR   Carr, Terry, Ed. *Terry Carr's Best Science Fiction of the Year.* NY: Tom Doherty Associates, 1985.

CARY Cary, Meredith. *Different Drummers: A Study of Cultural Alternatives in Fiction.* Metuchen NJ: Scarecrow, 1984.

CASS Cassill, R.V., Ed. *The Norton Anthology of Short Fiction.* 2nd Ed. NY: Norton, 1981.

CEDA Cedar and Nelly, Eds. *A Woman's Touch.* Eugene OR: Amazon Reality, 1979.

CHIN Chinoy, Helen and Linda W. Jenkins, Eds. *Women in American Theatre: Careers, Images, Movements: An Illustrated Anthology and Sourcebook.* NY: Crown, 1981.

CHRA Christ, Carol P. *Diving Deep and Surfacing: Women Writers on Spiritual Quest.* Boston: Beacon, 1980.

CHRF Christian, Barbara. *Black Feminist Criticism: Perspectives on Black Women Writers.* NY: Pergamon, 1985.

CHRW Christian, Barbara. *Black Women Novelists: The Development of a Tradition, 1892–1976.* Westport CT: Greenwood, 1980.

CO09 Commire, Anne, Ed. *Something About the Author, Facts and Pictures About Authors and Illustrators of Books for Young People.* Detroit: Gale, 1976.

CO10 Commire, Anne, Ed. *Something About the Author.* 1976.

CO12 Commire, Anne, Ed. *Something About the Author.* 1977.

CO14 Commire, Anne, Ed. *Something About the Author.* 1978.

CO15 Commire, Anne, Ed. *Something About the Author.* 1979.

CO16 Commire, Anne, Ed. *Something About the Author.* 1979.

CO20 Commire, Anne, Ed. *Something About the Author.* 1980.

CO24 Commire, Anne, Ed. *Something About the Author.* 1981.

CO31 Commire, Anne, Ed. *Something About the Author.* 1983.

CO40 Commire, Anne, Ed. *Something About the Author.* 1985.

CO48 Commire, Anne, Ed. *Something About the Author.* 1987.

CO49 Commire, Anne, Ed. *Something About the Author.* 1987.

COHN Cohn, Ruby. *New American Dramatists, 1960–1980.* NY: Grove, 1982.

COLL Collins, David R. and Evelyn Witter. *Notable Illinois Women.* Rock Island IL: Quest, 1982.

COOK Cooke, Michael G. *Afro-American Literature in the Twentieth Century: The Achievement of Intimacy.* New Haven: Yale UP, 1984.

COOP Cooper, Jane, *et al.,* Eds. *Extended Outlooks: The Iowa Review Collection of Contemporary Women Writers.* NY: Collier-Macmillan, 1982.

COOR Cooper-Clark, Diana. *Interviews with Contemporary Novelists.* NY: St. Martin's, 1986.

CRUA Cruikshank, Margaret, Ed. *The Lesbian Path.* Monterey CA: Angel, 1980.

CRUG Cruikshank, Margaret, Ed. *The Lesbian Path.* San Francisco: Grey Fox, 1985.

CRUI Cruikshank, Margaret, Ed. *Lesbian Studies, Present and Future.* Old Westbury NY: Feminist, 1982.

CRUW Cruikshank, Margaret, Ed. *New Lesbian Writing: An Anthology.* San Francisco: Grey Fox, 1984.

DAHL Dahlstrom, JoAnn Wolf and Deborah E. Ryel. *Promises to Keep: Reading and Writing About Values.* Englewood Cliffs NJ: Prentice-Hall, 1977.

DALE Dallman, Elaine, *et al.,* Eds. *Woman Poet, the East.* Reno NV: Women-in-Literature, 1980.

DALL Dallman, Elaine, *et al.,* Eds. *Woman Poet, the Midwest.* Reno NV: Women-in-Literature, 1985.

DALW   Dallman, Elaine, *et al., Eds. Woman Poet, the West.* Reno NV: Women-in-Literature, 1980.

DAVC   Davis, Charles T. and Henry Louis Gates, Jr. *The Slave's Narrative.* NY: Oxford, 1985.

DAVE   Davis, Enid. *The Liberty Cap: A Catalogue of Non-Sexist Materials for Children.* Chicago: Academy, 1977.

DAVI   Davis, Marianna W., Ed. *Contributions of Black Women to America (Vol. 1).* Columbia SC: Kenday, 1982.

DELA   Delacoste, Frédérique and Felice Newman, Eds. *Fight Back! Feminist Resistance to Male Violence.* Minneapolis: Cleis, 1981.

DEMO   DeMontreville, Doris and Elizabeth D. Crawford, Eds. *Fourth Book of Junior Authors and Illustrators.* NY: H.W. Wilson, 1978.

DESH   DeShazer, Mary K. *Inspiring Women: Reimagining the Muse.* NY: Pergamon, 1986.

DL05   Greiner, Donald J., Ed. *American Poets Since World War II (Dictionary of Literary Biography, Vol. 5).* Detroit: Gale, 1980.

DL06   Kibler, James E., Jr., Ed. *American Novelists Since World War II, Second Series (Dictionary of Literary Biography, Vol. 6).* Detroit: Gale, 1980.

DL07   Curb, Rosemary, Ed. *Twentieth-Century American Dramatists (Dictionary of Literary Biography, Vol. 7).* Detroit: Gale, 1981.

DL33   Davis, Thadious M. and Trudier Harris, Eds. *Afro-American Fiction Writers After 1955 (Dictionary of Literary Biography, Vol. 33).* Detroit: Gale, 1984.

DL38   Davis, Thadious M. and Trudier Harris, Eds. *Afro-American Writers After 1955: Dramatists and Prose Writers (Dictionary of Literary Biography, Vol. 38).* Detroit: Gale, 1985.

DL41   Harris, Trudier and Thadious M. Davis, Eds. *Afro-American Poets Since 1955 (Dictionary of Literary Biography, Vol. 41).* Detroit: Gale, 1985.

DL50   Harris, Trudier, Ed. and Thadious M. Davis, Assoc. Ed. *Afro-American Writers Before the Harlem Renaissance (Dictionary of Literary Biography, Vol. 50).* Detroit: Gale, 1986.

DL51   Harris, Trudier, Ed. and Thadious M. Davis, Assoc. Ed. *Afro-American Writers from the Harlem Renaissance to 1940 (Dictionary of Literary Biography, Vol. 51).* Detroit: Gale, 1987.

DL54   Quartermain, Peter, Ed. *American Poets, 1880–1945, Third Series (Dictionary of Literary Biography, Vol. 54).* Detroit: Gale, 1987.

DUKE   Duke, Maurice; Jackson R. Bryer; M. Thomas Inge, Eds. *American Women Writers: Bibliographical Essays.* Westport CT: Greenwood, 1983.

DY81   *Dictionary of Literary Biography Yearbook: 1981.* Detroit: Gale, 1982.

ENSO   Ensor, Allison R. and Thomas J.A. Heffernan, Eds. *Tennessee Studies in Literature, Vol. 26 (Southern Literature Issue).* Knoxville: Univ. of Tennessee, 1981–1982.

EVAN   Evans, Mari, Ed. *Black Women Writers (1950–1980): A Critical Evaluation.* NY: Anchor-Doubleday, 1984.

FANN   Fannin, Alice; Rebecca Lukens; Catherine Hoyser Mann, Eds. *Woman: An Affirmation.* Lexington MA: Heath, 1979.

FER2   Ferguson, Mary Anne, Ed. *Images of Women in Literature.* 2nd Ed. Boston: Houghton-Mifflin, 1977.

FER3   Ferguson, Mary Anne, Ed. *Images of Women in Literature.* 3rd Ed. Boston: Houghton-Mifflin, 1981.

FISH   Fisher, Dexter, Ed. *The Third Woman: Minority Women Writers of the United States.* Boston: Houghton-Mifflin, 1980.

FISS   Fisher, Dexter and Robert B. Stepto, Eds. *Afro-American Literature: The Reconstruction of Instruction.* NY: Modern Language Association, 1979.

FLEI   Fleischmann, Fritz, Ed. *American Novelists Revisited: Essays in Feminist Criticism.* Boston: G.K. Hall, 1982.

FLOR   Flora, Joseph M. and Robert Bain, Eds. *Fifty Southern Writers After 1900: A Bio-Bibliographical Sourcebook.* Westport CT: Greenwood, 1987.

FORK   Forkner, Ben and Patrick Samway, S.J., Eds. *A Modern Southern Reader: Major Stories, Drama, Poetry, Essays, Interviews and Reminiscences from the Twentieth-Century South.* Atlanta GA: Peachtree, 1986.

FRAN   France, Rachel, Ed. *A Century of Plays by American Women.* NY: Richards Rosen, 1979.

FREN   French, Warren, Introduction by. *Twentieth-Century American Literature.* NY: St. Martin's, 1980.

FRYE   Frye, Joanne S. *Living Stories, Telling Lives: Women and the Novel in Contemporary Experience.* Ann Arbor: Univ. of Michigan, 1986.

GAES   Gaess, Roger, Ed. *Leaving the Bough: Fifty American Poets of the Eighties.* NY: International, 1982.

GAIL   Gaillard, Dawson and John Mosier, Comps. *Women and Men Together: An Anthology of Short Fiction.* Boston: Houghton-Mifflin, 1978.

GATE   Gates, Henry Louis, Jr. *Black Literature and Literary Theory.* NY: Methuen, 1984.

GATP   Gates, Henry Louis, Jr. *Figures in Black: Words, Signs, and the "Racial" Self.* NY: Oxford UP, 1987.

GIBB   Gibbs, Joan and Sara Bennett, Eds. *Top Ranking: A Collection of Articles on Racism and Classism in the Lesbian Community.* Brooklyn: February 3, 1980.

GILN   Gilbert, Sandra M. and Susan Gubar. *The Norton Anthology of Literature by Women.* NY: Norton, 1985.

GILS   Gilbert, Sandra M. and Susan Gubar, Eds. *Shakespeare's Sisters: Feminist Essays on Women Poets.* Bloomington: Indiana UP, 1979.

GOUL   Gould, Jean. *Modern American Women Poets.* NY: Dodd, 1984.

GRAB   Grabes, Herbert, Ed. *Das Amerikanische Drama der Gegenwart.* Kronberg: Athenaeum, 1976.

GRAH   Grahn, Judy, Ed. *True-to-Life Adventure Stories. (Vol. 1).* Oakland CA: Diana, 1978.

GREE   Greene, Gayle and Coppélia Kahn, Eds. *Making a Difference: Feminist Literary Criticism.* NY: Methuen, 1985.

GRIE   Grier, Barbara and Coletta Reid, Eds. *The Lavender Herring: Lesbian Essays from* The Ladder. Baltimore: Diana, 1976.

GWIN   Gwin, Minrose C. *Black and White Women of the Old South: The Peculiar Sisterhood in American Literature.* Knoxville: Univ. of Tennessee, 1985.

HAMA   Hamalian, Linda and Leo Hamalian, Eds. *Solo: Women on Woman Alone.* NY: Dell, 1977.

HARL   Harley, Sharon and Rosalyn T. Penn. *The Afro-American Woman: Struggles and Images.* Port Washington NY: Kennikat, 1978.

HARP   Harper, Michael S. and Robert B. Stepto, Eds. *Chant of Saints: A Gathering of Afro-American Literature, Art, and Scholarship.* Urbana: Univ. of Illinois, 1979.

HARQ   Harris, Marie and Kathleen Aguero, Eds. *A Gift of Tongues: Critical Challenges in Contemporary American Poetry.* Athens: Univ. of Georgia, 1987.

HARR   Harris, Trudier. *Exorcising Blackness: Historical and Literary Lynching and Burning Rituals.* Bloomington: Indiana UP, 1984.

HARS   Harris, Trudier. *From Mammies to Militants: Domestics in Black American Literature.* Philadelphia: Temple UP, 1982.

HASL   Haslauer, Wilfried. *A Salzburg Miscellany: English and American Studies, 1964–1984. (Vol. 1).* Salzburg, Austria: Univ. of Salzburg, 1984.

HATC   Hatch, James V. *Black Playwrights, 1823–1977.* NY: Bowker, 1977.

HEAR   Hearne, Betsy and Marilyn Kaye, Eds. *Celebrating Children's Books: Essays on Children's Literature in Honor of Zena Sutherland.* NY: Lothrop, Lee and Shepard, 1981.

HERN   Hernton, Calvin C. *The Sexual Mountain and Black Women Writers: Adventures in Sex, Literature and Real Life.* NY: Anchor-Doubleday, 1987.

HEYE   Heyen, William, Ed. *The Generation of 2000: Contemporary American Poets.* Princeton NJ: Ontario Review, 1984.

HOFF   Hoffman, Nancy and Florence Howe, Eds. *Women Working: An Anthology of Stories and Poems.* Old Westbury NY: Feminist, 1979.

HOFM   Hoffman, Leonore and Deborah Rosenfelt, Eds. *Teaching Women's Literature from a Regional Perspective.* NY: Modern Language Association, 1982.

HOLL   Holloway, Karla F.C. and Stephanie A. Demetrakopoulos. *New Dimensions of Spirituality: A Biracial and Bicultural Reading of the Novels of Toni Morrison.* Westport CT: Greenwood, 1987.

HOLT   Holtze, Sally Holmes, Ed. *Fifth Book of Junior Authors and Illustrators.* NY: H.W. Wilson, 1983.

HOWI   Howink, Eda. *Wives of Famous Men.* Francestown NH: Golden Quill, 1982.

HULL   Hull, Gloria T.; Patricia Bell Scott; Barbara Smith, Eds. *All the Women Are White, All the Blacks Are Men, but Some of Us Are Brave: Black Women's Studies.* Old Westbury NY: Feminist, 1982.

INGE   Inge, M. Thomas; Maurice Duke; Jackson R. Bryer. *Black American Writers: Bibliographical Essays (Vol. 1, The Beginnings Through the Harlem Renaissance and Langston Hughes).* NY: St. Martin's, 1978.

JAYE   Jaye, Michael and Ann Chambers Watts, Eds. *Literature and the Urban Experience: Essays on the City and Literature.* New Brunswick NJ: Rutgers UP, 1981.

JAYK   Jay, Karla and Allen Young, Eds. *Lavender Culture.* NY: Harcourt, 1978.

JELI   Jelinek, Estelle C., Ed. *Women's Autobiography: Essays in Criticism.* Bloomington: Indiana UP, 1980.

JONE   Jones, Richard, Ed. *Poetry and Politics: An Anthology of Essays.* NY: Quill, 1985.

JUHA   Juhasz, Suzanne. *Naked and Fiery Forms: Modern American Poetry by Women, a New Tradition.* NY: Octagon, 1976.

KEYS   Keyssar, Helene. *The Curtain and the Veil: Strategies in Black Drama.* NY: Franklin, 1981.

KONE   Konek, Carol and Dorothy Walters, Eds. *I Hear My Sisters Saying: Poems by Twentieth-Century Women.* NY: Crowell, 1976.

KOPB   Koppelman, Susan, Ed. *Between Mothers and Daughters: Stories Across a Generation.* Old Westbury NY: Feminist, 1985.

KOPM   Koppelman, Susan, Comp. *Old Maids: Short Stories by Nineteenth Century U.S. Women Writers.* Boston: Pandora, 1984.

KOPO   Koppelman, Susan, Ed. *The Other Woman: Stories of Two Women and a Man.* Old Westbury NY: Feminist, 1984.

KUFR   Kufrin, Joan. *Uncommon Women.* Piscataway NJ: New Century, 1981.

LECL   LeClair, Tom and Larry McCaffery, Eds. *Anything Can Happen: Interviews with Contemporary American Novelists.* Urbana: Univ. of Illinois, 1983.

LEDE Lederer, Laura, Ed. *Take Back the Night: Women on Pornography.* NY: Morrow, 1980.

LEEE Lee, A. Robert, Ed. *Black Fiction: New Studies in the Afro-American Novel Since 1945.* Totawa NJ: Barnes and Noble, 1980.

LIFS Lifshin, Lyn, Ed. *Ariadne's Thread: A Collection of Contemporary Women's Journals.* NY: Harper, 1982.

LONG Long, Richard A. and Eugenia W. Collier, Eds. *Afro-American Writing: An Anthology of Prose and Poetry.* University Park: Pennsylvania State UP, 1985.

MA82 Magill, Frank N. *Magill's Literary Annual.* Englewood Cliffs NJ: Salem, 1982.

MA83 Magill, Frank N. *Magill's Literary Annual.* 1983.

MA84 Magill, Frank N. *Magill's Literary Annual.* 1984.

MA85 Magill, Frank N. *Magill's Literary Annual.* 1985.

MA86 Magill, Frank N. *Magill's Literary Annual.* 1986.

MA87 Magill, Frank N. *Magill's Literary Annual.* 1987.

MACC MacCann, Donnarae and Gloria Woodard, Eds. *The Black American in Books for Children: Readings in Racism.* Metuchen NJ: Scarecrow, 1985.

MACD MacCann, Donnarae and Gloria Woodard, Eds. *Cultural Conformity in Books for Children: Further Readings in Racism.* Metuchen NJ: Scarecrow, 1977.

MAIN Mainiero, Lina, Ed. *American Women Writers: A Critical Reference Guide from Colonial Times to the Present (4 Vols.).* NY: Ungar, 1979.

MCAL McAllister, Pam. *Reweaving the Web of Life: Feminism and Nonviolence.* Philadelphia: New Society, 1982.

MEES Meese, Elizabeth A. *Crossing the Double-Cross: The Practice of Feminist Criticism.* Chapel Hill: Univ. of North Carolina, 1986.

MESS Hartman, Joan E. and Ellen Messer-Davidow, Eds. *Women in Print, One: Opportunities for Women's Studies Research in Language and Literature.* NY: Modern Language Association, 1982.

MICK Mickelson, Anne Z. *Reaching Out: Sensitivity and Order in Recent American Fiction by Women.* Metuchen NJ: Scarecrow, 1979.

MIDD Middlebrook, Diane Wood and Marilyn Yalom, Eds. *Coming to Light: American Women Poets in the Twentieth Century.* Ann Arbor: Univ. of Michigan, 1985.

MILA Miles, Julia, Ed. *The Women's Project 2.* NY: Performing Arts Journal Publications, 1984.

MILB Miles, Julia, Ed. *The Women's Project: Seven New Plays by Women.* NY: Performing Arts Journal Publications, 1980.

MILE Miles, Sara, *et al.,* Eds. *Ordinary Women: Mujeres Comunes: An Anthology of Poetry by New York City Women.* NY: Ordinary Women, 1978.

MILL Miller, R. Baxter, Ed. *Black American Literature and Humanism.* Lexington: UP of Kentucky, 1981.

MILP Miller, R. Baxter, Ed. *Black American Poets Between Worlds, 1940–1960.* Knoxville: Univ. of Tennessee, 1986.

MOOR Moore, Honor, Ed. *The New Women's Theatre: Ten Plays by Contemporary American Women.* NY: Vintage, 1977.

MORA Moraga, Cherríe and Gloria Anzaldúa, Eds. *This Bridge Called My Back: Writings by Radical Women of Color.* Watertown MA: Persephone, 1981.

NEWT Newton, Judith and Deborah Rosenfelt. *Feminist Criticism and Social Change: Sex, Class and Race in Literature and Culture.* NY: Methuen, 1985.

NOBL   Noble, Jeanne. *Beautiful, Also, Are the Souls of My Black Sisters: A History of the Black Woman in America.* Englewood Cliffs NJ: Prentice-Hall, 1978.

OCON   O'Connor, Karen. *Contributions of Women: Literature.* Minneapolis: Dillon, 1984.

ODAN   O'Daniel, Therman B., Ed. *James Baldwin: A Critical Evaluation.* Washington DC: Howard Univ., 1977.

OLAU   Olauson, Judith. *The American Woman Playwright: A View of Criticism and Characterization.* Troy NY: Whitston, 1981.

OSTR   Ostrow, Eileen J., Ed. *Center Stage: An Anthology of Twenty-One Contemporary Black-American Plays.* Oakland CA: Sea Urchin, 1981.

PAGE   Page, James A. *Selected Black American Authors: An Illustrated Bio-Bibliography.* Boston: G.K. Hall, 1977.

PATT   Patterson, Lindsay, Ed. *Anthology of the Afro-American in the Theatre: A Critical Approach.* Cornwells Heights PA: Publishers Agency, 1978.

PERH   Perry, Margaret. *The Harlem Renaissance: An Annotated Bibliography and Commentary.* NY: Garland, 1982.

PERM   Perry, Margaret. *Silence to the Drums: A Survey of the Literature of the Harlem Renaissance.* Westport CT: Greenwood, 1976.

PERR   Perry, Ruth and Martine Watson Brownley, Eds. *Mothering of the Mind: Twelve Studies of Writers and Their Silent Partners.* NY: Holmes and Meier, 1984.

PESE   Peseroff, Joyce, Ed. *The Ploughshares Poetry Reader.* Watertown MA: Ploughshares, 1986.

PREN   Prenshaw, Peggy Whitman, Ed. *Women Writers of the Contemporary South.* Jackson: Univ. of Mississippi, 1984.

PRYS   Pryse, Marjorie and Hortense J. Spillers, Eds. *Conjuring: Black Women, Fiction, and Literary Tradition.* Bloomington: Indiana UP, 1985.

RAIN   Rainwater, Catherine and William J. Scheick, Eds. *Contemporary American Women Writers: Narrative Strategies.* Lexington: UP of Kentucky, 1985.

REDM   Redmond, Eugene B. *Drumvoices: The Mission of Afro-American Poetry, A Critical History.* Garden City NY: Anchor-Doubleday, 1976.

REEM   Rees, David. *Marble in the Water: Essays on Contemporary Writers of Fiction for Children and Young Adults.* Boston: Horn Book, 1980.

REES   Rees, David. *Painted Desert, Green Shade: Essays on Contemporary Writers of Fiction for Children and Young Adults.* Boston: Horn Book, 1984.

REIT   Reit, Ann, Ed. *Alone Amid All This Noise: A Collection of Women's Poetry.* NY: Four Winds, 1976.

ROBI   Robinson, William H., Jr. *Black New England Letters: The Uses of Writing in Black New England.* Boston: Trustees of the Public Library of the City of Boston, 1979.

ROCK   Rockwell, Jeanne, Ed. *Good Company: Poets at Michigan.* Ann Arbor: Noon Rock, 1977.

RODG   Rodgers-Rose, La Frances, Ed. *The Black Woman.* Beverly Hills CA: Sage, 1980.

ROGI   Roginski, Jim, Comp. *Newbery and Caldecott Medalists and Honor Book Winners: Bibliographies and Resource Material Through 1977.* Littleton CO: Libraries Unlimited, 1983.

RUAS   Ruas, Charles. *Conversations with American Writers.* NY: Knopf, 1985.

RUBI   Rubin, Louis D., Jr., *et al.,* Eds. *The History of Southern Literature.* Baton Rouge: Louisiana State Univ., 1985.

RUDD   Ruddick, Sara and Pamela Daniels, Eds. *Working It Out: Twenty-Three*

Women Writers, Artists, Scientists, and Scholars Talk About Their Lives and Work. NY: Pantheon, 1977.

SCAN   Scanlan, Tom. *Family, Drama, and American Dreams.* Westport CT: Greenwood, 1978.

SHOW   Showalter, Elaine, Ed. *The New Feminist Criticism: Essays on Women, Literature, and Theory.* NY: Pantheon, 1985.

SICH   Sicherman, Barbara and Carol H. Green, Eds. *Notable American Women, the Modern Period: A Biographical Dictionary.* Cambridge MA: Harvard UP, 1980.

SIMC   Simcox, Helen Earle, Ed. *Dear Dark Faces: Portraits of a People.* Detroit: Lotus, 1980.

SING   Singh, Amritjit. *The Novels of the Harlem Renaissance: Twelve Black Writers, 1923–1933.* University Park: Pennsylvania State UP, 1976.

SKLA   Sklar, Morty and Mary Biggs. *Editor's Choice II: Fiction, Poetry and Art from the U.S. Small Press.* Iowa City IA: The Spirit That Moves Us, 1987.

SMIT   Smith, Barbara, Ed. *Home Girls: A Black Feminist Anthology.* NY: Kitchen Table: Women of Color, 1983.

SMTC   Smith, Curtis, C., Ed. *Twentieth-Century Science-Fiction Writers.* 2nd Ed. Chicago: St. James, 1986.

SMTD   Smith, Dave and David Bottoms, Eds. *The Morrow Anthology of Younger American Poets.* NY: Quill, 1985.

SMTV   Smith, Valerie. *Self-Discovery and Authority in Afro-American Narrative.* Cambridge MA: Harvard UP, 1987.

SOUT   Southgate, Robert L. *Black Plots and Black Characters: A Handbook for Afro-American Literature.* Syracuse NY: Gaylord Professional, 1979.

SPAC   Spacks, Patricia Meyer, Ed. *Contemporary Women Novelists: A Collection of Critical Essays.* Englewood Cliffs NJ: Prentice-Hall, 1977.

SPIN   Spinner, Stephanie, Ed. *Motherlove: Stories by Women About Motherhood.* NY: Dell, 1978.

SQUI   Squier, Susan Merrill, Ed. *Women Writers and the City: Essays in Feminist Literary Criticism.* Knoxville: Univ. of Tennessee, 1984.

STER   Sternburg, Janet, Ed. *The Writer on Her Work.* NY: Norton, 1980.

STET   Stetson, Erlene, Ed. *Black Sister: Poetry by Black American Women, 1746–1980.* Bloomington: Indiana UP, 1981.

STRE   Street, Douglas, Ed. *Children's Novels and the Movies.* NY: Ungar, 1983.

TATE   Tate, Claudia, Ed. *Black Women Writers at Work.* NY: Continuum, 1983.

THOM   Thomas, Arthur E. *Like It Is: Arthur E. Thomas Interviews Leaders on Black America.* NY: Dutton, 1981.

TODD   Todd, Janet, Ed. *Women Writers Talking.* NY: Holmes and Meier, 1983.

TOTH   Toth, Emily, Ed. *Regionalism and the Female Imagination: A Collection of Essays.* NY: Human Sciences, 1985.

TOWN   Townsend, John Rowe. *A Sounding of Storytellers: New and Revised Essays on Contemporary Writers for Children.* Harmondsworth, Middlesex, England: Kestrel Books (published by Penguin), 1979.

VEND   Vendler, Helen, Ed. *The Harvard Book of Contemporary American Poetry.* Cambridge MA: Harvard UP, 1985.

VIDA   Vida, Ginny, Ed. *Our Right to Love: A Lesbian Resource Book.* Englewood Cliffs NJ: Prentice-Hall, 1978.

WADE   Wade-Gayles, Gloria. *No Crystal Stair: Visions of Race and Sex in Black Women's Fiction.* NY: Pilgrim, 1984.

WASA   Washington, Mary Helen, Ed. *Invented Lives: Narratives of Black Women 1860–1960.* Garden City NY: Doubleday, 1987.

WASH   Washington, Mary Helen, Ed. *Midnight Birds: Stories of Contemporary Black Women Writers.* NY: Anchor-Doubleday, 1980.

WEIB   Weixlmann, Joe and Chester J. Fontenot, Eds. *Belief vs. Theory in Black American Literary Criticism.* Greenwood FL: Penkevill, 1986.

WERN   Werner, Craig Hansen. *Paradoxical Resolutions: American Fiction Since James Joyce.* Urbana: Univ. of Illinois, 1982.

WETH   Wetherby, Terry, Ed. *New Poets: Women: An Anthology.* Millbrae CA: Les Femmes, 1976.

WHEE   Wheeler, Kenneth W. and Virginia Lee Lussier, Eds. *Women, the Arts, and the 1920's in Paris and New York.* New Brunswick NJ: Transaction, 1982.

WILK   Wilkerson, Margaret B., Ed. *Nine Plays by Black Women.* NY: New American Library, 1986.

WILL   Willis, Susan. *Specifying: Black Women Writing the American Experience.* Madison: Univ. of Wisconsin, 1987.

WINT   Winter, Nina. *Interview with the Muse: Remarkable Women Speak on Creativity and Power.* Berkeley: Moon, 1978.

WORD   *Wordplays 3: An Anthology of New American Drama.* NY: Performing Arts Journal Publications, 1984.

YALO   Yalom, Marilyn, Ed. *Women Writers of the West Coast: Speaking of Their Lives and Careers.* Santa Barbara CA: Capra, 1983.

ZINS   Zinsser, William, Ed. *Inventing the Truth: The Art and Craft of Memoir.* Boston: Houghton-Mifflin, 1987.

Index

A

G

I

K

L

O

S